THE GOLDEN NORTH

A Vast Country of Inexhaustible Gold Fields, and a Land of Illimitable Cereal and Stock Raising Capabilities.

BY C. R. TUTTLE,

Author "Canadian North Land," Meteorological Observer of Canadian Government Expeditions to Hudson's Bay and Strait, and the Far Northwest.

ILLUSTRATED WITH MAPS AND ENGRAVINGS.

CHICAGO:
Rand, McNally & Co., Publishers,
1897.

PREFACE.

The rush after the rich deposits of virgin gold in the far northwest will be doubly rewarded. Those who go in seach of the precious metal, with proper equipment, will not return empty handed. Experiments already made warrant the statement that gold may be found there in great abundance, and that it may be separated from the baser material with which it is associated, at slight cost, although of course, only be enduring the hardships incident to a miner's life in a frozen country. To those willing, and physically able to make the necessary sacrifices, the Golden North offers a Golden Prize.

But it offers more than this. Hard by the vast auriferous slopes which hang down from the summit of the watershed that divides the two great river systems of the north, are vast alluvial plains stretching up to the 65th parallel, where stock raising, dairying and the cultivation of cereals may be carried on without limit and with great profit.

When the northwest routes to the gold fields have been opened for travel as they will be in a short time, returning gold hunters will not only exhibit the fortunes taken from the banks of creek and gulch of the higher elevations, but they will tell of the mighty valleys and prairies of the basins of the Peace, Athabasca and Mackenzie rivers; and, their telling will result in the colonization and development of the greatest agricultural and stock raising El Dorado on the face of the earth.

The north is a country of gold. It will become a land of golden harvests. For centuries Nature has been pushing back the cold, farther and farther towards the pole, and been preparing a new land for the over-crowded populations of these lower latitudes. The Klondike bells are now ringing out the glory of that land. The march of the weary, the disappointed, and the oppressed is to be into higher latitudes, where the bounties of Providence have been spread with a lavish hand.

CHARLES R. TUTTLE.

Chicago, Sept. 15, 1897.

CONTENTS.

CHAPTER I.

GOLD AND COLONIZATION.

Northwesterly trend of progress—Gradual advance of soil, forests, cereals, population, commerce and civilization towards the Arctic—Extent of the gold-bearing districts of the great North—History repeating itself—Prospects of the Golden North.

CHAPTER II.

VASTNESS OF THE NORTH LAND.

Its mighty river systems and basins—Basin of the Yukon —The wonderful Peace River country—Fertile plains and prairies extending up to the 64th parellel—The great plains of the Saskatchewan basin—The Churchill country and the basins of James' and Ungava Bay.

CHAPTER III.

TRADING POSTS OF THE NORTH.

Trails across the continent in the sub-Arctic belt—Many that have been traveled for two centuries—Short cut to the gold fields of the Klondike from Edmonton via Lake Athabaska and the Upper Mackenzie—The quicker and cheaper route—List of North Land trading stations—Hints on map study.

CHAPTER IV.

THE YUKON DISTRICT—ALASKA.

From Bering Sea to the junction of the Pelly and Lewis rivers—Cereal, vegetable and stock capabilities—The forests and climate—Value of the white spruce.

CHAPTER V.

UPPER YUKON OR KLONDIKE REGION.

Auriferous areas lying west of the Mackenzie watershed—Territory is duplicated in extent and gold bearing riches on the slopes east of the summit—Three great routes to the Klondike—Reasons why the all-overland route will become most favored.

CHAPTER VI.

UPPER YUKON OR KLONDIKE REGION. (Continued.)

Pioneers of the Klondike country—Administration of mining laws, tariff regulations and homestead entry rules extended to the district by the Canadian government—Explorations of Dr. Dawson and Surveyor Ogilvie—Increase of mining camps.

CHAPTER VII.

THE ALEUTIAN DISTRICT—ALASKA.

A mountainous and volcanic country—Broad meadows and sloping hillsides—Stock raising and cereal capabilities—Altitude limit of vegetation.

CHAPTER VIII.

SITKAN DISTRICT—ALASKA.

Channels, natural canals, rivers and lakes—The water highways of the country—Great timber resources of Southern Alaska—Wild berries abundant—Pest of mosquitoes and flies—Stock and agriculture.

CHAPTER IX.

UPPER YUKON—LEWIS RIVER.

From Lake Bennett to the head of the Lewis—Down the Lewis to the Yukon—A country of lakes and rivers—The Klondike region proper—Its extent—Rich gold discoveries eastward from the Klondike—Dr. Dawson's opinion of the Klondike—Surveyor Ogilvie's explorations.

CHAPTER X.

UPPER YUKON AND TRIBUTARIES.

The North Country from the International boundary to the junction of the Lewis and Pelly—The Stewart River—Other streams—Sixty Mile River—The Klondike River and tributary creeks—Forty Mile River.

CHAPTER XI.

UPPER YUKON—AGRICULTURE AND TIMBER.

Only a small proportion of the region available for cereal and vegetable crops—Considerable areas of timber suitable for manufacturing purposes—An abundance of trees for firewood and for all mining necessities.

CHAPTER XII.

WEALTH OF THE KLONDIKE.

Inexhaustible deposits of placer and quartz gold—The silver-bearing rock—Vast coal fields—Reports of government officials that read like tales of the Arabian Nights—Sensational reports of Surveyor Ogilvie.

CHAPTER XIII.

PROCESS OF PLACER MINING.

Methods of the prospector—Use of the pan, the rocker and the sluice—Mining in the far north—Continuous daylight in summer and almost perpetual darkness in winter—Filling the hours of summer with hard work—"Burning" in winter—Vast Peace River gold discoveries.

CHAPTER XIV.

FURS, FISH AND GAME OF THE KLONDIKE.

The silver gray, black and red fox—Abundance of game—The Caribou, moose and the grizzly, brown, black and silver-tip bears—Salmon and other fish.

CHAPTER XV.

IMPORTANT INTERNATIONAL QUESTIONS.

Verified reports of rich gold discoveries and the arrival of the precious metal in this country likely to send a vast population from the United States to the Klondike regions—Might possibly lead to a war between England and this country—The feeling in London—Chicago and London competitors—Routes for railroad communication—Settlement of the boundary question.

CHAPTER XVI.

THE GREAT FERTILE NORTH.

A boundless territory of inexhaustible bread, meat and dairy capabilities—Coal and other resources—How the lower levels are sheltered from storms and cold.

CHAPTER XVII.

CANADIAN NORTHWEST.

Districts of Assiniboia, Saskatchewan, Alberta and Athabaska—The vast fertile plains to the north of these—Greatest agricultural and stock raising region on earth.

CHAPTER XVIII.

RESOURCES OF BRITISH COLUMBIA.

Excellent climate—Abundance of coal—Gold in inexhaustible quantities—Iron, copper, galena, mercury, platinum, plumbago, mica, salt and many other valuable deposits—Progress of the mines.

CHAPTER XIX.

COUNTRY OF THE SKEENA.

Trip from Port Simpson on the Pacific to the summit of Pine River Pass—Wonderful mountain and valley scenery—Resources of the mighty valleys.

CHAPTER XX.

FROM THE ROCKIES TO CHURCHILL.

A transcontinental route from Atlantic to Pacific through Hudson's Bay and Strait—Across the rich, fertile prairies, through the Pine River Pass—Vast areas of rich lands.

CHAPTER XXI.

METROPOLIS OF THE KLONDIKE.

Description of the immediate Klondike country—Life at Dawson City—Boom in real estate—Trading and the high price of supplies—Saloons and gambling—The future of Dawson City.

CHAPTER XXII.

NORTHWEST ROUTES TO GOLD FIELDS.

Description of trail by the Lewis and Peace rivers—Short and cheap cut to the Klondike—Route by the Pelly and Liard rivers.

CHAPTER XXIII.

YUKON AND JUNEAU ROUTES.

Description of St. Michaels—Temperature and ice—Season of navigation on the Yukon—"Fort Get There"—The Dyea and Skaguay passes.

CHAPTER XXIV.

ALASKAN BOUNDARY QUESTION.

Alaskan boundary controversy and correspondence between the United States and Dominion of Canada—Population of Alaska—Increase owing to gold discoveries.

CHAPTER XXV.

TOWNS AND TRADING POSTS OF ALASKA.

Sitka and Juneau—St. Michaels and the trading posts of the Aleutian Islands—Douglas City and the great Treadwell gold mine—Trade and traffic.

CHAPTER XXVI.

THE FUR SEAL CONTROVERSY.

Account of the fur sealing grounds and their great value—The annual catch—Pelagic sealing—History of the great controversy—Solution of all difficulties practically accomplished.

CHAPTER XXVII.

SALMON, WHALES, COD AND HERRING.

Extent of the Alaskan fisheries—Statistics of the salmon catch—Product of oil, bone and ivory—Cod and herring fisheries.

CHAPTER XXVIII.

COMMERCE, GOVERNMENT, TRANSPORTATION.

Transportation facilities—Exports and imports—Territorial government—The civil list of Alaska.

CHAPTER XXIX.

RESOURCES OF HUDSON'S BAY.

Mountains of pure mica—The salmon fisheries of Ungava—The Eskimos and their language—Extracts from prayer and hymn books—On to Churchill.

CHAPTER XXX.

IN HUDSON'S STRAIT.

Its length, width and islands—Height of its tides, and velocity of its tidal currents—Talks with Eskimos.

CHAPTER XXXI.

CAPTURING A WHALE.

Scenes and impressions of Marble Island—Visit to the Rose Welcome—The "crow's nest" and Lookout-man—Harpooning a whale—An exciting contest—A "flurry."

CHAPTER XXXII.

DAY AT FORT CHURCHILL.

Rev. Mr. Lofthouse—A curious courtship by photograph and letter—An intended bride starts from the old country for Hudson's Bay to become the wife of a missionary—The porpoise fishery.

CHAPTER XXXIII.

OBSERVATIONS AT YORK FACTORY.

Buildings at the trading post—The Churchill and the school—An interesting murder trial.

CHAPTER XXXIV.

PORPOISE, WALRUS AND SEAL.

Character and value of these animals—The porpoise fisheries—The Walrus hunt—Peculiarities of Narwhal—Probabilities of a seal breeding ground in Hudson's Strait—Great possibilities of the oil industry.

CHAPTER XXXV.

FUR BEARING ANIMALS.

The silver, blue, gray, red and white foxes—The ermine—The marten—The otter—The varying hare—The lynx—The wolf—The sable, musk ox, etc.—The fur trade.

CHAPTER XXXVI.

OBSERVATIONS ON THE ESKIMOS.

Romance of the marriage of an Eskimo Princess—Habits of life—The Kayak.

CHAPTER XXXVII.

NATURE'S NEWEST LAND.

Wonders of the new north—Product of natural laws for the last one thousand years—Specific work of glaziers—New areas for many millions—Probable gold and other products—Hard times to disappear as dew before an advancing sun.

CHAPTER XXXVIII.

GOLD OUTPUT OF THE WORLD.

Interesting article by Director Preston of the United States Mint—Statistics.

CHAPTER XXXIX.

HON. CLIFFORD SEFTON.

Minister of the Interior of the Canadian Government—Head Official in charge of the New El Dorado.

CHAPTER XL.

THE PEACE-LIARD-PELLY ROUTE.

Detailed description of the Northwest Route, via the Peace, Liard and Pelly rivers from Edmonton to the Yukon.

APPENDIX.

I.—Routes and distances.
II.—Facts about gold.
III.—Canadian and Alaskan mining laws and regulations.
IV.—Canadian land regulations.
V.—Cost of supplies and outfits.

THE GOLDEN NORTH.

CHAPTER I.

GOLD AND COLONIZATION.

Northwesterly trend of progress—Gradual advance of soil, forests, cereals, population, commerce and civilization towards the Arctic—Extent of the gold-bearing districts of the great North—History repeating itself—Prospects of the Golden North.

The gold deposits of the Klondike are probably unequalled in any part of the world either as to their extent or the significance of their discovery. It is evident to those acquainted with the character and geological formation of that region, including the whole country traversed by the gulches and creeks flowing into the upper waters of the Yukon and the Mackenzie, that still richer strikes will be made in the near future, and that the gold fever of 1897 will be eclipsed by that of 1898.

Beyond doubt the efforts of the prospector will be richly rewarded in both placer and quartz diggings throughout nearly the whole country between the 55th and 65th parallels and the 125th and 145th degrees, an auriferous area of nearly 600,000 square miles, and sufficient to profitably engage 250,000 miners. This does not include the gold fields of southern Alaska, nor the extensive yellow metal deposits in the greater part of British Columbia, but it does cover the Kootenai discoveries.

This vast gold bearing tract consists of the watershed or great summit-divide between the main upper tributaries of the Yukon and the Mackenzie rivers, the lower depressions of which are from 1,500 to 3,000 feet above sea level. It is well timbered and is subject to a snow fall of from two to five feet according to altitude, the higher elevations receiving the heaviest snow mantle during the winter season, which extends from the middle of September or first of October to the latter part of April, or between seven and eight months, leaving but a little more than four months of summer and autumn. There is no spring season, properly speaking, in that country. These four months, however, contain in the aggregate, as many hours of sunshine as six summer months in the latitude of Chicago.

The country is rugged, traversed everywhere by deep gulches and mountain streams, the formations almost invariably indicating the presence of gold deposits in both gravel and quartz. Those best acquainted with the region expect that far richer strikes will be made considerably east of the Klondike and on both sides of the summit dividing the two great river systems.

These gold discoveries which are now engrossing the attention of the people everywhere are significant. They will undoubtedly mark a new epoch in the progress and development of this continent. Thousands upon thousands will push northward after gold. Transportation facilities will have to be provided so that supplies will be cheaper and more abundant, and the cost, in time and money, of reaching the country be greatly reduced. In this way the vast extent and wonderful resources of the whole north country will become generally known, and hundreds of thousands will rush into it, not only to dig gold, but to produce bread and meat from the broad fertile plains, valleys and prairies, to exchange for it.

It is difficult for one who has traveled extensively in this great golden north land to write in what those ignorant of its character will concede to be conservative terms. The natural history surveyors of the United

States and Canada, who are best acquainted with the capabilities of the north, persist in making their reports in what those who have never visited the country characterize as extravagant terms.

It is left for the Hudson's Bay Company's trading post officials to speak disparagingly of the land. They have practiced in that line of policy for more than three generations, under instructions from London, in order that the company might be left to enjoy a monopoly of the fur trade. But all others who have seen the wonderful north, talk of its resources in words of irrepressible enthusiasm. It is impossible for them to do otherwise.

Gold discoveries have led to the settlement and development of many countries. The great cereal and fruit resources of California would probably have remained unknown for one or two generations longer than they did, had it not been that the discovery of rich deposits of the yellow metal attracted an army of prospectors thither in 1849.

In the Golden North the early history of California is repeating itself on more than one line. Thousands will become wealthy in the diggings of the Klondike and the creek and gulch regions of the upper Yukon and the Mackenzie, but many hundreds of thousands will find happy homes of peace and plenty in the vast agricultural and stock raising valleys, and on the fertile plains and prairies of the wonderful north land, as a result of information concerning the resources of that country which the gold hunters are sure to disseminate. Without this agency the resources of the north would probably remain a sealed book for an indefinite period.

Indeed the thoughtful reader will ask, what means this wild clanging of the Klondike bells? Is it the yellow dust that is being washed from bars and banks of river and gulch?

Yes, that and more.

It is the voice of the mighty north calling to the over-crowded and depressed centers of population in the United States to march into higher latitudes and there to take possession of boundless riches.

May it not be the ringing up the dawn of an area of prosperity that shall banish economic heresies in this country, and ultimately change the political map of a hemisphere?

The voice of the Klondike may be regarded as the class bell of the World's University calling the people to the study of a new problem and of a new country. The nation's schoolmaster has opened the text-book of the north, and the struggling, discontented masses are to lay aside their threadbare delusions of silver restoration, the social democracy, and the co-operative commonwealth. They are now to repudiate false teachers, turn their backs upon false gods, and realize the saving truth that the earth possesses "enough for each, enough for all, enough forever more."

People will come to their right senses. They will cease to contend for the bone that has already been gnawed bare, and will flock into new pastures, rich not only in precious metals, but in illimitable possibilities of bread and meat.

And what a text-book!

From its pages pupils of an older growth than those who fill our school houses will learn how nature is gradually extending her mantle of soil and vegetation over the rocks of the north towards the shores of the Arctic Sea. They will read and dream of a receding pole and a slow but portentous revolution of the earth from north to south, placing the northern habitable boundary of the continent about one hundred miles nearer the axis with each century. Nor are they to be left to theory as to these phenomena. Hudson's Bay trading posts from 100 to 200 years standing, stretching from the rugged upper Labrador to Bering Sea, are to give testimony and to declare that in the brief period of their existence, soil and vegetation and forests and cereal growth have come to them from the south and have grown up around them on the once barren rocks.

From that wonderful text-book of the north, they are to realize that altitude far more than latitude governs thermal conditions of the Arctic zone, and that while the rocks, mountains, hills, and gulches abound in practically inexhaustible deposits of gold and other mineral treasures, the valleys and plains and broad prairies of the region await the directing touch of man to yield cereals and cattle sufficient to glut all the bread and meat markets of earth. From the pages of that book they are to be told of the innumerable herds of sea-faring mammals, including oil and fur-bearing seals, walruses, porpoises and whales, from the products of which two hemispheres may be abundantly supplied with oil, hides, bone and ivory; and they will hear of the millions of tons of the best salmon caught in any waters, and of all the many other resources of the rugged land so well calculated to yield brain and muscle and wealth to all who will go up to inhabit its mighty basins and treasure-bearing summits.

Before a dozen pages of that wonderful text-book of the north are gone over and understood, thousands and hundreds of thousands will flock to that land "flowing with milk and honey," hitherto hidden from immigration and yet hard by our doors. Gold is there in abundance, but resources of even greater intrinsic value are there, and these will eventually outweigh the importance of the gold.

And all this is but another stride in the northwestward progress of man.

The world's march of commerce, and science and skill
In errands of blessing its work to fulfill
Moves in the same course,—northwesterly still.

The directive magnetic force that controls the needle is not a more attractive problem than is the unerring northwesterly trend of human progress. Westward and northward have been the marching orders until the people of the present generation must look southward and eastward for the homes of their ancestors. The greatest deeds have always been performed in high latitude, because the highest habitable latitudes produce the greatest men. And yet, strange as it may appear, the north is always underrated.

Go to the Eastern hemisphere for examples of this. Half a century before Christ, Caesar concluded a series of great victories in the northwest, by subjugating the hardy inhabitants of Britain; but this was regarded by the Romans as placing the Imperial standard on the utmost confines of the north rather than as a conquest of valuable territory. A few centuries and the island camping-ground of the Roman Conqueror became mistress of the world. Upon those northern shores a mighty commerce began to develop, and vast industrial enterprises grew up, until, in every part of the earth, England was hailed as the greatest nation under the sun. But there was no prophet to foretell England's greatness, nor was there anything in the general appearance of the country to attract attention. Its high latitude is one of the secrets of Britain's importance.

History is ever repeating itself, and the political transformations of the old world may yet, to a great extent, be re-enacted in the new. Here on this continent the trend of all material progress is northwesterly. The flow of immigration is northwesterly, and the Creator, as if to make way for its latest advance, has pushed back, as it were, the cold of the sub-arctic regions nearer to the pole, and extended the vast fertile belt of the northern temperate zone from the great lakes to the head waters of the Mackenzie and the Yukon.

CHAPTER II.

VASTNESS OF THE NORTH LAND.

Its mighty river systems and basins—Basin of the Yukon —The wonderful Peace River country—Fertile plains and prairies extending up to the 64th parallel—The great plains of the Saskatchewan basin—The Churchill country and the basins of James' and Ungava Bay.

In order to form a correct idea of the extent of the north country, it will be advisable to briefly glance at the whole continental plain which stretches north and south between the Gulf of Mexico and the Arctic Ocean. This plain is bounded on the west by the Rocky Mountains throughout its whole extent, and on the east side by a less elevated plateau known as the Appalachian Range. This great plain occupies the whole of the continent between the western and eastern mountain ranges, and in the far north it broadens, stretching from the western shores of Hudson's Bay and James' Bay to the head waters of the Mackenzie and the Yukon, where the mountain passes do not reach an elevation of more than from 1,000 to 2,500 feet. This vast plain is divided by its river system into three perfectly distinct drainage basins. One drains to the south into the Gulf of Mexico; another into the Atlantic by the channel of the great river St. Lawrence; and the third, north into the arctic and sub-arctic waters.

Of these three great basins that of the St. Lawrence is decidedly the smallest, while the northern is larger than the other two together. The St. Lawrence basin, divided by the boundary between the United States and Canada, occupies part of both countries. The southern basin is wholly in the United States, while a greater portion of the northern basin is in British Canadian territory.

The north and south basins are separated by the 49th parallel of latitude, which in addition to marking the international boundary line between central Canada and the United States, runs along very close to what is known as the watershed. It will thus be seen that the great continental plain of North America is divided naturally as well as politically near its center.

Our attention must be confined to the northern basin, or basins, for the region is physically subdivided by several extensive river systems. Beginning at the western coast of Alaska, we have first the Yukon basin, which is over 2,000 miles long, extending up into the Canadian northwest from the 141st degree to considerably beyond the 130th, until its upper waters interlock with those of the upper Mackenzie River, on the summit of the northern Rockies. This vast area of the Yukon, consisting of about 400,000 square miles, or nearly the whole of Alaska, is a rugged, mountainous, snowbound country, which will be more fully described later on.

Crossing the mountains through any of the passes between the 55th and 65th parallels, we come to perhaps the largest and most fertile subdivision of the great northern basin, known as the Peace River country. This vast area is drained by the Peace and Athabasca rivers and their numerous tributaries, flowing into Lake Athabasca, which is only 400 feet above the level of the sea; and by the Peace River and its numerous tributaries stretching far up into the mountains, flowing also into Lake Athabasca; by the Great Slave River, flowing from Lake Athabasca into Great Slave Lake at Fort Resolution; and by the Mackenzie River, the Mountain River and the many branches which flow into it. This mighty valley, comprising the largest area of cereal and stock-producing lands in one body to be found anywhere in the world, has an elevation above sea level from 400 to 1,500 feet, and enjoys a climate equal in all respects to that of Maryland, although of course its winters are longer, and its summers are shorter as to number of days, but not as to aggregate number of hours of sunshine. This almost illimitable territory, rich beyond description in agricultural, fruit, and meat-producing resources, lies between the 55th and 64th parallels of latitude and the 105th and 120th degrees of longitude, and comprises nearly 500,000 square miles. This great plain, prairie, or park country, is but slightly timbered, although there are forests of considerable growth all along the foot-hills of the Rocky Mountains which are everywhere penetrated by the creeks and tributary streams of the upper Mackenzie, the Peace and the Athabasca rivers. According to the reports of the natural history surveys of the Canadian Dominion, there are as rich gold deposits on the eastern slopes of the Rockies in the quartz formation and river banks and bars of the upper western branches of the Mackenzie as on the western slope in the Klondike region.

Passing from the Peace River country southeastward, we come to the higher plain, almost as extensive, of the north and south branches of the Saskatchewan and the Battle and Deer rivers, which are located between them, and the Saskatchewan itself, from the confluence of the two principal branches to Lake Winnipeg. The Saskatchewan system of rivers, which drain the basin between Lake Winnipeg and the Rocky Mountains, aggregate an almost incredible length. The country has an elevation above sea level of from 900 to 4,000 feet and is quite heavily timbered not only in the neighborhood of Lake Winnipeg but along the foot-hills of the Rockies and on the borders of most of the streams, especially in the more northerly and westernly districts. This area of cereal and stock-sustaining country lies between the 49th and 55th parallels of latitude and between the 90th and 115th, and farther to the north, 120th degrees of longitude, and comprises about 500,000 square miles. This region is already quite well known and is being rapidly settled and developed both as to its agricultural and stock-raising capabilities. It includes the province of Manitoba and the territories of Kewatin, Saskatchewan, Assiniboia, and Alberta. The territory of Athabasca lies to the north of Alberta at the threshold of the great Peace River country, which is yet unsettled, and of course undeveloped in any way. Our knowledge of that extensive territory is derived from traveling through it, and from reports and meteorological data gathered and given out by Hudson's Bay trading-post officials.

There is a smaller basin, practically within and between the two great districts mentioned, lying to the north of the latter and to the west of the former. This is the basin of the Churchill, flowing from Reindeer Lake to Hudson's Bay. There are a large number of Hudson's Bay trading posts in this territory, and from the reports of those in charge of them, we learn that while a century ago there were no forests bordering any of the lakes and rivers thereabouts, there is now well developed tamarac ranging from five to fifteen inches in diameter extending almost down to Fort Churchill on the western shores of Hudson's Bay.

The outlet for the drainage of the great Saskatchewan country from Lake Winnipeg to Hudson's Bay is by way of the Nelson, the Hayes, and the Severn rivers, the first and the last being about 550 miles in length and the second finding its way into the northern waters of Lake Winnipeg at Norway House through a series of smaller lakes to the northwest. This country between Lake Winnipeg and the Hudson's Bay is all pretty heavily timbered, both the soil and the forests having been largely developed within the last century.

There is another basin in the north drained by the rivers flowing into James' Bay, the Albany, the Moose and the Abittibi being the principal streams, some of them reaching nearly as far south as Lake Superior. This section is heavily timbered.

Eastward from the east-main coast of Hudson's Bay and extending half way across the great peninsula between that inland sea and the Labrador coast is another vast basin drained by the Whale, Big and East Main rivers. This basin is all heavily timbered with tamarac as far north as the 53d parallel of north latitude, and is said to contain rich mineral deposits consisting of gold and copper. There is still another basin farther to the eastward, drained by the Ungava and Whale rivers, which flow into Ungava Bay at Fort Chimo. Near the mouth of the Ungava River, in the Laurentian formation, there are mountains of pure mica, sufficiently extensive, perhaps, to supply the whole world with that commodity. The streams flowing into Ungava Bay are filled with salmon of the very finest quality, and for several years back two refrigerator steamers have been plying between these waters and the English metropolis in the salmon trade. It is a remarkable fact that with the traps used to catch these valuable fish, a moderate sized steamship can be loaded in a single tide. This basin is also heavily timbered. The upper portion of it has been so for many years back; and the lower portion, extending down to Fort Chimo, has begun to produce timber within the last three-quarters of a century.

In addition to the extensive areas mentioned, there are Southern Alaska and British Columbia. Both possess vast resources in gold, coal, and on agricultural lines.

From these observations the reader must have acquired a pretty good idea of the vast extent of the north country. We have already given the boundaries of an area nearly as large as the whole of the United States, and contained within it are 1,250,000 square miles of the most fertile and productive park prairie and plain region to be found anywhere on the face of the earth. The elevations of this rich plain range from

400 to 4,000 feet above sea level, the lowest winter temperatures prevailing on the highest latitudes, and the highest temperature readings during the same season are, of course, found in the greatest depressions. Most of this vast territory is favorably affected by the Chinook winds which find their way through all the passes of the Rockies north of the 53d parallel, and especially into the Peace River country, greatly improving the winter climate. The cold is very great in the southwestern portions of this plain where the elevations are from 2,500 to 4,000 feet, and the cattle on the ranches in that neighborhood have to be well sheltered during most of the winter. But in the far north, in the neighborhood of Lake Athabasca, and still farther north to Fort Simpson on the Mackenzie River, which is only 750 feet above the level of the sea, sunshine snow-storms are common and the snow melts almost as fast as it falls. In this region cattle may roam at large, winter and summer, without shelter of any kind. The hay cures on the stem and the pasturage is better in December, January and February than during any other months of the year. But of the climate and resources of this vast north country, we shall speak more in detail hereafter.

CHAPTER III.

TRADING POSTS OF THE NORTH.

Trails across the continent in the sub-Arctic belt—Many that have been traveled for a hundred and fifty years—Short cut to the gold fields of the Klondike from Edmonton via Lake Athabaska and the Upper Mackenzie—The quicker and cheaper route—Lis of Northern trading stations—Hints on map study.

It is already well understood by the reader that the object of this volume is to provide an accurate account of the vast extent of territory and rich resources of the Golden North. The foregoing chapters shed some light upon the vast area and physical features of the country. It may now be observed that there is an important sense in which this whole North Land has been settled, though not to any extent developed, during a period reaching back to the middle, and beyond it, of the eighteenth century. There is a chain of trading posts belonging to the Hudson's Bay Company extending from the Atlantic to the eastern borders of Alaska, and covering the whole belt of territory lying between the 55th parallel and the Arctic Circle; and in Alaska, covering the whole of that territory, there are similar trading posts under the control of American companies.

For more than one hundred and fifty years these trading stations have been supplied from three points, namely: Fort Garry, near the mouth of the Red River, York Factory, and Fort Churchill on the western shores of Hudson's Bay. Supplies for the trading posts in Alaska have for many years been distributed from St. Michaels by way of the Yukon and from Sitka for those in the Southern Alaskan district. From the points named the products of the northern region have been shipped to foreign markets. These products formerly consisted of valuable furs, reindeer tongues, oil from the marine mammals, ivory from the walrus, fish, and other commodities. At one time this trade was carried on very extensively, but of late years it has dwindled away, in some portions of the north, to almost nothing. A little over thirty years ago the Hudson's Bay Company sold its interests in the North country to the Canadian Government, reserving certain portions of the lands, and it has since that time become quite as much interested in the colonization and development of the country—in order to realize from its landed interests—as it is in the fur trade.

The Hudson's Bay Company still maintains about one hundred and seventy-five trading posts in the belt mentioned, and it is interesting to note that there are trails, well known to Indian and Esquimo runners, and hunters, and to the Hudson's Bay trading post officials, leading from one to another of these little marts of trade, throughout the entire region. For instance: One may leave Fort Churchill on the western shore of Hudson's Bay and travel by way of Reindeer Lake up the Churchill, across to Lake Athabasca, thence to Great Slave Lake, down the Mackenzie River to Fort Simpson, across the country through one of the passes of the Rockies to the head waters of the Yukon, and down that river to St. Michaels, over a route which has been known and traveled more than a century and a half. Again, one may leave Edmonton, on the north branch of the Saskatchewan River, at the most northern extension of the Canadian Pacific Railway, and follow a well known trail across the height of land, thence to Athabasca River, and across it to the south shores of Little Slave Lake, thence northwestward to Landing at the confluence of the Smoky and Peace rivers, thence by way of the Peace River, the Pine River pass, and down the Skeena to Port Simpson on the Pacific coast; or, from the confluence of the Peace and Smoky rivers, northwestward to the upper Mackenzie and across it through any of the convenient passes of the lower Rocky Mountain ranges of the far north to the Klondike country, and in all of these journeys he will follow trails which have been well known and constantly traveled for more than a century.

By the way, it is the belief of many who have traveled extensively in the far northwest country, that the better and less expensive way of reaching the gold fields of the upper Yukon and Mackenzie rivers is to go by rail to Edmonton, and thence along one of the trails leading overland to any of the mountain passes which extend across the plateau from the southwest branches of the Mackenzie to the southeast tributaries of the Yukon, of which the Klondike is one. Certainly this route can be covered in as short a time as either that by Juneau or the Yukon, while on the other hand, the expense of transporting supplies will not be nearly as great as by any of the Pacific routes.

The Hudson's Bay trading posts of the whole North country, including the trading stations of Alaska, constitute an important feature of that region. The traveler in any of the overland routes always journeys from one trading post to another and follows a well defined trail. He may not always be able to purchase supplies at these stations in large quantities, but the posts are generally pretty well stocked, and those in charge of them are noted for liberality in extending relief and shelter and assistance to persons going through the country. Our knowledge of the North is largely due to the existence of these trading stations, and to the information carried to them by Indian and Esquimo hunters and traders.

It will be an interesting and instructive exercise for the reader to lay before him a reliable map of the North country and to locate thereon the following list of Hudson's Bay trading posts, which comprise all, except temporary winter stations, from the Atlantic to Rampart House, located just above the Arctic circle near the international boundary line between the Canadian northwest and Alaska:

Fort Chippewayan.
Fort McMurray.
Fond du Lac.
Red River.
Fort Vermillion.
Fort Smith.
Fort Resolution.
Fort Dunvegan.
Fort St. John's.
Hudson's Hope.
Battle River.
Lesser Slave Lake.
Whitefish Lake.
Grand Prairie.
Fort Simpson.
Rampart House.
Lapierre's House.
Wabigoon.
Whitefish Bay.
White Dog (Lake Winnipeg).
Trout Lake.
Seine River.
North-West Angle.
Norway House.
Nelson River.
Behrens River.
Grand Rapid.
Poplar River.
Oxford House.
Island Lake.
York Factory.
Severn.
Trout Lake (Keewatin).
Churchill.
Winnipeg.
Lower Fort Garry.
Doghead.
Fort Alexander.
Indian Settlement.
Portage la Prairie.
Isle a la Crosse.
Portage la Loche.
Green Lake (English River).
Souris River.
Cumberland House.
Moose Lake.
Pas.
Pelican Narrows.
Lac du Brochets.
Rapid River.
Grand Rapids.
Calgary.
Edmonton.
Lac la Biche.
Jasper House.
Lac Ste. Anne's.
Victoria.
Battle River.
Peel's River.
Fort Good Hope.
Fort Liard.
Fort Nelson.
Fort Providence.
Fort Rae.
Fort Norman.
Nut Lake.
Manitoba House.
Fairford.
Waterhen River.
Shoal River.
Duck Bay.

Rat Portage.
Fort Frances.
Lac Seul.
Eagle Lake.
Prince Albert.
Carleton House.
Battleford.
South Branch.
Fort Pitt.
Turtle Lake.
Fort a la Corne.
Frog Lake.
Fort Qu'Appelle.
Fort Ellice.
Riding Mountain.
Fort Pelly.
Russell.
Touchwood Hills.
Egg Lake.
Cariboo.
Barkerville.
Quesnel.
New Caledonia.
Stuart's Lake.
Skeena.
Fraser's Lake.
Babine.
Conolly's Lake.
Fort George.
McLeod's Lake.
Montreal.
Michipicoten.
Aquawah River.
Pic.
Nepigon House.
Long Lake.
Red Rock.
Lake Missanabie.
Sand Lake.
Pine Portage.
La Cloche.
Whitefish Lake (Huron).
Mississaque.
Green Lake (Huron).
Wahnapitaeping.
Pagamasing.
Mattawa.
Temiscaminque.
Hunter's Lodge.
Grand Lake.
Barriere.
Trout Lake.
Totogan.
Pembina.
Oak Point.
Moose Factory.
Albany.
Henley.
English River.
Marten's Falls.
Osnaburgh.
Rupert's House.
Woswonaby.
Mechiskim.
Mustassing.
Nichequon.
Eastmain.
Fort George.
Great Whale River.
Little Whale River.
Fort Trial.
Long Portage.
Kinoqumisse.
Matawagaminque.
Natachewan.
New Brunswick.
Victoria.
Massett.

Hazelton.
Fort Langley.
Fort Hope.
Fort Yale.
Kamloops.
Thompson's River.
Temagiminque.
Nepissinque.
Abittibi.
Winawaya.
Weymoutachinque.
Coocache.
Kickendach.
Manoman.
Pointe Blin.
Bersamis.
Seven Islands.
Moisie.
Mungan.
Musquarro.
Rigolet.
North-West River.
Davis Inlet.
Nachoak.
Fort Chimo.
George's River.

One may obtain a vast deal of information as to the character and extent of the country from a carefully prepared map, but in the matter of distances there are some lessons in mathematical geography with which the reader should be familiar before beginning his map studies. One is always inclined to measure distances upon a spherical map by the degrees of latitude and longitude marked thereon. This, however, will prove a very misleading procedure unless the map student is sufficiently acquainted with the decrease in the length of the degrees of longitude on different parallels of latitude. For instance: the length of a degree of longitude on the equator is 69.16 statute miles, whereas, a degree of longitude in latitude 42 is 51.47 statute miles. Again, a degree of longitude on the 60th parallel is but 34.67 statute miles, and a degree of longitude on the 82nd parallel of latitude is but 9.66 statute miles.

The question of distances is deeply involved in a study of the great North, and for the benefit of the reader and student of this volume the following table of lengths, in common land or statute miles of 5,280 feet each, of a degree of longitude in the different latitudes north of the equator is here presented:

Deg. of Lat.	Stat. Miles.	Deg. of Lat.	Stat. Miles
0	69.16	42	51.47
2	69.12	44	49.83
4	68.99	46	48.12
6	68.78	48	46.36
8	68.49	50	44.54
10	68.12	52	42.67
12	67.66	54	40.74
14	67.12	56	38.76
16	66.50	58	36.74
18	65.80	60	34.67
20	65.02	62	32.55
22	64.15	64	30.40
24	63.21	66	28.21
26	62.20	68	25.98
28	61.11	70	23.72
30	59.94	72	21.43
32	58.70	74	19.12
34	57.35	76	16.78
36	56.01	78	14.42
38	54.56	80	12.05
40	53.05	82	9.66

The above table will be useful to those who attempt to determine east and west distances on a map from the meridian lines of longitude. Of course the degrees of latitude are always of the same length no matter on what part of the earth's surface the parallels are drawn.

CHAPTER IV.

THE YUKON DISTRICT—ALASKA.

From Bering Sea to the junction of the Pelly and Lewis rivers—Cereal, vegetable and stock capabilities—The forests and climate—Value of the white spruce.

From the foregoing general observations on the North country, the reader is now prepared to take up the several physical divisions mentioned and to study them more carefully as to character, climate, elevations and resources.

First, as to Alaska and that portion of the Canadian Northwest north of the 60th parallel and east of the great watershed dividing the Yukon and Mackenzie River systems. This interesting stretch of country comprises about 1,500,000 square miles and is physically divided into three principal districts. These may be called the Yukon territory, the Aleutian district and the Sitkan district. The first, which is the more northern territory, is bounded on the south by the Alaskan Mountains, on the east by the Rocky Mountains and by the 60th parallel, which is the northern boundary of British Columbia; on the north by the Arctic Ocean and on the west by Bering Sea and Strait.

The Yukon River proper extends through this territory from Bering Sea to the confluence of the Pelly and Lewis rivers, which is about one hundred and fifty miles east of the international boundary line, and about 1,750 miles from its mouth. The Pelly and Lewis rivers, their many tributaries, and the hundreds of creeks and gulches which drain the mountain region into these tributary streams, throughout this immense gold-bearing territory, reach out over 500 miles further to the east from their junction, and cover over 400 miles of territory north and south.

The character of the country of the Yukon district proper varies from low, rolling and somewhat rocky hills, usually quite easy of ascent, to broad and sometimes marshy plains, extending for many miles on either side of the river, especially for about 100 or 200 miles from the coast. There are no roads leading from the mountains and uplands down to this great river, and but few well defined trails. In fact, the river itself and its tributary streams constitute the highways of the country.

The rocks along the Yukon River and in the whole Yukon district below the junction of the Pelly and Lewis rivers, consist for the most part of conglomerate, sienite, quartzite and sandstone. From the confluence of the two last named rivers to the Rockies, quartzite prevails. This formation and the sands, gravel and dirt overlaying it, are generally more or less auriferous, or gold-bearing.

Over a very large extent of this country, except upon the summits of the higher elevations, the soil is a rich alluvial, composed of very fine sand, mud and vegetable matter, brought down by the river and forming deposits of a considerable depth.

During the winter seasons frost penetrates the soil to the depth of from two to six feet, and in the majority of situations it does not more than half thaw out during the summer months. This, however, is due to the want of sufficient drainage, combined with the non-conductive covering of moss which prevents the hot sun of midsummer from warming the surface to any considerable depth. In locations where the soil is not covered with this moss, and where the drainage is good, as in the extensive areas near the mouth of the river, frost is generally thawed out of the ground completely during the warm season.

It must not be supposed, however, that a layer of frozen ground below the surface, say two or three feet thick, is destructive to cereal or vegetable growth. As a matter of experience in Manitoba and the Canadian

Northwest, east of the Rockies, such has been found to facilitate the growth and ripening development of cereals.

There are along the banks of the Yukon, in the neighborhood of Escholtz Bay, bluffs or banks of apparently solid ice fronting the water. These continuous banks of ice, strange to say, are covered with a heavy layer of soil and vegetable matter, where herbs and shrubs flourish with a luxuriance only equalled in latitudes more than two thousand miles to the southeast.

The lesson to be learned from these facts is that heavy and luxuriant vegetation may exist, develop and ripen above a layer of frozen ground and in the immediate vicinity of permanent ice. Hence it is proper to conclude that a large extent of territory in Alaska, even in this Yukon district, long considered valueless, will yet furnish not only to the trader and fisherman, but also to the farmer, an abundant harvest.

The climate of the interior of the Yukon district differs from that of the sea coast, where the temperature is greatly improved by the vast body of water contained in Bering Sea, and by the many currents from the south bringing warm water from the Pacific, making the winter climate of an extensive region of the coast much milder than that of the interior. The summers, however, owing to the quantity of rain and prevailing cloudy weather of the coast, are cooler and less inviting than those of the interior. Near the coast, the months of May and June are delightful, being sunny, warm and clear. As soon as the snow disappears, and even before it is gone from the summits of the foothills, an immense growth of herbage springs up very rapidly, and large areas, which a few days before presented nothing but a white sheet of snow, are teeming with a rapidly developing vegetation, producing leaves, flowers and fruits in rapid succession.

At St. Michaels, on the coast of Norton Sound, in latitude 63.28; at the Mission, on the Yukon River,

150 miles from its mouth, in latitude 61.47; at Nulato, 450 miles further up the river, in latitude 64.40; and at Fort Yukon, 1,200 miles from the mouth of the river and in latitude 66.34, the mean temperatures for the four seasons of the year are as follows:

Means for	St. Michaels.	Mission.	Nulato.	Ft. Yukon
Spring	29.3	19.62	29.3	14.22
Summer	53.0	59.32	60.0	59.67
Autumn	26.3	36.05	36.0	17.37
Winter	8.6	0.95	—14.0	—23.80
Year	29.3	26.48	27.8	16.92

It must not be supposed, however, that the agricultural capabilities of Alaska are to be measured by mean temperatures alone. Much depends upon the heat of the summer months, the duration of that season and the length of the days of sunshine. At Fort Yukon the thermometer often rises, at noon, not in the direct rays of the sun, to 112 degrees above zero, and in some instances the mercury has been known to rise to 120. It is almost impossible to calculate the rapid growth of vegetation under these conditions. In mid-summer on the upper Yukon, the only relief from the intense heat, under which the vegetation attains an almost tropical luxuriance, is the brief space during which the sun hovers just under the northern horizon.

The annual rainfall of this district is quite large, but not excessive, while the snowfall for November to the end of April will average from three to six feet and sometimes eight feet, although in the district of the upper Yukon, or territory drained by the Pelly and Lewis rivers and their tributaries, the snowfall ranges from two to three and a half feet. There is very little snow near the coast, but in this region high winds prevail, while in the interior there is less wind. The whole country except in the lower valleys is well timbered, and towards spring the gullies and brush-wood are well filled or covered up with snow, and transportation with dogs and sleds is easy and pleasant. The warm sun at noon melts the surface of the snow, which freezes at night and forms a hard crust, rendering snowshoes almost unnecessary. The rainfall is much greater near the coast than it is in the interior. In the months of May, June and part of July, it is bright delightful weather at St. Michaels, and all along the coast, but the remainder of the season, or for four days in the week, at least, it is rainy, until October, when the north winds set in, bringing fine weather. The valley of the lower Yukon is often foggy in the latter part of the summer, but as one ascends the river the climate improves, and the short summer at Fort Yukon is always dry, hot, but pleasant withal, being varied by occasional showers.

The largest and most valuable tree found in the district is the white spruce, which abounds over the whole country, but is always largest in the vicinity of running streams. This tree attains a height of from fifty to one hundred feet, with a diameter at the butt of from three to four feet. The most common size, however, is thirty or forty feet high, with fourteen or eighteen inches at the butt. This wood is white, clear, close and straight-grained, easily worked, light and yet very tough. It is to be greatly preferred over the Oregon pine. For spars it has no superior. It is very durable and many houses twenty years old, built of this timber, still contain a majority of sound logs. These trees decrease in size and grow more sparsely as one approaches Fort Yukon, but they are still large enough for many purposes. The northern limit of this tree is about 66.44 north latitude, and it occupies the same place in the physical development of the country in Alaska as does the tamarac on the southern and western basins of Hudson's and James' bays. In the interior of Alaska the white spruce is found often above the 70th parallel, and as in the north country to the east of the Rocky Mountains, the forests in the Yukon district are steadily pushing their advance towards the shores of the Arctic Ocean. Forests consisting mostly of the spruce are abundant at Fort Yukon in latitude 66.34, and the waters of the Tananah River bring down the largest logs of this tree in the spring freshets. The number of these logs annually floated down the northern Alaskan rivers is almost beyond calçulation. Freshets prevail in the rivers for about three weeks, and although the period of their duration is short, sufficient is brought down to supply the demand of the Arctic coast and Bering Sea, as well as the numerous islands.*

The tree of next importance in the forests of northern Alaska is the birch, which, however, rarely grows over eighteen inches in diameter and forty feet in height. The wood of this tree is hard and tough. The treeless coasts of the territory, as well as the lowlands of the Yukon, are covered in spring with a most luxuriant growth of grass and flowers, including the well known Kentucky bluegrass, which grows luxuriantly as far north as Kotzebue Sound, and, to some extent, at Port Barrow. The wild meadow grass is also abundant and furnishes good, fattening pasturage for cattle. The blue-joint grass also abounds, and sometimes grows four or five feet in height. Its average is three feet.

Grain has never been sown to any extent in the Yukon territory until within the last few years, in which tests have been successfully made in barley and other cereals. Turnips and radishes flourish, and cattle thrive, but require shelter during the long winter months.

The agricultural capabilities of the Yukon territory, though not great, are gradually enlarging and improving, and will be utilized to the great advantage of the inhabitants in the near future.

*** Capt. W. H. Doll.**

The points and posts of interest on the Yukon from St. Michaels to Fort Selkirk, at the junction of the Pelly and Lewis rivers, are: Andreafski, Cogmute, Koserefski, Hamilton's Lodge, Nulato, Weare, Fort Yukon, and Circle City.

CHAPTER V.

UPPER YUKON OR KLONDIKE REGION.

Auriferous districts lying west of the Mackenzie—Territory is duplicated in extent and gold bearing riches on the slopes east of the summit—Three great routes to the Klondike—Reasons why the all-overland route will become most favored.

We now come to consider the most interesting subdivision of the whole north region, the upper Yukon country—the El Dorado of our hopes—that vast extent of country stretching away from the confluence of the Lewis and Pelly rivers to the summit of the watershed of the Mackenzie River, and west of it to Circle City.

This is the Klondike.

This is the auriferous land where gold lies hidden in sand, dirt, gravel and quartz, in quantities sufficiently great to enrich half the people of this nation.

It is a vast country too, all more or less gold-bearing, containing at least 240,000 square miles, and yellow metal probably to the extent of billions of dollars in value.

And let it be stated here and now that this wonderful region to the west of the watershed of the Mackenzie is beyond all question duplicated, both in extent and gold-bearing value, on the eastern slopes of the same watershed in the country of the southwestern tributaries, creeks and gulches of the upper Mackenzie River. Only a small corner of the Klondike country has yet been explored. There are hundreds of river branches, creeks and gulches, in that section yet without a name, and unknown to the hardy miner-pioneer. It will no doubt consume the whole of 1898 to complete anything like a perfect exploration of this territory; and during the coming eighteen months the reader may be prepared to hear of more wonderful discoveries of gold, in both placer and quartz mines, in this region, than have yet been reported. Not only so, but the mining prospector and the gold hunter will either cross the watershed of the Mackenzie, and develop the rich gold fields of the more eastern district, or enter it overland by way of the northwest trails from Edmonton. The data at hand, including the writer's own observations in that country, fully justify the statement that there is just as much gold east of the watershed as there is west of it. This applies not only to the far north, but to the more southerly areas in northern British Columbia south of the 60th parallel. This statement is supported by the natural history survey reports of the Canadian Government as well as the information gained by explorers and surveyors sent out from time to time under the auspices of the Department of the Interior of the Dominion Government.

The gold-bearing district on the eastern slopes of the Mackenzie and Yukon watershed contains an area of 250,000 square miles, and like its neighboring district on the slopes west of the summit, it is not only richly gold-bearing, but contains inexhaustible deposits of silver and coal.

It is probably idle at this time to attempt to forecast the future of this wonderful region, but it may be said that the paying gold discoveries which have already been made cannot possibly yield up all their treasure in a few months and be forgotten, nor give way to something more interesting in any near future. On the contrary, one is warranted in the belief that the five or ten thousand gold hunters now in that territory will be increased to fifty or one hundred thousand in 1898, and possibly to two hundred thousand before the close of the present century.

The vast cereal, vegetable, stock-raising and dairy possibilties of the alluvial plains which lie on the one hand in the mighty valleys eastward of the auriferous

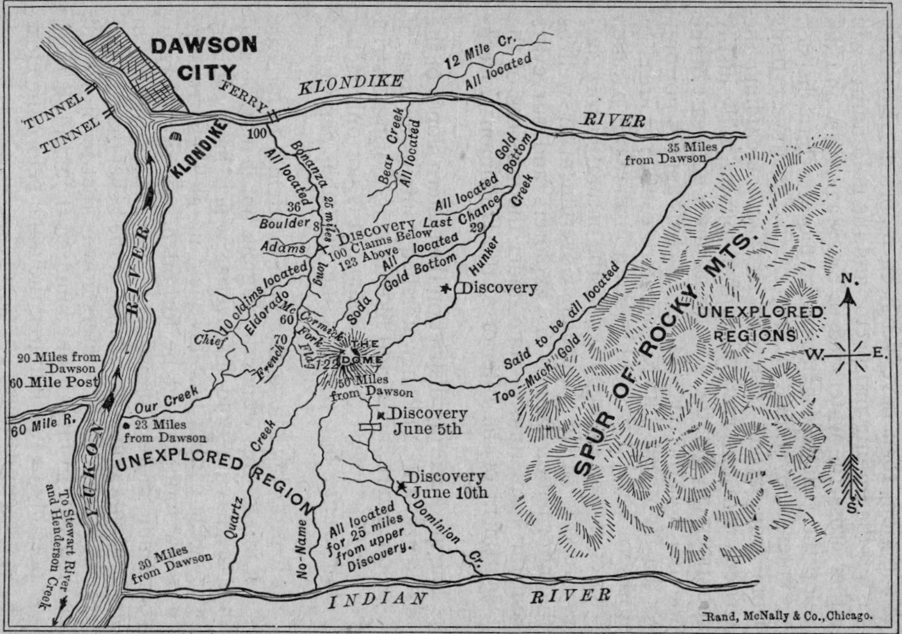

MAP OF THE UPPER YUKON AND KLONDIKE REGIONS.

slopes on this side the great watershed, and on the Alaskan lowlands to the west, will in a short time be sufficiently developed to abundantly supply all the gold, silver and coal diggers that may go into the mining districts. Hence it will not always be necessary to transport supplies, at the cost of two or three times their value, from southeastern markets, to support the treasure hunters of the north. The time is not far distant when the adjacent fertile plains will produce all that will be necessary, and the miner will be required to transport from eastern markets only tools and implements necessary for the proper development of the diggings.

The upper Yukon, of which we are speaking, lies wholly within British territory. In fact it may be divided, for convenience, from the district of the Yukon proper by the international boundary line, which in this region lies along the 141st degree of longitude, from the Arctic Ocean to the northern base of Mt. St. Elias.

Between this international boundary line which crosses the Yukon where Seventy Mile Creek enters that stream, and at the junction of the Pelly and Lewis rivers, there are, in this order, from the northwest, Fort Cudahy, Forty Mile Post, Old Fort Reliance, Dawson City, and most of the mining camps now in active operation, including those on the Klondike and the creeks flowing into it. Fort Selkirk is located at the junction of the rivers last named, and there the Yukon ceases as such. This is in longitude 137.30 west in the British Northwest territory. The Pelly River, starting from this point, reaches far to the westward, taking its rise in the almost innumerable creeks and gulches in the Rocky Mountains. The Lewis River reaches far away to the southeast, taking its rise northeast of Chilcat Pass, in a large number of long narrow lakes imbedded in that mountainous region. The head waters of both of these rivers comprise an undefinable and only very partially explored region of creeks and brooks. Hundreds of these are yet without names, having never been visited by white men, but that which is known of the district in a general way, as to its auriferous formation, fully justifies the statement, on a geological basis, that the whole country thereabouts is about equal, one section with the other, as to its gold-bearing resources. Dr. Dawson, chief of the Natural History and Geological Survey of Canada; William Ogilvie, of the Geographical Survey of the same country, and many others have made official reports which justify this general statement as to the resources of the whole region. Dr. Dawson verified the discoveries of coal and silver in that neighborhood, and also far to the south of it.

Both the Pelly and Lewis are large rivers. The latter is the best known, having been used for the past six years as the highway from Southern Alaska to the gold diggings of the Yukon in the neighborhood of the boundary line. Its length from Lake Lindeman, one of its chief sources, to its junction with the Pelly, is about 375 miles. As already stated, the river lies wholly in British territory. This applies to the greater portion of the lakes which constitute its source. Some of these lakes, however, extend into Southern Alaska, to a point not far north of Dyea.

The Pelly River takes its rise in and about Dease Lake, near the head waters of the Stikine River. It has a length of fully 500 miles before uniting with the Lewis to form the Yukon. The latter river at the junction, and for miles below, varies from three-quarters of a mile to a mile in width. For many miles along the northern bank there is a solid wall of lava. For convenience we may refer to the whole gold-bearing region west of the Rocky Mountains and down the Yukon to the international boundary line, and even beyond it, as the Klondike country.

There are three general routes by which this new El Dorado may be reached. One is a all-water route by way of St. Michaels and along the great Yukon River, the longest and, at present, probably the most expensive journey. This may be called the summer route, for the river is not navigable during the winter season. The second route, and that which is now being most generally traveled, is by Juneau and Dyea, through the several passes to the Lewis River beyond the mountains, the principal of these being the Chilcat and Chilkoot passes. These passes are being rapidly improved, so that it is possible to make the journey, though with considerable hardship, during the winter season. The third route has not yet been traveled to any extent by gold hunters, but it is predicted that it will, in a short time, become the most favored highway by which the gold-bearing regions of the great North will be reached. It is from Edmonton, in the Canadian Northwest, by way of the Athabasca, Great Slave Lake and the upper Mackenzie and across the watershed to the head waters of the Pelly or the McMillan, the latter being a northeasterly branch of the Pelly. One reason, and an important one, why this is likely to become a favored route is because of the well-grounded belief that gold exists in quantities equally as great east of the watershed, on the upper creeks and tributaries of the Mackenzie, as on the western slopes, or in the Klondike region.

Of course the trip is one of difficulties, taxing the endurance and nerve of the traveler, no matter which route is taken. Only persons can expect to make the journey successfully who can endure the work of packing supplies over the precipitous and somewhat pathless mountains, towing boats against strong currents, and sleeping anywhere night overtakes them, and in the summer season, fighting the veritable pestilence of gnats and mosquitoes. However, the climate is unequaled for health in both summer and winter, provided one enjoys anything like reasonable supplies of the necessaries of life in that region.

But as to transportation facilities, there will no doubt be great improvements within the next few months. Wagon-roads and trails will be constructed through the coast range mountains. More commodious steamers will be placed on lakes and rivers, passable roads will be constructed over the northwest route, and the whole vast upper country on both sides of the Rockies will be made reasonably accessible to all who desire to enter it. Then thousands will flock there. The writer of this book, who has traveled extensively over the region and acquired a considerable knowledge of its wonderful resources, predicts that in ten years there will be a population of over 250,000 in these territories.

CHAPTER VI.

UPPER YUKON OR KLONDIKE REGION.

(Continued.)

Pioneers of the Klondike country—Administration of mining laws, tariff regulations and homestead entry rules extended to the district by the Canadian Government—Explorations of Dr. Dawson and Surveyor Ogilvie—Increase of mining camps.

Continuing our account of the upper Yukon or Klondike country, the work becomes partly historical and partly descriptive. We find that the first representatives of civilization to enter the region were the traders of the Hudson's Bay Company. In the year 1840 a Mr. Campbell was sent out by Sir George Simpson to explore the upper Liard, one of the branches of the Mackenzie River, and to cross the watershed in search of any rivers flowing to the westward. After ascending the river to its head waters, he had no difficulty in crossing one of the many convenient passes of the Rocky Mountain range to the head waters of the Pelly River. Thence he descended the Pelly to the confluence of the Lewis. From this point he returned, his men having become discouraged by reports of the hostile character of the Wood Indians encamped near there. From these reports he represented that the lower portion of the river was inhabited by a large tribe of cannibals. In 1847 Fort Yukon was established at the mouth of the Porcupine River on the northern banks of the Yukon by A. H. Murray, another representative of the Hudson's Bay Company. It was in 1848 that Campbell established Fort Selkirk at the junction of the Pelly and Lewis rivers. This fort was plundered and destroyed four years later by the coast Indians. At present only its ruins remain. It was at one time one of the most important trading posts of the Hudson's Bay Company west of the Rocky Mountains.

Coming down to more recent dates, it will be remembered that in 1869, two years after Alaska was acquired by the United States Government, the Hudson's Bay Company's officers and traders were expelled from Fort Yukon by our Government, it having been determined by astronomical observations that the post was located within United States territory. At this time the Hudson's Bay Company's representatives left Fort Yukon, ascended the Porcupine River to a point which they believed to be within British jurisdiction, where they established Rampart House; but as ill-luck would have it, the international boundary line was further determined in 1890, and the new trading station was found to be twenty miles within Uncle Sam's domain. Therefore, in 1891, the post was moved twenty miles farther up the river, where it was located on British territory.

According to the best information at hand, the next people to enter the Klondike country were Harper and McQuestion. They established several trading posts, most of which they afterwards abandoned; later Mr. Harper located as a trader at Fort Selkirk, and Mr. McQuestion entered the employ of the Alaska Commercial Company at Circle City, which is a distributing point for a vast region of territory.

In 1882 quite a number of miners entered the Yukon country by the Taiya Pass, which was then the best and most traveled route. It is still largely used, and is said to be shorter than any of the other passes, though it is by no means the lowest. It will be remembered that in 1883 Lieut. Schwatka went into the Yukon country through this pass, and descended the Lewis and Yukon rivers to Bering Sea. In 1887 the Canadian Government fitted out an expedition, having for its object the exploration of the far northwest territory of Canada, which is drained by the Pelly and

Lewis rivers. This expedition was entrusted to Dr. George M. Dawson, then, as now, the chief director of the Geological and Natural History Survey of the Canadian Dominion. His chief assistant in the work was Dominion Land Surveyor William Ogilvie, from whose pen the people of this country have had the most recent official information regarding the gold fields of the Klondike country. Mr. Ogilvie, who has long been known in Canada as a Dominion Land Surveyor, now ranks equal with Dr. Dawson himself as an explorer of the far north country, especially of that portion of it along the northern Rocky Mountain summit and the slopes on either side of it. Dr. Dawson devoted the whole of that season to exploring, locating and defining the lakes and rivers of the upper Yukon region, and Mr. Ogilvie remained in the country for two years gathering geological and topographical information concerning the country lying adjacent to the 141st degree of longitude, which is the international boundary line, and the country east of it.

This expedition found that the whole country as far as they traveled over it contained valuable gold mines, and they were surprised at meeting at least 300 miners who were at work digging and washing out the gold. Mr. Ogilvie, by a series of observations, determined the point at which the Yukon River is crossed by the international boundary line, and also that at which Forty Mile Creek is crossed by the same; and this survey proved that the place which had then been selected as a convenient point for the distribution of supplies for the various mining camps, namely, Fort Cudahy, which is situated where Forty Mile Creek enters the Yukon, was in British Canadian territory. Even at that date it was discovered that the greater proportion of the mines being worked was on the British side. Since that date the best paying mines have been discovered still further to the east, and it is evident, from the official and other reports at hand, that the further east the prospecting is conducted the greater the rewards to those engaged in that work. As before intimated, the reports of Dr. Dawson which cover a period of more than twenty years, support the belief that the most productive gold deposits will yet be found considerably to the east of the Klondike, and even beyond the summit of the mountains, on the eastern slopes.

The number of persons who had entered the Klondike country to engage in mining had reached over 1,000 up to the year 1895, and the additions to that number between 1895 and 1896 were considerable. During the present year there has, of course, been a very large increase to the mining population.

We learn from Canadian official reports that for many years subsequent to the retirement of the Hudson's Bay Company from Alaska, the Alaska Commercial Company enjoyed a monopoly of the trade of the Yukon, carrying into the country and delivering at various points along the river, without regard to the international boundary line or to customs laws, such commodities and supplies as were required for the prosecution of the fur trade, and later on, of placer mining. Of course these were the only two industries known to the country.

It may be noted here that with the discovery of gold in larger quantities, there followed the organization of a company to compete with the Alaska Commercial Company, known as the North American Transportation and Trading Company, having its headquarters in Chicago, and its chief trading center at Fort Cudahy, on the Yukon. This company has now been engaged in this trade for about five years, and owns and operates lines of steamers plying between Pacific ports and St. Michaels at the mouth of the Yukon, and trading to Juneau and Dyea in southeastern Alaska. By means of these steamers the Company transports merchandise to the first mentioned point, trans-shipping it into river steamers at the mouth of the Yukon to points inland, notably to Fort Cudahy at the western borders of the Klondike country. This route has been the principal highway of the carrying trade of the upper Yukon, but more recently importations of some value consisting of miners' supplies and their tools have reached the Klondike district from Juneau by way of Dyea and the mountain passes to the chain of waterways leading therefrom to the Lewis River, thence to Cudahy on the Yukon.

Up to within a year past, although civil government had been fully established by the United States in all parts of Alaska, no governmental authority of any kind had been set up in any portion of the Canadian Northwest between the international boundary line and the Rocky Mountains north of the 60th parallel. As a result importations of considerable value were taken into the country without the payment of duty, except that, in 1894, the North American Transportation and Trading Company paid customs charges on the merchandise which it carried into the country, to the amount of $3,240. Recently, however, the Canadian Government has extended its administration, both as to the collecting of customs and the enforcing of mining regulations and homestead laws in that territory. The officials sent out there to administer these branches of the Canadian Government are now backed up by a considerable force of the Canadian Northwest mounted police. As a result, customs duties are being collected on merchandise taken across the international boundary line, the Canadian mining laws are being enforced, and the door has been opened for the settlement of Canadian lands under the free entry system, as fast as they can be surveyed into townships and sections for that purpose. The miners have made some complaints as to the alleged excessive customs charges by the Canadian officials, but in the main, those who have gone into the country, and those contemplating going, will appreciate the value of the fact that the Canadian Government has taken ample steps for the enforcement of law, maintenance of order and the administration of justice in the upper Yukon territory. Without this step the placer mining of gold, which is now being carried forward on an extensive scale east of the international boundary, would be attended with great danger and much insecurity. It was clearly in the interests of humanity, and absolutely necessary for the security and safety of the lives and property of the citizens of the United States as well as of Canadian subjects.

The exploration and surveys made by Dr. Dawson and Mr. Ogilvie in the upper Yukon region in 1887 and the years immediately following are among the most important official documents describing the topography and resources of that country, and form the basis of nearly everything that has been printed concerning it since. Mr. Ogilvie returned to the northwest and continued his explorations and surveys, of which we have printed accounts as late as the latter part of January of the present year. Some of his letters to the Canadian Minister of the Interior, dated in the latter part of 1896 and the early portion of the present year, give almost sensational accounts of gold discoveries in the Klondike. This fully substantiates the unofficial reports which have come from the miners themselves by way of letters to friends in different parts of this country.

CHAPTER VII.

THE ALEUTIAN DISTRICT—ALASKA.

A mountainous and volcanic country—Broad meadows and sloping hillsides capable of cereal and stock-raising development—A mountainous country—Altitude limit of vegetation.

Before proceeding to further details concerning the gold regions of the great north country, let us turn aside to glance at the interesting features of the other physical divisions of Alaska. This step leads us to the Aleutian district, which comprises the Aleutian Islands and part of the Peninsula of Alaska. Owing to the presence of trees, the Island of Kadiak and those adjacent belong rather to the Sitkan division.

These islands contain many high mountains, some of them volcanic, a few still showing activity by emitting smoke and steam. Between them and the sea are extensive rolling hills and meadows. Much of the soil is rich, consisting of vegetable mold and dark-colored clays, with here and there light loam formed of decomposed rocks and rich in tertiary fossils. In many parts of these meadows the drainage is insufficient, but may be improved at little cost. In some places the soil is composed of decayed volcanic products, but much of this is rich and productive.

From the evidence at hand one is warranted in the statement that vast areas of this soil will produce cereals and vegetables. The mercury ranges from zero to 75 above. The following statistics will show the range of the thermometer, by means, for four years within the last decade, although there are readings at hand extending as far back as 1830:

7 A. M.	1 P. M.	9 P. M.	Ex. Heat.	Ex. Cold.
35	38	34	77	Zero.
36	40	34	64	7
39	42	38	77	7
38	41	36	76	5

The average for the four years is 37 above at 7 A. M.; 40.5 above at 1 P. M.; 36 above at 9 P. M. The average extreme heat for the four years is 77 above, and the extreme cold for the same period is zero.

The average weather statistics for seven years out of the last ten is as follows: January, 11 all-clear days; 111 half-clear days; 95 all-cloudy days; February, 9 all-clear days, 86 half-clear days, and 103 all-cloudy days; March, 3 all-clear days, 112 half-clear days, 102 all-cloudy days; April, 4 all-clear days, 104 half-clear days, 102 all-cloudy days; May, 2 all-clear days, 105 half-clear days, and 104 all-cloudy days; June, 6 all-clear days, 118 half-clear days, 99 all-cloudy days; July, no all-clear days, 118 half-clear days, and 99 all-cloudy days; August, 5 all-clear days, 106 half-clear days, 106 all-cloudy days; September, 2 all-clear days, 107 half-clear days, 100 all-cloudy days; October, 2 all-clear days, 115 half-clear days, 100 all-cloudy days; November, 3 all-clear days, 88 half-clear days, 119 all-cloudy days; December, 6 all-clear days, 116 half-clear days, 95 all-cloudy days. The total for the seven years records 53 all-clear days, 1,263 half-clear days, and 1,235 all-cloudy days.

It will be seen that there is a great proportion of cloudy and half-cloudy weather in this district. The average number of rainy days for seven years in this district is 150, but it will be seen that the precipitation is light, as during that whole period the rainfall measured but 45 inches. This is about the average for the whole district in question.

There is no timber of any kind on the islands except shrub, but the grasses in this climate—which is warmer than that of the Yukon district, and drier than that of the Sitkan—attain almost an incredible luxuriance. For example, Unalaska, in the vicinity of Captain's Harbor, abounds in fertile meadows, with a climate better adapted for haying than many districts 2,000 miles southeast of it. Here and in this vicinity cattle may be raised by the hundreds of thousands, without trouble or any considerable expense. They become remarkably fat, and the beef is tender and delicate, rarely surpassed by any stock-fed beef. The milk is of excellent quality and dairy products may be easily made profitable in this quarter.

It may be noted that the best and most available arable lands lie near the coast, formed by the debris of the mountains and valleys mingling with the sea sands, which together form a remarkably rich soil, excellently adapted for cereal and vegetable culture. These things, considered together with the extraordinarily favorable climate, warrant the statement that these broad meadows and sloping, sunny hillsides, will produce good crops under the thrifty hand of enterprise, while on the rolling meadows stock raising and dairying may be carried on with great profit.

The broad areas are all cleared for the plow, and cultivation may proceed as on the prairies of any of the northwestern states. Many of the grasses found on these meadows are cereal-like, and their nature leads one to infer that oats and barley will thrive and ripen in this quarter excellently. The great length of the days and the many hours of sunshine during the summer months, as compared with the districts thousands of miles to the southeast, go very far to warrant the belief that the climate is capable of producing almost all kinds of cereals, though the early heavy frosts may somewhat interfere with ripening wheat harvests.

From the best information obtainable from Russian traders, and others, it may be said that potatoes may be cultivated on almost all the Aleutian Islands, and upon the rolling meadows and sloping hillsides of the mainland. At False Pass, or Isanotski Strait, potatoes have been raised and the seed preserved for planting from year to year. The products of the islands to the westward of this district are about the same as those of Unalaska. Turnips grow very large in size, and are excellent in quality. In this district vegetation ceases about 2,000 feet above the level of the sea. It is impossible, from the data at hand, to estimate the extent of the productive areas of the Aleutian territory, but they are sufficiently great to support a considerable population.

CHAPTER VIII.

SITKAN DISTRICT—ALASKA.

Channels, natural canals, rivers and lakes—The water highways of the country—Great timber resources of Southern Alaska—Wild berries abundant—Pest of mosquitoes and flies—Stock and agriculture.

As we have defined it, from physical features, the Sitkan district of Alaska includes the mainland and the islands from the southern boundary of the peninsula, and also Kadiak and the adjacent islands. The surface of this part of the country is rugged and mountainous in the extreme. It is only in the northern portion that one meets with arable lands that are level and adapted to cultivation. Small patches are found in the southern portion, here and there, but not extensive enough for any but very small farms. As a rule the mountains descend precipitously into the sea, with their steep sides covered with dense and almost impenetrable forests, and their summits, in many cases, crowned with eternal snow and ice.

Channels and natural canals constitute the highways of the country, and these are so numerous and intricate, and penetrate the region so completely, that they afford means of communication with all sections. The elevations average about 1,500 feet above these channels. Here and there a wide, glittering, mammoth glacier stands out picturesquely in some ravine, contrasting strangely with the dense foliage on either side of it.

The soil is principally alluvial, with substrata of gravel and clay. That of Cook's Inlet and Kadiak is of the same character, but from a mixture of volcanic sand, and an underlying of limestone stratum, it is lighter and drier and better adapted for cultivation.

In the southern part of this district there is little beside timber, from an agricultural point of view. At Sitka a considerable variety of vegetables do fairly well. Turnips, beans, peas, carrots, beets, lettuce and radishes flourish. Potatoes are small and do not reach a healthy maturity. This is owing to the excessive moisture. Cabbages grow luxuriantly, but do not head properly. Cereals are not successful to any extent in this locality. Cattle, however, may be successfully kept, and the dairy product is excellent. Kadiak and Cook's Inlet, northeast of Fort Alexander, have, comparatively, colder winters and drier and warmer summers than the islands and coasts to the south. Here haying can be successfully carried on. The native grasses are good for fodder, whether cut and cured, or on the stem. Barley and oats have been successfully raised in this neighborhood, and the evidence we have indicates that cereals may be raised with considerable profit.

There is an abundance of wood in this neighborhood, but it is not to be found on the lowlands, which for the greater part are bare of both brush and trees. The summer climate in the neighborhood of Cook's Inlet and Kadiak, unlike that of Sitka, furnishes an excellent haying season. There are broad valleys from which an extensive supply of hay, consisting of native grasses, can be annually secured, and this industry may be developed to almost any extent. The cattle existing here are fat and healthy, and the milk is abundant. The butter is yellow and remarkably rich. Potatoes do well in this neighborhood—much better than at Sitka, but do not grow very large. Cattle were first brought to this district by the Russian-American Company, and have been maintained there ever since in a thriving condition. It may be said, therefore, that the stock-raising capabilities, and the possibilities of dairy products in Alaska are more than sufficient for the needs of any population that is likely ever to inhabit the country. At present, however, the great

4

agricultural staple of the southern Sitkan district is timber. Yellow cedar is the finest tree of these forests, and the most profitable wood of the Pacific coast. The next in order is the Sitka spruce, or white pine, which is well known in the lumber trade of the coast. Like the yellow cedar, it attains a large size, and is remarkable for its straight and beautifully tapering trunk. This wood is not as durable as yellow cedar, but is valuable for many purposes. Hemlock also abounds in many sections. So does the balsam fir, and a considerable variety of less noteworthy trees. In Kadiak the growth of timber is confined to the eastern valleys and slopes of the islands, but it is gradually extending all over its surface, except upon the highest summits. The largest sized trees seen there are three feet in diameter and 90 to 100 feet in height. The wooded districts comprise the whole of the Alexandrian Archipelago, and the mainland of the North Lituya Bay. From this point to Prince William's Sound the country is fairly well timbered.

And now, speaking of the physical features of Alaska, as a whole, it is not so large a country in area as some suppose. It contains, in the aggregate, a little less than 600,000 square miles, and is pre-eminently a land of mountains, streams, and lakes. It may be said that, while the Yukon territory does not present extended agricultural resources, its stock-raising capabilities, provided cattle have good winter shelter, are considerable. Nevertheless the future settlers of that vast country may have an abundance of milk, butter, fresh beef and fresh vegetables, if they use the skill and do the work necessary to produce them. During the summer months cattle may roam and fatten on the meadows and slopes and hillsides, and ample fodder, consisting of the perennial grasses, may be gathered for their winter supplies.

In the Aleutian district, of course, the greatest extent of arable land is found. In the northern part of the Sitkan territory the climate is most favorable for agriculture and stock-raising. Indeed, the capabilities of this district and the islands mentioned are much better than have heretofore been reported. Oats and barley, wheat and rye, and a very wide range of vegetables will succeed well on these islands. There is now no doubt of the great stock-raising capabilities of this section of the country. Sheep, goats and swine may do well, but of this experiments have not yet furnished us any reliable information.

A great variety of berries abound in unlimited quantities, both in the Yukon and Aleutian territories, and in the northern Sitkan district. It is believed that fruit trees may be successfully cultivated in the drier sections of the territory mentioned.

The soil product of the southern Sitkan district consists entirely in timber. No better lumber district can well be imagined, and it is interlaced everywhere with means of water transportation. The mountain sides are so steep that slides for delivering the timber to the watercourses can easily be made. Once afloat, it is readily formed into rafts and towed to mill or market, as may be desired.

One of the most remarkable characteristics of Alaska is the network of rivers and lakes and channels that intersect its surface, and that offers a most available means of transportation. In fact, land travel is almost impossible in many parts of the territory. Only the savages travel by land. The whites go by water almost exclusively, except where they are forced to use convenient passes and portages in making the distances between the rivers and lakes. In the more northern regions—between the mountain ranges—are vast areas of meadows, sloping uplands and bogs, and these are dotted with thousands of lakes, large and small, and threaded in all directions by innumerable rivers and channels.

Beginning at the south the Sitkine is the first stream of large size. This river has become well known on account of the gold diggings on its banks, all of which, however, are in British territory. It is over 250 miles in length and is navigable only by small boats, except during the spring freshets. The north fork, about 40 miles long, rises on the east of Bald Mountain, near the headwaters of the Yukon. A small stream called the Taku flows into a glacier arm of St. Stephen's Strait. Chilkoot, a much larger river, enters the northern extremity of Lynn channel, its general direction being from the north. From its upper waters one passes through the Chilkoot Pass, and by means of lakes and rivers and portages, reaches Lewis River, one of the great tributaries of the Yukon.

The Yukon can be reached from Norton sound by way of Unalakeik and Antrokakat rivers, or by way of the Kaltag. The latter is the usual route from St. Michaels. The Yukon River also connects by way of the Koynkuk with Kotzebue Sound; and it is now well known that there are routes of travel between the north tributaries of the Yukon or the Noatak, and many of the rivers that empty into the Arctic Ocean.

The Yukon is a mighty river, larger than the Mississippi, and empties about one-third more water into Bering Sea every hour than does the Father of Waters into the Gulf of Mexico. The sea is very shallow at the mouth of this river, varying in depth from two to three fathoms for 50 miles out. It is a mournful, desolate country to the traveler, and as he ascends the mighty stream there are vast areas on either side of low, boggy country, covered everywhere with a mountainous cloak of willows and rank grasses. Wherever the banks raise to any considerable height they are being constantly undermined and washed away by the floods. So precipitate are the landslides caused in this way, that at times travelers are fortunate to escape with their lives. This is the general character of the country until Kusilvak is reached, and until the bluffs at Andriewsky and Chatinakh give evidence that all the land of Alaska is not under water.

The Yukon impresses one as a vast inland sea with

expansive, water-charged, boggy areas on either side as far up as 700 or 800 miles above its mouth. There are many points at which this river extends to a breadth of 20 miles from shore to shore, even as high up as 800 miles above St. Michaels. For over 2,000 miles, or up to a considerable distance above the junction of the Lewis and the Pelly, the river is navigable for flat-bottomed steamers, of say 500 tons each. White River, a portion of whose waters flow through Alaskan territory, empties into the Yukon on the British side. Forty Mile Creek, and Birch and Beaver creeks join the river between Fort Yukon and Dawson City. During the summer months the whole population, native and civilized, excepting, of course, the miners, flock to the many rivers and lakes, attracted by the myriads of salmon, which they catch, dry and cure for the winter's stock of food. During this season the banks of the river are lined with the camps of the fishermen, who project their basket traps far out into the eddies of the streams.

One of the natural features of Alaska amounts to a veritable pestilence. This consists of the clouds of bloodthirsty mosquitoes, and poisonous black flies. Swarms of these pests fairly darken the sky, and often render life miserable to the traveler, who is obliged to cover his face even in the hottest weather in order to shield himself from his tormentors. They infest the country from May to September. They breed in the vast network of slough and swamp. Perhaps the most discouraging feature of the whole country is presented in a truthful report of this almost intolerable infliction. The way they swarm in rear and front, and on every side, and the torture they inflict on the explorers, is beyond all adequate description. The traveler who exposes his face will very soon lose his natural appearance. From their stings and bites the eyelids swell up and close, and the face becomes one mass of lumps and fiery pimples.

The glaciers, and other ice phenomena of Alaska,

will be considered in connection with the entire glacier regions of the great north country, and, with these exceptions, we shall now bid adieu to Alaska so far as its physical features and agricultural and stock-raising capabilities are concerned, and turn our attention once more to the Golden North, lying east of the international boundary line. We shall return to Alaska later, however, to study its seal and other fisheries, its furs and its gold fields, and to speak of its educational growth, government, and general industries.

CHAPTER IX.

UPPER YUKON—LEWIS RIVER.

From Lake Bennett to the head of the Lewis—Down the Lewis to the Yukon—A country of lakes and rivers—The Klondike region proper—Its extent—Rich gold discoveries eastward from the Klondike—Dr. Dawson's opinion of the Klondike—Surveyor Oglivie's explorations.

The reader is now invited to leave Alaska behind for the present, and all together, so far as its physical features and natural resources are concerned, and to accompany the writer into that golden northland lying between the international boundary line and the sources of the Mackenzie. We have already seen much of this country, but must now study it at greater length, not only from the standpoint of its natural features, but also with a view to the development of its gold and other mineral resources.

It has already been intimated in this volume that the gold discoveries of the Klondike are likely to be eclipsed or many times duplicated by equal or richer strikes in the vast country to the east of that immediate district, and even beyond the watershed, among the many creeks and river-branches on the eastern slopes of the Rockies, and throughout the foothills at their base. This statement has been several times repeated for the purpose of impressing the reader with its importance. It has gone out from some quarters that all the paying sections or claims of the Klondike, have already been taken up or staked out, and that there are more miners in the country than there are paying gold claims to be worked. This is sheer nonsense.

Dr. G. M. Dawson, president of the Geological section of the British Association for the Advancement of Science, and chief director of the natural history and geological survey of the Dominion of Canada, who has traveled more extensively throughout the upper Yukon and the upper Mackenzie regions than any other explorer, with the possible exception of William Ogilvie, gave his opinion of the extent of the gold, and mineral deposits generally, of the far northwest, a few days ago at Toronto, Ontario.

Dr. Dawson, although a man of conservative views on almost all subjects, has become an enthusiast on the question of the resources of the Golden North. Speaking of the Klondike country, he said:

"The Klondike has a glorious future, a period to grow bright with the luster of unlimited gold, white with the sheen of enormous quantities of silver and glittering with the brilliancy of hundreds of valuable mineral deposits."

This is the opinion of an expert; but of course it is the language of an enthusiast. It is seldom that one hears such extravagant words from the tongue of a geologist of such eminence as Dr. Dawson, but it is impossible for one who is able to read lessons in natural history from the rocks and the borders of rivers and lakes, to travel through the north land, comprehending its wonderful resources as he must, without becoming enthusiastic, and writing and talking in extravagant terms. Here he beholds a country greater in its capabilities of sustaining a population in high latitudes than any other, in any part of the earth. And in addition to this, he is inspired by the presence of vast deposits of precious metals, and by the existence of inexhaustible coal areas.

On the occasion referred to Dr. Dawson made the following interesting and instructive statement:

"Ten years ago I was in the Klondike region as the head of the Royal Survey of the Dominion. At that time the gold-producing qualities of the locality were but little known, and we did not pay especial attention to the locality now known as the Klondike. Our survey included the country drained by the Upper Yukon River, however. We spent one complete summer there. There was a little bar-mining in the rivers, but no great strikes had been made, although just after we left the richness of Forty Mile Creek was found out.

"Speaking on the general characteristics of the region, I should not hesitate to say it is extremely rich in gold. It is like other great mining districts in that the alluvial metal washed down by the streams has been first discovered and collected. But the mountains from which these streams rise must also be rich in gold. There, some day, the great lodes and veins of auriferous quartz will be found and worked, while stamp mills and plants of machinery will be scattered thickly about the mountains. But this quartz must yet be discovered.

"The western part of British Columbia in the neighborhood of Alaska is a region of extraordinarily complex and varied geological conditions. Our survey, of course, merely noted the general features in evidence there. It would take years of labor to complete the task down to the details. But all kinds of minerals, judging from what we saw, are certain to be discovered there, and, while I am unwilling to predict special finds of any one metal, I have no doubt but that all the more common ones will be found in abundance. Already, silver bearing lead ores have been found, and others are certain to follow. I have no doubt but that some day the Klondike will be a great silver-mining field.

"As for the story published in the newspapers of the discovery of a great petroleum lake surrounded by hills of coal, it is a joke to a scientific man. I not only do not think there is any such, but think none will ever be found. But coal does exist in the Klondike region. I found it there myself.

"The Yukon is not such a bad country as is imagined by a great many people, except in winter. The summer climate is good, though it does not last very long. The country is pretty and green, and pleasant to work in. But the winters are long and extremely cold. Altogether, the weather conditions are likely to prove far from being rigorous enough to prevent the mineral development of the region.

"The task is a tremendous one. With the extremely large area to be covered and the difficulties in the way of locomotion and transportation, it is going to require considerable time and great labor to thoroughly develop the region. But such great finds of auriferous gold as those recently made, give rise to the belief that the coming work of development will be extraordinarily profitable."

In further proof of the rich gold deposits eastward from the Klondike, and in support of the contention that the farther the prospector penetrates the foothills of the western, and even the eastern slopes of the Mackenzie watershed, the richer gold strikes he will meet with, the following information is submitted, gleaned from a letter sent out by one of the miners from Dawson City, under date of June 22, 1897.

A summary of this letter is to the effect that "A strike that is credited with showing fabulously rich dirt has been made on an unnamed creek 60 miles above Klondike. Forty-seven pounds of gold were taken from the hole, and there has been a rush of the luckless ones from Klondike to the new diggings. News of the discovery reached Juneau on August 7 in a letter written by James O'Brien to W. H. Hindle. O'Brien, in his brief letter, declares that six of the streams tributary to the Klondike have proved richer than the most sanguine had predicted, and that the output in the new field more than redeemed the golden promise of the Klondike. O'Brien says that the news of the find above Klondike had only reached Dawson City, but that he saw one steamer pull out for the new diggings with 170 men on board."

And so it will be. Still richer gold fields will be met

with as the mining progresses eastward, until placer and quartz will be profitably carried on everywhere, on both sides of the Rockies in that golden northland.

An account of the expedition to the far northwest in 1887 and the years following, headed by Dr. Dawson and Mr. Ogilvie, has already been given. However, Mr. Ogilvie returned to the country in 1890 and is still there, continuing his valuable work of survey and exploration. A description of the region, gleaned from his reports, will prove of considerable value. Our attention is first directed to the Lewis River, its affluent streams and the resources of the adjacent country. Starting at the head of Lake Bennett, one may traverse the whole Lewis River Basin. Above that point and between it and Lake Lindeman, there is only about three-quarters of a mile of river which is not more than fifty or sixty yards wide and two or three feet deep, and is so swift and rough that navigation is rendered very difficult and almost impossible. Lake Lindeman is about five miles long, and a half mile wide, and is deep enough for all the demands of navigation in that country. Lake Bennett, at the head of which a saw-mill has been established, and where lumber for boat building is now being sold at $100 per thousand feet, is over twenty-six miles long, the upper portion being very narrow—not more than a half mile wide. Near the center a vast arm comes in from the west. This Schwatka mistook for a river and named it Wheaton River. This arm has its source or head in a glacier, which lies in the pass at the head of Chilkoot Inlet. It is surrounded by high mountains. A deep, wide valley extends northwards from the north end of Lake Bennett, extending to the canyon a short distance above it. The waters of the lake empty at the extreme northeast angle through a channel not more than one hundred yards wide, and later it expands into what Schwatka called Lake Nares. This channel has a swift current and is about seven feet deep. The ice breaks up in Lake Bennett early in June, frequently by the first of the month. The connecting waters between Lake Bennett and Tagish Lake constitute what is now called Cariboo Crossing.

Lake Nares is only two and one-half miles long and its greatest width is only a mile. It is not deep, but is navigable for boats drawing a little over five feet of water. It is separated from Lake Bennett by a shallow sand-point of not more than 200 yards in length. Strange to say, no streams of any consequence flow into either of these lakes. Lake Nares flows through a narrow, curved channel into Bove Lake, a channel not more than 600 or 700 yards long, but the water in it is sufficiently deep for boats that can navigate either of the lakes. This Bove Lake is the Tagish Lake of Dr. Dawson. It is about a mile wide for the first two miles of its length, where it is joined by what the miners have properly called the Windy Arm. Here the lake expands to a width of about two miles for a distance of some three miles, when it suddenly narrows to about a half a mile, for a distance of a little over a mile, after which it widens again. Ten miles from the head of the lake it is joined by the Taku Arm from the south, which is of considerable length. Dr. Dawson included Bove Lake and both of these arms under the name of Tagish Lake.

From the junction with the Taku Arm to the north end of the lake, the distance is about six miles, the greater part being over two miles wide. Where the river leaves the lake it is about 150 yards wide and for a short distance not more than five or six feet deep. It soon increases to ten feet or more, and so continues down to Mud Lake.

Marsh Lake, the next in order, is about nineteen miles long and two miles wide. The piece of river connecting Mud Lake with Marsh Lake is about five miles long and nearly 200 yards wide. Along its banks are situated a considerable number of Indian houses showing some pretension and skill in construction. They are now in ruins.

The Lewis River, where it leaves Marsh Lake, is about 200 yards wide, and averages this width as far as the canyon. It is very deep. From the head of Lake Bennett to the canyon, the distance is ninety-five miles, all of which is navigable for boats drawing five feet of water. Below the canyon proper there is a stretch of rapids about a mile in length, then about a half mile of smooth water. Following these are the White Horse Rapids, which are nearly half a mile long and unsafe for boats. The total fall in the canyon and succeeding rapids is thirty-two feet. For some distance below the White Horse Rapids the current is swift and the river wide, with many gravel bars. But little prospecting has yet been done on these bars, but they undoubtedly contain valuable gold deposits.

The reach between these rapids and Lake Labarge, a distance of some twenty-seven miles, is smooth water but with a strong current. The average width throughout this distance is about 150 yards. About midway in this stretch the Tahkeena River joins the Lewis. It is about half the size of the latter. It runs through a clayey district. It has its source in a lake of considerable size, and may be navigated up to that point. Lake Labarge is thirty-one miles long and is of various widths—from four miles to one. The width of the Lewis River where it leaves this lake is about the same as its entrance, namely, 200 yards. After leaving Lake Labarge, the river for a distance of about five miles preserves a uniform width and an easy current of about four miles an hour. It then turns around a low gravel point and flows in exactly the opposite to its general course, for a mile, when it again resumes its general direction. The current around this bend is very swift, reaching several miles an hour. Not far below, the Teslintoo enters the Lewis. This is a very large stream, wider, though not deeper, than the Lewis above the junction. There are a considerable number of Indians located at this junction. The Teslintoo is about 175 miles long, taking its rise in a lake which has not yet been explored, but which is said to be fully 150 miles long.

Between the Teslintoo and the Big Salmon the distance is thirty-three miles, throughout which the Lewis preserves a uniform width and current. The Big Salmon is about a hundred yards wide at its mouth, and about five feet deep. Its valley is wide and affords some magnificent scenery. The mountains on either side tower very high and are covered with perpetual snow. Some of them are 5,000 feet above the valley. The river is about 190 miles long to its lake sources. The course of the Lewis River from the Tahkeena to the Big Salmon is a little east of north. At the latter point it turns to nearly west, and so continues for some distance, when its course to the confluence with the Pelly becomes northeast. Thirty-six miles below the Big Salmon, the Little Salmon River enters the Lewis. It is about sixty yards wide at its mouth, but not more than two or three feet deep. Eight miles below Little Salmon River a large rock, called the Eagle's Nest, rises from a gravel slope on the eastward bank of the river to a height of about 500 feet. Thirty-two miles below Eagle's Nest rock, Nordenskiold River enters from the west. It is an unimportant river. A curious feature of the Lewis River, some distance below the mouth of the last stream named, is the Five Finger Rapids, so called from the fact that five large masses of rock stand in mid-channel. About two miles below these rapids the Tatshum River enters from the east. It is an unimportant stream. The Indians are generally engaged hereabouts, during the season, in the salmon catch. It is 58 miles from the Five Finger Rapids to the mouth of the Pelly River. In all this distance no streams of importance enter the Lewis. At the junction with the Pelly, the Lewis is about half a mile wide. At this point there are many islands. A mile below the junction of the Pelly and Lewis, at the ruins of Fort Selkirk, the Yukon is 565 yards wide. About two thirds of this width is over ten feet deep, with a current of nearly five miles an hour. Pelly River at its mouth is about 200 yards wide. A complete description of the Pelly River basin is given by Dr. Dawson in his report entitled "Yukon District and Northern British Columbia."

The character of the country along the Yukon River, from the junction of the Lewis and Pelly to the international boundary line at Seventy Mile Creek, has already been partially described. For this distance the river flows in a generally northwesterly direction. On the southwest side, in part, but principally on the northeast side, is the Klondike country proper. The chief settlements on the river, proceeding from the boundary, are Fort Cudahy, Forty Mile Post, Dawson City, near the junction of the Klondike River with the Yukon, and Sixty Mile Post, at the junction of Sixty Mile Creek with the river. There are a vast number of creeks flowing into the Klondike, all of them gold-bearing. These rivers and creeks, including the Stewart River, the Indian River, the Klondike and its branches, find their sources in the foothills of the Rocky Mountains north of the Pelly and McMillan rivers. This stretch of gold-bearing country lies between the 136th and 140th degrees of longitude, and between the parallels of 63.30 and 65 north latitude. In these latitudes the length of the degrees of longitude is about thirty-two miles, thus making the Klondike country proper about 130 miles from east to west, by a little over a hundred miles from north to south. Only a very small portion of this territory has yet been searched by the prospectors; and, of course, the vast gold-bearing regions, both north and south and principally to the east of this section, have, as yet, been but partially explored by surveyors.

CHAPTER X.

UPPER YUKON AND TRIBUTARIES.

The North Country from the International Boundary to the junction of the Lewis and Pelly—The Stewart River—Other streams—Sixty Mile River—The Klondike River and tributary creeks—Forty Mile River.

It will prove useful to one studying the physical features of the auriferous areas of the Klondike region to make some further observations on the country lying between the international boundary line and the junction of the Lewis and Pelly rivers, before ascending the basin of the latter stream.

It is ninety-six miles from Selkirk to White River. On this stretch islands are numerous. Some of them are of considerable size, and the greater part are well timbered. Bars are numerous, nearly all being composed of gravel. White River enters the main stream from the west. At its mouth it is about 200 yards wide. A great portion of it here, however, is filled with constantly shifting sand-bars, the main current being confined to a channel not more than 100 yards in width. The current is very strong. The valley of this river runs due west for over eight miles; thence it bears to the southwest. It is about two miles wide and holds that width for most of its length.

There is much clay soil along the White River banks. The stream takes its rise further up than the source of Forty Mile River, but near the same valley, and probably in the Mentasia Pass, between which and the head waters of the Tanana River there are mountain ranges. The length of this stream is not yet fully determined.

Between White and Stewart rivers, a distance of ten miles, the Yukon is a mile wide and is a maze of islands and bars. The main channel is along the westerly shore. Stewart River enters from the east, from the center of a wide valley with low hills on both sides rising in steps or terraces. The river, a little distance above its mouth, is two hundred yards wide. The current is not strong. A miner named Alexander McDonald, of New Brunswick, spent a whole summer on this river and its vicinity, prospecting with good results. He states that about seventy miles up the Stewart a large creek enters from the south, to which he gave the name of Rose Bud River, and that about forty miles further up a large stream flows from the northeast. This is no doubt Beaver River. From the head of this stream one may float down to the mouth, in a canoe or on a raft, in five days, which indicates that the stream is over 200 miles in length. It is from sixty to seventy yards wide and is about four or five feet deep. The current is not strong. Above this stream the Stewart is considerably over one hundred yards wide, with an even current, and clear water. Sixty or seventy miles above the branch mentioned a large river joins it, though Mr. Ogilvie thinks this may be the main stream. At the head of it is a lake thirty miles long and about a mile and a half in width, which has been called Mayhew Lake. Thirty miles on the other branch there are falls estimated to be two hundred feet in height. Overcoming these falls by a portage, one may proceed to the head of this stream where are terraced gravel hills which are filled with virgin gold in paying quantities. Crossing these, the traveler will find a river flowing to the north. On this, he may embark and float down to some point, no one yet knows where, as the stream has not been explored.

Returning to the head waters of the stream in the gold bearing hills just mentioned, the prospector may travel westward over a high range of mountains, composed of shales with many thin seams of gold bearing quartz. On the west side of this range there is a river flowing out of a large lake. Crossing this to the head of Beaver River, one may descend to the main stream, and to the Yukon. It is supposed that the river flowing to the north over the gold hills mentioned, is one of the branches of the Peel River. It is evident that light draught steamers can navigate the whole of Stewart River and its principal tributaries.

From Stewart River to the site of Fort Reliance, on the Yukon, a little over seventy-three miles, the great river is broad and full of islands. Its average width is half a mile, but there are many expansions where it is over a mile in breadth.

There are many islands in these wide stretches of the Yukon. About twenty miles below the Stewart, Sixty Mile Creek enters. The banks of this stream are well stocked with virgin gold, and from the gravel much of the treasure has already been taken by miners. Sixty Mile Creek is a hundred miles in length, very crooked, and has a swift current. Miller, Glacier, Gold, Little Gold, and Bed Rock creeks are all tributaries of Sixty Mile. Very rich discoveries of gold have been made on these streams, but much of it has already been mined. There is a claim on Miller Creek, from which over $100,000 worth of gold has been taken. Freight for this mining district is taken up Forty Mile Creek in summer, for a distance of over thirty miles, and is then portaged across to the head of Miller and Glacier creeks. In winter it is hauled in by dogs. The trip from Cudahy to the Post at the mouth of Sixty Mile River, is made by ascending Forty Mile Creek a little distance, making a short portage to Sixty Mile River, and running down with its swift current. Coming back on the Yukon, nearly the whole round trip is made down stream.

Indian Creek enters the Yukon from the east about thirty miles below Sixty Mile River. It is rich in gold and has already been extensively mined. It was neglected for some time, owing to the difficulty of getting supplies to the mining camps. At the mouth of Sixty Mile River a town site has been laid out, called

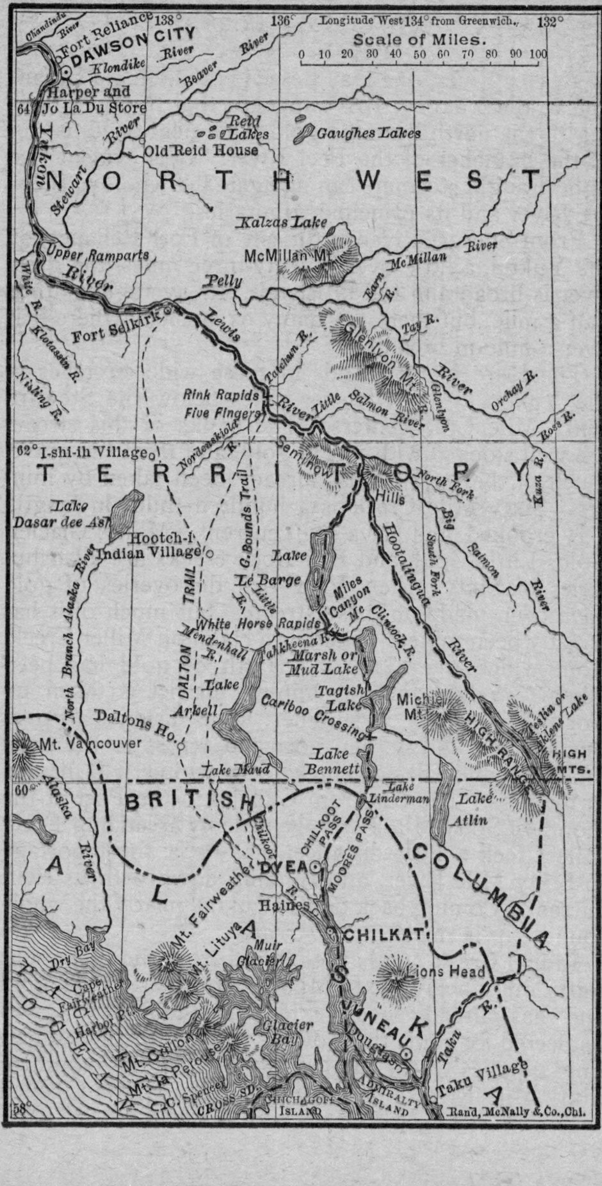

Longitude West 134° from Greenwich.
138°
136°
132°
Scale of Miles.
0 10 20 30 40 50 60 70 80 90 100
Chandindu River
Fort Reliance
DAWSON CITY
Klondike River
Beaver River
Harper and
64° Jo La Du Store
Stewart River
Reid Lakes
Gaughes Lakes
Old Reid House
Yukon
NORTH WEST
Kalzas Lake
McMillan Mt.
McMillan River
Upper Ramparts
River
Pelly
White R.
Earn R.
Fort Selkirk
Lewis
Tay R.
Klotassin R.
Glenlyon Mt.
River
Nisling R.
Tatchun R.
Orchay R.
Rink Rapids
Five Fingers
River
Little Salmon River
Glenlyon
Ross R.
Nordenskiold R.
Seminow
62° I-shi-ih Village
TERRITORY
North Fork
Hills
Kuza R.
Lake
Dasar dee Ash
Big
Hootch-i
Indian Village
G. Bounds Trail
Lake
Le Barge
Hootalinqua
South Fork
Salmon
River
North Branch Alaska River
TRAIL
Little R.
Miles Canyon
Mc Clintock R.
White Horse Rapids
Mendenhall R.
Takkheena R.
Marsh or Mud Lake
River
DALTON
Lake
Tagish Lake
Michie Mt.
Arkell
Cariboo Crossing
HIGH RANGE
Teslin or Aklene Lake
Daltons Ho.
Mt. Vancouver
Lake Bennett
HIGH MTS.
Lake Maud
60°
Alaska
BRITISH
Lake Linderman
Lake
Atlin
Chilkoot
CHILKOOT PASS
MOORES PASS
A
River
DYEA
COLUMBIA
L
Mt. Fairweather
Haines
R.
CHILKAT
A
Mt. Lituya
Muir Glacier
Dry Bay
Lions Head
S
Cape Fairweather
Harbor Pt.
JUNEAU
K
Taku R.
Glacier Bay
Douglas
Mt. Cillon
Mt. la Perouse
Taku Village
A
C. Spencer
CROSS SD.
CHICHAGOFF ISLAND
ADMIRALTY ISLAND
58°
PACIFIC
Rand, McNally & Co., Chi.

Sixty Mile. It has been the headquarters of many miners, most of whom, however, have recently moved further to the east. There is a saw mill and trading post at the mouth of the river.

Six and a half miles above Fort Reliance, the Klondike River enters the Yukon. It is a small stream—about forty yards wide at its mouth, and quite shallow. The water, however, is clear and transparent, and of a beautiful blue color. The stream is filled with salmon, and from it the Indians reap a rich harvest of the king of fish every season. This river and its creek tributaries have been fully explored by prospectors, and upon their banks and bottoms some of the richest gold claims ever located have been developed. It is all placer mining here. Many fortunes have been made in the Klondike within the past year, and as these lines are penned (August, 1897) gold is being taken from the gravel and dirt of the region, probably at the rate of $100,000 a day, or more.

Twelve and a half miles below Fort Reliance the Chandindu River, as it was named by Schwatka, enters from the east. It is thirty to forty yards wide at the mouth, very shallow, and for half a mile up is one continuous rapid. Its valley is wide and can be seen for a long distance looking north-eastward from the mouth.

Between Fort Reliance and Forty Mile River the Yukon assumes its normal appearance, having fewer islands and being narrower, averaging four to six hundred yards wide, and the current being more regular. This stretch is forty-six miles long, but was estimated by the traders at forty, from which the Forty Mile River took its name.

Forty Mile River joins the Yukon from the west. Forty Mile townsite is located at its mouth. The Alaska Commercial Company has a station here. There are also several blacksmith shops, restaurants, billiard halls, bakeries, an opera house and so on. Rather more than half a mile below Forty Mile townsite, the town of Cudahy was founded on the north side of Forty Mile River, in the summer of 1892. It is named after a well known member of the North American Transportation and Trading Company. In population and extent of business the town bears comparison with its neighbor across the river. The opposition in trade has been the means of very materially reducing the cost of supplies and living. The North American Transportation and Trading Company has erected a saw-mill and some extensive warehouses. Fort Constantine was established here immediately upon the arrival of the Mounted Police detachment in the latter part of July, 1895.

Forty Mile River has a general southwest course, as far up as the international boundary line, a distance of twenty-three miles. From this point it runs more from the south. The stream has been ascended for more than one hundred miles. It is only a short distance from the head of this river across to the Tanana, a large tributary of the Yukon. Only twenty-three miles of Forty Mile River are in Canada. The greater part of it is in Alaska. It is nearly a hundred and fifty yards wide at its mouth, and the current is generally strong, with many small rapids. There is a canyon about eight miles up this stream. At the lower end of it is a swift current in which are some rocks that cannot be seen by the descending voyager, owing to a sudden bend in the river. Several miners have been drowned in this rapid by their canoes or boats being dashed to pieces on the rocks. Between Forty Mile River and the boundary line, no streams of any size join the Yukon.

CHAPTER XI.

UPPER YUKON—AGRICULTURE AND TIMBER.

Only a small proportion of the region available for cereal and vegetable crops—Considerable areas of timber suitable for manufacturing purposes—An abundance of trees for firewood and for all mining necessities.

The agricultural capabilities of the upper Yukon basin are not great. Hence the miners in that region will be compelled to draw most of their supplies of bread and meat, vegetables and dairy products from markets far to the south, until the fertile valleys to east and west have been cultivated and developed. The land is not of a very good quality hereabouts, and the climate is not favorable to the growth of cereals or vegetables.

The temperature records show an average of 8 degrees of frost for August. The meteorological record for September places the mercury considerably below freezing point. Along the east side of Lake Bennett, opposite the Chilkoot, there are quite extensive flats of dry, gravelly soil, where farming can be carried on to a limited extent. On the west side, around the mouth of Wheaton River, there is a very extensive flat of sand and gravel, covered with pine and spruce of a small growth. The vegetation is poor and sparse. At the lower end of the lake there is another extensive flat of sandy soil, thinly covered with small poplars and pines.

There are great tracts of low, marshy land on the westerly shore of Tagish Lake, which will, no doubt, prove very productive. The same may be said of the western borders of Marsh Lake, which district is pretty well covered with native grasses. Along the head of the river below Marsh Lake, there are extensive flats on both sides. There the soil is good, and the growth of forest trees and under brush is healthy and well developed. In that region agriculture will thrive.

As we approach the canyon the banks become higher, and the bottom lands less extensive. Here the soil is light and sandy on both sides. Between the canyon and Lake Labarge there is not much land of value. At the head of the lake there is an extensive flat, pretty well covered with timber that is much larger and better than any met with above this point. Poplars eight and ten inches thick, are common, and there is a considerable quantity of spruce from fifteen to sixteen inches in diameter. The soil, however, is not very good, and vegetation is sparse. Some distance down the lake the soil and vegetation show great improvement. On the lower end of the lake there is a large plain well suited to agricultural pursuits. Northward from the end of the lake, Ogilvie Valley stretches out to a vast extent. Here the soil is good and the timber of large size. About forty miles above the mouth of the Pelly there are extensive flats on both sides of the Lewis River. The soil is poor and sandy, with small open timber consisting of spruce and popular. For many miles up the Pelly and down the Yukon, from the junction, there is an extensive plateau, two or three hundred feet above the river. On this, the soil is good for pasturage only. It is very lightly timbered.

Between Pelly and White rivers, there is an extensive flat of many thousand acres. It is quite heavily timbered, and as the surface is covered with a heavy layer of moss, the frost never leaves the ground. At Stewart River there is another large flat to which the same remarks will apply. Thence to Fort Reliance there are no flats of any size. Above the river, in most of this region, there are extensive wooded slopes, which, when cleared, will no doubt be quite well adapted to cereal and vegetable productions.

At Fort Reliance there is a flat of about 2,000 acres,

and at the mouth of Forty Mile River there is another, but not as large. All the rivers of this part of the country are cleared of ice from the 25th of May to the 1st of June. The extent of tillable lands in the upper Yukon region bears a very small proportion to the areas which are practically worthless for agricultural purposes, but the timber is sufficient in quantity and quality for the necessities of a mining country. Probably not more than 250,000 acres or 1,000 farms of workable lands could be located in that part of the country. This is exclusive of the available lands at the junction of the Pelly and Lewis rivers, where the tract is sufficiently large to lay out about 2,000 farms.

The amount of timber in the district suitable for building and manufacturing is considerable; for fire wood, and use in the mines, there is an abundance. There is a great deal of excellent timber on the islands in the Yukon. On these the soil is warmer and richer, the sun's rays striking the surface for a much longer time, and more directly, than on the banks.

At the confluence with the Pelly, on the east side of the river, there is a grove of spruce from which some very nice lumber could be made, and on the islands below this point, much of the same class of timber exists. Near White and Stewart rivers there is a good deal of nice clean timber, but it is small. There is more good timber on Stewart River, in proportion to the ground wooded, than on the main river. Between Stewart River and the boundary there is not so much surface covered with large trees as on many of the flats above it, the valley being generally narrower, and the sides steeper, than higher up the river. This, of course, precludes the growth of timber.

The whole country stretching from the international boundary line to the summit of the Rockies, including the basins of the upper Yukon, the Pelly and Lewis rivers, and the regions between them and to the north of the Pelly, is timbered in about the same manner. In some localities the trees are workable for building purposes; but the greater part of the forests is available only for fire wood, mining purposes, log houses, and the like. However, there is an abundance of it for these requirements.

CHAPTER XII.

WEALTH OF THE KLONDIKE.

Inexhaustible deposits of placer and quartz gold—The silver-bearing rock—Vast coal fields—Reports of government officials that read like tales of the Arabian Nights—Sensational reports of Explorer Ogilvie.

Probably no stretch of country of equal area on the earth is so rich in the precious metals, and minerals generally, including coal, as that of the upper Yukon and the basins of the Pelly and Lewis rivers. Only a small part of this vast region has yet been explored, but it has been sufficiently gone over by natural history and mining experts to demonstrate that the whole district is of the same auriferous and mineral bearing character. While some river-beds and banks are richer than others, there is scarcely a square mile of this great territory that cannot be profitably worked for some precious metal or other valuable mineral deposit.

Most of the region is rich in virgin gold. Silver predominates in some of the districts, and there is an abundance of good coal. Silver frequently abounds in the immediate neighborhood of rich placer-gold deposits. This is true of Forty Mile River. About two miles from its mouth, where there are extensive exposures of white and gray limestone, many seams and pockets of galena have been discovered. One of these seams has been traced and found to be of vast extent. Specimens assayed show nearly forty ounces of silver to the ton. The silver mines here, as elsewhere in that country, are known to be very rich. Specimens recently assayed show as high as two hundred ounces to the ton. All of these specimens were found by accident. A closer examination of the silver deposits will, no doubt, reveal more valuable seams. Dr. Dawson declares that almost fabulous silver deposits exist in that country.

Aside from the rich placer-gold deposits, which have yielded so much wealth during the past year, equally rich quartz gold strikes have been made; but as the region is still inaccessible for quartz mining machinery no development has yet been made on this line. Both gold and silver-bearing quartz has been discovered near Sixty Mile River. A specimen of gold-bearing quartz, found near White River, assayed the enormous value of $20,000 to the ton. This specimen was taken from a seam nearly 2,000 feet above the Yukon water-level. There is also an extensive ledge of gold-bearing quartz on the west side of the Yukon, not far above Stewart River. There is also an extensive exposure of gold-bearing rock not far from Lake Bennett. Specimens of this have assayed $9.00 of gold and $1.00 of silver to the ton. Mr. Ogilvie says, however, that this rock-area is near Lake Tagish.

So far as explorations have been made upon which a reasonable estimate can be based, there are 4,000 miles of stream in the upper Yukon district upon which placer-gold can be profitably worked. The unexplored regions will probably add 5,000 miles to this river and creek extent. Mr. Ogilvie, writing of his explorations in 1887, says:

"About eighteen miles below the Teslintoo, I saw the first place that had been worked for gold. Here a hut had been erected, and there were indications that a party had wintered there. Between it and Big Salmon River six other locations were met with. One of them named Cassiar Bar, was worked in the season of 1886, by a party of four, who took out $6,000 in thirty days. They were working there when I passed in 1887, but stated that all they could get that season was about $10 per day.

"Two of this party subsequently went down to Forty Mile River, where I met one of them. He was a Swede, and had been gold-mining for upwards of twenty-five years in California and British Columbia. He gave me his opinion on the district in these words: 'I never saw a country where there was so much gold, and so evenly distributed; no place is very rich, but no place is very poor; every man can make a "grub stake" (that is enough to feed and clothe him for a year), which is more than I can say of the other places I have been in.'

"In conversation with Mr. Boswell, who, as already stated, has prospected the Teslintoo, or Newberry River, in the summer of 1887, I learned that the whole length of that river yielded fine gold, generally at the rate of $8 to $10 per day; but as the miners' great desideratum is coarse gold, they do not remain long in a country in which only the fine gold is found—generally no longer than is necessary to make a 'grub stake,' unless gold is in unusually large quantities. Mr. Boswell therefore went to the lower part of the river, having heard the reports of rich finds. Stewart River was the first in the district on which mining to any extent was done. In 1886 there were quite a number of miners on it engaged in washing gold, and they all appear to have done fairly well.

"I have heard the amount of gold taken from Stewart River in 1885 and 1886 estimated at various amounts. One estimate was $300,000. The highest amount I heard as representing one man's earnings was about $6,000. This may be true, as many agree that $30 per day, per man, was common on many of the bars of the river, and instances of as high as $100 per day having been earned, were spoken of. The only mining done on Stewart River was on the bars in the river; the bench and bank bars were all timbered and frozen, so that to work them would entail a resort to hydraulic mining, for which there was no machinery in the country.

"During the fall of 1886, three or four miners combined and got the owners of the 'New Racket' steamboat to allow the use of her engines to work pumps for sluicing with. The boat was hauled up on a bar, her engines detached from the wheels, and made to drive a set of pumps manufactured on the ground, which supplied water for a set of sluicing boxes. With this crude machinery, in less than a month, the miners cleared $1,000 each and paid an equal amount to the owners of the boat as their share.

"Many of the miners who had spent 1886 on Stewart River, and 1887 on Forty Mile River, seemed to think the former the better all-round mining field, as there were no such failures there as on Forty Mile, and they declared their intention to make their way to the Stewart, for the season of 1888. Forty Mile River is the only river in the district on which, up to the fall of 1888, coarse gold had been found, and it may be said that much of it can hardly claim that distinctive title. The largest nugget found was worth about $39. It was lost on the body of a miner who was drowned at the canyon.

"The miners term Forty Mile a 'bed-rock' creek—that is, one in the bed of which there is little or no drift, or detrital matter, the bottom of the river being bed-rock. In many places this rock has been scraped with knives by the miners, in order to gather the small amount of detritus and its accompanying gold. Very little of the gold on this creek was found in Canadian territory, the coarsest gold being found well up the river. The river had been prospected in 1887 for upwards of one hundred miles, and gold found all the way up. The great point with a miner is to find where the gold comes from. To this end he has to reach a point on the river where there is none; then he knows he has passed the source, and will search in side valleys and gulches. The theory seems to be that the gold is stored up somewhere and dribbled out along the river. Pieces of gold-bearing quartz had frequently been picked up along the river in the shallow drift, but none had been found in place, nor did it appear to me that much search had been made for it.

Near the mouth of the river, there is an extensive flat of detrital matter through which a couple of small creeks flow. This is all said to be gold-bearing, and it was thought, would pay well for sluicing. Accordingly, a couple of claimants had staked off claims at the mouth of the creeks and intended to try sluicing in the season of 1888.

"I think it may, with confidence, be asserted that rich finds will yet be made of both coarse gold and gold-bearing quartz. It is not likely in the nature of things that such a vast extent of country should have all its fine gold deposited as sediment, brought from a distance in past ages. If this is not the case, the matrix, from which all gold on these streams has come, must still exist, in part at least, and will no doubt be discovered, and thus enrich this otherwise gloomy and desolate region. There are many bank and bench bars along the rivers, which would pay well if sluiced, but there is yet no convenient or economical way of getting water on them, and there is no pumping machinery as yet in the country."

It is now nine years since the above was written by this veteran explorer of the far northwest, and we, who study the region to-day, see how completely Mr. Ogilvie's predictions have been realized. This explorer and surveyor re-entered the country in 1895, and continued his work of locating the boundary line, and of defining the rivers and lakes of the Klondike district. He also surveyed several townsites, including Cudahy, Forty Mile and Dawson, and one or two mission posts. In 1895-6 he made full investigations as to the coal deposits, and found them to be of great extent and good quality. On Coal Creek one seam was found to be twelve feet six inches thick.

An extensive copper-bearing vein was found near the Klondike above Fort Reliance. Asbestos was also discovered in paying quantities. In 1895 the placer diggings had greatly increased. A survey of the Cone Hill quartz gold mine was made in 1895, and assays of the quartz taken from the mine proved exceedingly satisfactory. The quantity of gold-bearing rock in this mine will not be exhausted for generations. Its extent and richness place the great Treadwell mine of Juneau, Alaska, far in the shade. Other paying quartz gold claims were located on Twelve Mile Creek in the same year. These deposits are even richer than at Cone Hill. In 1895 it became evident that quartz gold mining would, in the near future, become a leading feature of the mining camps of the Klondike country.

By the middle of 1895 the Alaska Commercial Company had four powerful steamers on the Yukon, and the North American Trading and Transportation Company were preparing to increase its carrying capacity on the same water-way. Thus, on every side, the country showed signs of progress. There was then, as there still is a great demand for horses, which were being taken into the country at a cost of about $250 a head.

In 1896 coal was found in vast quantities all along Coal Creek, and from it up to Twelve Mile Creek, which flows into the Yukon thirty miles up the river. On the Cornell claim on Cliff Creek, the coal seam was ascertained to be nearly six feet thick. It was in 1896 that coarse gold was discovered in vast deposits on the Klondike, or Thron-Diuck, as it was first called. Concerning these finds Mr. Ogilvie wrote the Canadian Minister of the Interior, under date of September 6, 1896, as follows:

"I am very much pleased to be able to inform you that a most important discovery of gold has been made on a creek called Bonanza Creek, an affluent of the river known here as the Klondike. It is marked on the map extant as Deer River and joins the Yukon a few miles above the site of Fort Reliance.

"The discovery was made by G. W. Cormack, who worked with me in 1887 on the coast range. The indications are that it is very rich, indeed the richest yet found, and as far as work has been carried on, it realizes expectations. It is only two weeks since it was known, and already about 200 claims have been staked on it and the creek is not yet exhausted; it and its branches are considered good for 300 or 400 claims. Besides, there are two other creeks above it, which, it is confidently expected, will yield good pay, and if they do so, we have from 800 to 1,000 claims on this river which will require over 2,000 men for their proper working. Between Thron-Diuck River and Stewart River, a large creek called Indian Creek flows into the Yukon, and rich prospects have been found on it, and no doubt it is in the gold-bearing country between Thron-Diuck and Stewart rivers, which is considered by all the old miners the best and most extensive gold country yet found. Scores of them would prospect it but for the fact that they cannot get provisions up there, and it is too far to boat them from here in small boats.

"This new find will necessitate an upward step on the Yukon and help the Stewart River region.

"News has just arrived from Bonanza Creek that three men worked out $75 in four hours the other day and a $12 nugget has been found, which assured the character of the ground, namely, coarse gold and plenty of it, as three times this can be done with sluice boxes. You can fancy the excitement here. It is claimed that from $100 to $500 per day can be made off the ground that has been prospected so far. As we have about 100 claims on Glacier and Miller creeks, with three or four hundred in this vicinity, next year it is imperative that a man be sent in here to look after these claims and all land matters, and it is almost imperative that the agent be a surveyor. Already on Bonanza Creek they are disputing about the size of claims."

Speaking at further length of the rich Klondike region in the same year, 1896, Mr. Ogilvie said:

"As I have already intimated rich placer mines of gold were discovered on the branches of this stream.

The discovery, I believe, was due to the reports of Indians. A white man, named Geo. W. Cormack, who worked with me in 1887, was the first to take advantage of the rumors and locate a claim on the first branch, which was named by the miners Bonanza Creek. Cormack located late in August, but had to cut some logs for the mill here to get a few pounds of provisions to enable him to begin work on his claim. The fishing at Thron-Diuck having totally failed him, he returned with a few weeks' provisions for himself, his wife and brother-in-law (Indians) and another Indian, in the last days of August, and immediately set about working his claim. As he was very short of appliances, he could only put together a rather defective apparatus to wash the gravel with. The gravel itself, he had to carry in a box on his back from 30 to 100 feet; notwithstanding this, the three men working very irregularly, washed out $1,200 in eight days, and Cormack asserts with reason, that had he had proper facilities, it could have been done in two days, besides having several hundred dollars more gold, which was lost in the tailings through defective apparatus.

"On the same creek two men rocked out $75 in about four hours, and it is asserted that two men in the same creek took out $4,000 in two days with only two lengths of sluice boxes. Mr. Leduc assures me he weighed that much gold for them. They were new comers and had not done much in the country, so the probabilities are they got it on Bonanza Creek. A branch of Bonanza, named Eldorado, has prospected magnificently, and another branch named Tilly Creek has prospected well; in all there are some four or five branches to Bonanza which have given good prospects. There are about 170 claims staked on the main creek, and the branches are good for about as many more, aggregating say about 350 claims, which will require over 1,000 men to work properly.

"A few miles farther up Bear Creek enters Thron-Diuck, and it has been prospected and located on.

Compared with Bonanza, it is small, and will not afford more than 20 or 30 claims. About twelve miles above the mouth, Gold-bottom Creek joins Thron-Diuck, and on it and a branch named Hunker Creek, very rich ground has been found. One man showed me $22.75 he took out in a few hours on Hunker Creek with a gold pan, prospecting his claim on the surface, taking a handful here and there as fancy suggested. On Gold-bottom Creek and branches, there will probably be 200 or 300 claims. The Indians have reported another creek much farther up, which they call 'Too Much Gold Creek,' on which the gold is so plentiful that, as the miners say in joke, 'you have to mix gravel with it to sluice it.' Up to date, nothing definite has been heard from this creek.

"From all this we may, I think, infer that we have here a district which will give 1,000 claims of 500 feet in length each. Now, 1,000 such claims will require at least 3,000 men to work them properly, and as wages for working in the mines are from $8 to $10 per day without board, we have every reason to assume that this part of our territory will, in a year or two, contain 10,000 souls at least. For the news has gone out to the coast, and an unprecedented influx is expected next spring. And this is not all, for a large creek called Indian Creek joins the Yukon about midway between Thron-Diuck and Stewart rivers, and all along this creek good pay has been found. All that has stood in the way of working it heretofore, has been the scarcity of provisions, and the difficulty of getting them up there even when here. Indian Creek is quite a large stream and it is probable it will yield five to six hundred claims. Further south yet lies the head of several branches of Stewart River, on which some prospecting has been done this summer and good indications found, but the want of provisions prevented development. Now gold has been found in several of the streams joining Pelly River, and also all along the Hootalinqua. In the line of these finds farther south is the Cassiar gold field in British Columbia; so the presumption is that we have in our territory, along the easterly watershed of the Yukon, a gold-bearing belt of indefinite width, and upwards of three hundred miles long, exclusive of the British Columbia part of it. On the westerly side of the Yukon, prospecting has been done on a creek a short distance above Selkirk, with a fair amount of success, and on a large creek some thirty or forty miles below Selkirk, fair prospects have been found; but, as before remarked, the difficulty of getting supplies here prevents any extensive prospecting.

"Good quartz has been found in places just across the line on Davis Creek, but of what extent is unknown, as it is in the bed of the creek, and covered with gravel. Good quartz is also reported on the hills around Bonanza Creek. It is pretty certain from information I have got from prospectors, that all or nearly all of the northerly branch of White River, is on our side of the line, and copper is found on it, but more abundantly on the southerly branch, of which a great portion is in our territory also, so it is probable we have that metal too. I have seen here several lumps of copper, brought by the natives from White River, but just from what part is uncertain. I have also seen a specimen of silver ore said to have been picked up in a creek flowing into Lake Bennett, about fourteen miles down it on the east side. I think this is enough to show that we may look forward with confidence to a fairly bright future for this part of our territory.

"When it was fairly established that Bonanza Creek was rich in gold, which took a few days, for Thron-Diuck had been prospected several times with no encouraging result, there was a great rush from all over the country adjacent to Forty Mile. The town was almost deserted; men who had been in a chronic state of drunkenness for weeks were pitched into boats as ballast and taken up to stake themselves a claim, and claims were staked by men for their friends who were not in the country at the time. All this gave rise to such conflict and confusion, there being no one present to take charge of matters, the agent being unable to go up and attend to the thing, and myself not yet knowing what to do, that the miners held a meeting, and appointed one of themselves to measure off and stake the claims, and record the owners' names in connection therewith, for which he got a fee of $2, it being of course understood that each claim holder would have to record his claim with the Dominion agent and pay his fee of $15."

In December, 1896, Mr. Ogilvie wrote:

"Since my last, the prospects on Bonanza Creek and tributaries are increasing in richness and extent until now it is certain that millions will be taken out of the district in the next few days.

"On some of the claims prospected the pay dirt is of great extent and very rich. One man told me yesterday that he washed out a single pan of dirt on one of the claims on Bonanza, and found $14.25 in it. Of course that may be an exceptionally rich pan, but $5 to $7 per pan is the average on that claim it is reported, with five feet of pay dirt, and the width yet undetermined, but it is known to be thirty feet even at that; figure the result at nine to ten pans to the cubic foot, and 500 feet long; nearly $4,000,000 at $5 per pan. One-fourth of this would be enormous.

"Another claim has been prospected to such an extent that it is known there is about five feet pay dirt averaging $2 per pan, and width not less than thirty feet. Enough prospecting has been done to show that there are at least fifteen miles of this extraordinary richness; and the indications are that we will have three or four times that extent, if not all equal to the above, yet all, at least, very rich.

"It appears a great deal of staking for absentees has been done, some of whom have turned up and some have not. This has caused confusion, and leads to a good deal of what might be called fraud, for it is easy for a few in the inner circle to know what claims have been recorded in accordance with the law and what have not. They can then for themselves, directly or through the intervention of a friend, have the latter jumped for their whole or partial interest. It appears this has been done in several instances."

Again, under date of January, 1897, Mr. Ogilvie sent information to his government, in the following terms:

"The reports from the Thron-Diuck (Klondike) region are still very encouraging; so much so that all the other creeks around are practically abandoned, especially those on the head of Forty Mile in American territory, and nearly one hundred men have made their way up from Circle City, many of them hauling their sleds themselves. Those who cannot get claims are buying in on those already located. Men cannot be got to work for love or money, and development is consequently slow; one and a half dollars per hour is the wages paid the few men who have to work for hire, and work as many hours as they like. Some of the claims are so rich that every night a few pans of dirt suffices to pay the hired help when there is any; as high as $204 have been reported to a single pan. Claim owners are now very reticent about what they get, so you can hardly credit anything you hear; but one thing is certain, we have one of the richest mining areas ever found, with a fair prospect that we have not yet discovered its limits.

"Miller and Glacier creeks on the head of Sixty Mile River, which my survey of the 141st meridian determined to be in Canada, were thought to be very rich, but they are poor both in quality and quantity compared with Thron-Diuck.

"Chicken Creek on the head of Forty Mile, in Alaska, discovered a year ago and rated very high, is to-day practically abandoned.

"Some quartz prospecting has been done in the Thron-Diuck region, and it is probable that some good veins will be found there. Coal is found on the upper part of Thron-Diuck; so that the facilities for working it, if found, are good and convenient.

"A quartz lode showing free gold in paying quantities has been located on one of the creeks, but I cannot yet send particulars. I am confident from the nature of the gold found in the creeks that many more of them—and rich, too—will be found.

"I have just heard from a reliable source that the quartz mentioned above is rich, as tested—over one hundred dollars to the ton. The lode appears to run from three to eight feet in thickness, and is about nineteen miles from the Yukon River. I will likely be called on to survey it, and will be able to report fully.

"Placer prospects continue more and more encouraging and extraordinary. It is beyond doubt that three pans on different claims on Eldorado turned out $204, $212 and $216; but it must be borne in mind that there were only three such pans, though there are many running from $10 to $50."

This closes the official information of the Klondike country, up to the middle of August, 1897, but later news was received through private sources, which the foregoing fully substantiates.

CHAPTER XIII.

PROCESS OF PLACER MINING.

Methods of the prospector—Use of the Pan, the Rocker and the Sluice—Mining in the Far North—Continuous daylight in summer and almost perpetual darkness in winter—Filling the hours of summer with hard work—"Burning" in winter—Vast Peace River gold discoveries —The Northeast route.

As many of our readers understand little of the nomenclature of the mining craft, or of the methods employed to separate the very small particles of the precious metals from the baser material with which it is associated, a short description will be in place here.

First, as to prospecting. When a miner "strikes" a bar he "prospects" it by washing a few panfuls of the gravel or sand of which it is composed. He is guided as to the value of the "dirt" by "colors;" in other words by the number of specs of gold he can see in his pan after all the dirt has been washed out. Most of these prospectors have had sufficient experience to determine the value of sand or gravel in a few minutes, and to estimate, at once, how much a bar will yield per day and per man.

The process of placer mining has been described as follows: "After clearing all the coarse gravel and stone off a patch of ground the miner lifts a little of the finer gravel or sand in his pan, which is a broad, shallow dish, made of strong sheet iron; he then puts in water enough to fill the pan, and gives it a few rapid whirls and shakes; this tends to bring the gold to the bottom on account of its greater specific gravity. The dish is then shaken and held in such a way that the gravel and sand are gradually washed out, care being taken as the process nears completion to avoid letting out the finer and heavier parts that have settled to the bottom. Finally all that is left in the pan is whatever gold may have been in the dish and some black sand which almost invariably accompanies it.

"This black sand is nothing but pulverized magnetic iron ore. Should the gold thus found be fine, the contents of the pan are thrown into a barrel containing water and a pound or two of mercury. As soon as the gold comes in contact with the mercury it combines with it and forms an amalgam. The process is continued until enough amalgam has been formed to pay for 'roasting' or 'firing.' It is then squeezed through a buckskin bag, all the mercury that comes through the bag being put back into the barrel to serve again, and what remains in the bag is placed in a retort, if the miner has one, or if not, on a shovel, and heated until nearly all the mercury is vaporized. The gold then remains in a lump with some mercury still held in combination with it.

"This is called the 'pan' or 'hand' method, and is never, on account of its slowness and laboriousness, continued for any length of time when it is possible to procure a 'rocker,' or to make and work sluices.

"A 'rocker' is simply a box about three feet long and two wide, made in two parts, the top part being shallow, with a heavy sheet iron bottom, which is punched full of quarter-inch holes. The other part of the box is fitted with an inclined shelf about midway in its depth, which is six or eight inches lower at its lower end than at its upper. Over this is placed a piece of heavy woolen blanket. The whole is then mounted on two rockers, much resembling those of an ordinary cradle, and when in use they are placed on two blocks of wood so that the whole may be readily rocked. After the miner has selected his claim, he looks for the most convenient place to set up his 'rocker,' which must be near a good supply of water. Then he proceeds to clear away all the stones and coarse gravel, gathering the finer gravel and sand in a heap near the 'rocker.' The shallow box on top is filled with this, and with one hand the miner rocks it through, while with the other he ladles in water. The finer matter with the gold falls through the holes onto the blanket, which checks its progress, and holds the fine particles of gold while the sand and other matter pass over it to the bottom of the box, which is sloped so that what comes through is washed downwards and finally out of the box. Across the bottom of the box are fixed thin slats, behind which some mercury is placed to catch any particles of gold which may escape the blanket. If the gold is nuggety, the large nuggets are found in the upper box, their weight detaining them until all the lighter stuff has passed through, and the smaller ones are held by a deeper slat at the outward end of the bottom of the box. The piece of blanket is, at intervals, taken out and rinsed into a barrel; if the gold is fine, mercury is placed at the bottom of the barrel, as already mentioned.

"Sluicing is always employed when possible. It requires a good supply of water with sufficient head or fall. The process is as follows: Planks are procured and formed into a box of suitable width and depth. Slats are fixed across the bottom of the box at suitable intervals, or shallow holes bored in the bottom in such order that no particle could run along the bottom in a straight line and escape without running over a hole. Several of these boxes are then set up with a considerable slope and are fitted into one another at the ends like a stovepipe. A stream of water is now directed into the upper end of the highest box. The gravel having been collected, as in the case of the rocker, it is shoveled into the upper box and is washed downwards by the strong current of water. The gold is detained by its weight and is held by the slats or in the holes mentioned; if it is fine, mercury is placed behind the slats or in these holes to catch it. In this way about three times as much dirt can be washed as by the rocker, and consequently three times as much gold is secured in a given time. After the boxes are done with they are burned, and the ashes washed for the gold held in the wood.

"A great many of the miners spend their time in the summer prospecting and in the winter resort to a method lately adopted and which is called 'burning.' They make fires on the surface, thus thawing the ground until the bed rock is reached, then drift and tunnel. The pay dirt is brought to the surface and heaped in a pile until spring, when water can be obtained. The sluice boxes are then set up and the dirt is washed out, thus enabling the miner to work advantageously and profitably the year round. This method has been found very satisfactory in places where the pay streak is at any great depth from the surface. In this way the complaint is overcome which has been so commonly advanced by miners and others that in the Yukon several months of the year are lost in idleness. Winter usually sets in very soon after the middle of September and continues until the beginning of June, and is decidedly cold. The mercury frequently falls to 60 degrees below zero, but in the interior there is so little humidity in the atmosphere that the cold is more easily endured than on the coast. In the absence of thermometers, miners, it is said, leave their mercury out all night; when they find it frozen solid in the morning they conclude that it is too cold to work, and stay at home. The temperature runs to great extremes in summer as well as in winter. It is quite a common thing for the thermometer to register 100 degrees in the shade."

There is continuous daylight from the middle of June until the early part of August; but in the middle of winter there is little more than three hours of partial daylight in the twenty-four. Hence constant daylight for a portion of the year, and almost total darkness for another portion, might very well create doubts in one's mind as to what portion of the day in either case should be given to sleep. In the summer months it is possible for a miner to put in as many hours as he has the power to endure. Constant daylight admits of several shifts of men being employed, and in this way mining operations may go on continuously.

In this connection additional reports of the Klondike country, circulated by returning lucky miners, and told in newspapers to fire the spirit of adventure in the American people, may be mentioned. This one was given out in Chicago in August:

"One year ago Fred Phiscator was a poor man engaged in the lumber business at Barodo, Mich. He arrived in Chicago on his way home from Alaska. In a big red pocketbook which he carried in the inside pocket of his vest there reposed a certificate of deposit for $120,000, beside which Mr. Phiscator had sufficient loose change to keep him from borrowing whenever he wanted a cigar. And just as though he had been used to counting his money in six figures all his life, he remarked that he had refused $200,000 for the claim he left behind, and thought it was worth $1,000,000. Mr. Phiscator dropped his traveling bag before the clerk's desk in the Great Northern hotel and said that nothing was too good for him. It is his intention to spend the winter with his family and friends and in the spring he will lead a party of friends to the scene of his fortune making.

"Mr. Phiscator was one of a party of four that followed the discoveries on Bonanza Creek, and he and another man located the claims that have been reported as being so rich on Eldorado Creek. Mr. Phiscator said the party was nearly out of food and was about ready to turn back to the nearest trading post when it met another party that had more flour that it needed and sold his party some. That evening, while the cook was preparing supper, Phiscator suggested to an old man named Whipple that they go a mile up the Klondike and wash a pan of Eldorado Creek dirt. They did so, and were amazed when they found between $6 and $7 in yellow metal in the bottom of the pan. They immediately staked claims and went back and told what they had found. The others in the party then staked claims and all have become rich. He said:

"'This was a little over a year ago, and in that time I have taken out more than $150,000, and have hardly made a hole in my claim. In one hole 35 by 50 feet, I took out $49,000. Most people I meet have a wrong impression of what the claims are, and the reports of fabulous wealth being taken out of them are exaggerated.

"'To work a claim a hole about 6 by 3½ feet, or about the size of an ordinary mining shaft, is started down. As the ground never thaws out to a depth of more than two feet, this is not easy work. As it is not brittle, it can not be shot out, so it is necessary to use a pick until a certain depth is reached. Then fires are built and the ground thawed out. A fire over night will soften about three feet of earth. This is taken out the next day and another fire built. The rich dirt is at bed rock, and after this is reached the fire process is continued, and the excavation is carried on laterally, the dirt being taken out to about the height of a man. It is necessary to do this work during the winter months, for the reason that the gas fumes are so great in the summer that it is impossible to work. All the earth taken out in the winter is piled up, and when summer comes it is panned for the gold.'"

In further confirmation of the contention of the author, who has traveled extensively through that region, the following additional proof of the existence of pay gold on the eastern slopes of the Rockies is submitted. The evidence is not the less valuable because it comes in a second-hand, or round about way:

"Tacoma, Wash., Aug. 22.—The next mining excitement will be on Peace River, in Northwest territory. Mining has been carried on there in a slow way for years, but discoveries made this summer leave no room to doubt that an immense amount of gold will be taken out of that river and its tributaries during the next two years. Men who are now taking out gold in large quantities there are not trying to create a boom, but are quietly sending for their friends to come into the country and secure claims.

"A. D. Kitchen, a prominent mining broker of this city, has just returned from British Columbia. At Vancouver he met a young man named Johnson, who had just come down from Peace River with his partner, bringing $18,000. A third partner was left at the mines. The two came out with part of the season's output to secure supplies for the winter. The money brought out was placed in a Vancouver bank. Part of it was drawn out for the purchase of supplies, which were at once shipped to Edmonton, Northwest territory, whence they were to be sent to the mines by a large pack train.

"The $18,000 brought out had been cleaned up by the three men in three months. They went to Peace River early in the spring, and Johnson started out in July. Johnson said that all the miners on Peace River were making a great deal of money with the crudest of appliances. Up to the time he left only pans and twelve-foot sluices had been used. Most of the miners were not coming out this fall, because it was possible to purchase supplies at the trading posts of the Hudson's Bay Company near the mouth of the river. Johnson told Mr. Kitchen that if he wanted gold all he had to do was to go to Peace River.

"The Peace River country is reached most easily from Edmonton, which is 833 miles from Vancouver, being 191 miles north of Calgary, on the Canadian Pacific Railroad. Fort Chippewyan, on Athabasca Lake, at the mouth of Peace River, is reached by taking a stage from Edmonton to Athabasca landing, forty miles, and thence down Athabasca River and lake by boat. Chippewyan is 465 miles from Edmonton. Steamboats go up the Peace River for a considerable distance. A number of its tributaries, including the Loon and Deer rivers, are as rich as the main stream.

"The Peace River rises in the eastern slopes of the Rocky Mountains, a little north of the center of British Columbia. In the northern continuation of the same mountains rise the Klondike, Pelly, Stewart, and other gold-bearing tributaries of the Yukon. There is this difference, that Peace River rises on the eastern slope of the mountains, while the Yukon's tributaries rise on the west side. Along Peace River on the north are the Reindeer or Caribou mountains, which have been found this summer to be rich in gold-bearing quartz.

"Mr. Kitchen found that other miners had recently arrived at Vancouver, bringing large amounts of gold from Peace River. He is accordingly arranging to organize a company which will put steamers on the Athabasca River and lake and on Peace River next spring, and establish three trading posts. He will go to Lincoln, Neb., where he formerly lived, to get part of the necessary capital."

The Edmonton and Athabasca route will not only be available for travel to the rich mining areas on the eastern slopes of the Rockies—it will be found preferable to any other in reaching the Klondike territory as well. This trail is both shorter—affording a much cheaper route—and practicable for the transportation of horses, machinery and supplies into the whole northwest country, without hardship or serious difficulty.

CHAPTER XIV.

FURS, FISH AND GAME OF THE KLONDIKE.

The silver, gray, black and red fox—Abundance of game—The caribou, moose and the grizzly, brown, black and silver-tip bears—Salmon and other fish, etc.

The principal fur procured in the Canadian Northwest, west of the Rockies and north of the 60th parallel, which is just now being called the Klondike country, are the silver, gray and black fox, the number of which bears a greater ratio to the red foxes than in any other part of the north. The red fox is, of course, very common, and a species called the blue is abundant further towards the coast. Marten or sable, and lynx, are quite numerous. Otter are far more scarce than to the east of the Rockies, and beaver do not exist to any extent. It is estimated that the value of the gray and black fox skins taken out of the country annually more than equals the value of all other furs secured.

Game is very abundant, but owing to the presence of miners most of it has been driven back from the rivers occupied by them. The Indians have to ascend the tributary streams ten or twenty miles to secure furs or game worth going after. Here on the uplands are vast herds of caribou, although in some seasons they disappear altogether. The Indians slaughter them without regard to their meat necessities. Some years ago moose were numerous along the principal rivers, but are now seldom seen except at a considerable distance from the regions occupied by miners. Eighteen moose were killed on Coal Creek in one day in 1888. The Indians sell much of this meat to the miners.

There are two species of caribou in the country. One—the ordinary kind—is found in most parts of the north. This much resembles and is generally spoken of as the reindeer. The other is known as the "Wood caribou," being a much larger and more beautiful animal. The ordinary caribou runs in herds, often numbering hundreds. They are easily approached and may be killed without much difficulty. When the Indians overtake a herd they surround it, gradually driving them into a bunch, when the animals, being panic-stricken, are slaughtered in a wholesale manner.

There are four species of bear in this region. These are the grizzly, brown, black, and a small kind called the "silver-tip." The latter are of a gray color, and are very fierce. There are a few of the common gray wolves, but these are seldom met with. The arctic rabbit is scarce, except once in seven years, when they may be seen in myriads. They are plentiful for about four years, and then disappear for about three years. The marten is also subject to periodical increase. The mountain sheep and mountain goats exist everywhere in this country, but are most numerous on the mountain sides.

Birds are rarely seen. A few ravens are met with along the rivers. They are very active and noisy on stormy days. Once in awhile the magpie and white-headed eagle are seen. Partridges are very scarce, but ptarmigan, or the arctic partridge, is abundant. Wild geese and ducks are plentiful in season. The ducks abound in endless variety.

Fish are numerous in all the streams. Lake trout are caught in most of the lakes. They take a troll bait readily. Salmon abound in all the principal streams flowing into the Yukon. One can easily trace their presence by the slight ripple they make on the surface, and they can be taken by gently placing a scoop net in their way and lifting them out when they enter it.

Indians inhabit the country, but the tribes are not very numerous, nor of any special interest.

CHAPTER XV.

IMPORTANT INTERNATIONAL QUESTIONS.

Verified reports of rich gold discoveries and the arrival of the precious metal in this country likely to send a vast population from the United States to the Klondike regions—Might possibly lead to war between England and this country—The feeling in London—Chicago and London competitors—Routes for railroad communication with the upper Yukon—The boundary question practically settled.

It is not impossible that the great influx of citizens of the United States to the Klondike country, which lies almost wholly within British territory, may lead to serious international complications. There will be in the neighborhood of 10,000 Americans in that region by the spring of 1898, and the number is likely to be quadrupled before the beginning of 1899. Some authorities estimate that 250,000, all told, will have gone into the country before the beginning of the 20th century.

The excitement over the rich gold fields there is being daily augmented by the return of miners with bags of coarse gold and nuggets. Nearly all of these pioneers of the new country bring fortunes, of greater or less dimensions, with them, and leave behind them gold claims worth millions, to which they propose to return in the spring. Reports of this kind, all fully verified, cannot fail to cause many thousands to leave the United States for the Golden North. Reports similar to the following are now, August, 1897, of almost daily occurrence:

"Tacoma, Wash, Aug. 21.—T. P. Riley, formerly section foreman of the Northern Pacific at Alderton, twelve miles from Tacoma, returned to-day from the Klondike and weighed out in front of a Ledger reporter $85,000 in gold nuggets, the result of two years of hardships and toil in frozen regions of the North.

"His partners, Flannigan and O'Brien, have an equal share with him, and are now speeding across the continent to Pennsylvania with $85,000 apiece of Klondike gold. Mr. Riley and his party left the Klondike on July 6, and were twenty-three days at Dyea. They carried their golden gleanings themselves, and, to evade notoriety, told no one of their good fortune. 'All of my life, I have had to work like a slave for small wages,' said Mr. Riley, 'but I am now independent for life. Two years ago I was a section foreman on the Northern Pacific, twelve miles from Tacoma. I was a hard drinker, and for that I was discharged. It was the best thing ever happened to me. I went to Alaska, and was near Circle City when the richness of the Klondike was discovered. I at once went over, and with my partners (Flannigan and O'Brien) took up two claims. We worked all winter, and when the clean-up came in the spring we had $85,000 apiece. Here is mine. How does it look?

"'It means no more hard work for me. I have all I want, and more too. I am going to Ireland to see some of my relatives, and next March I will return to Tacoma, buy me a good big farm, and live for the rest of my days on what it will bring in. I left the Klondike July 6th, and after a rapid though hard trip we landed at Dyea on July 29th. Thousands of rich strikes have been made there this spring and summer, and I would not take $5,000,000 for my share in our two claims. There is gold enough in the district to supply the world and make everybody rich. A man who never had a pick or shovel in his hand in his life stands just as good a chance as an old, experienced miner. When I left, there were nearly six tons of gold waiting to be shipped down on the Portland, at St. Michaels, which I heard will be here in a few days. On Stewart River, 180 miles from the Klondike diggings, rich strikes have been made, and the people of the district are wild with excitement and many are rushing to the new diggings. Dawson City is now quite a town, and has about 3,500 people. The best buildings are given up to saloons and gambling houses, and every one gambles and drinks. Though the country is rich and the strikes are numerous, I fear for the thousands who are trying to rush over the passes at this season of the year. They will many of them fail in their attempt, and will leave their bones along the trail. I would advise all who intend going to wait until spring and then go in over the ice or Hudson's Bay route. If they go over the latter, let them take plenty of horses and cattle with them and they will have no trouble.'"

Mr. Riley talks about six tons of gold. That appears to be fabulous, but it is impressed upon the minds of the people as true; for word came from Washington on even date with the above that when the steamer Portland comes out into Bering Sea with her load of virgin gold, on her last trip, she will be convoyed to a place of safety by one of the revenue cutters belonging to the United States government, now on duty in northern waters. It is certain that instructions were sent to Captain Tuttle, who commands the Bear, to act as convoy to the treasure steamer.

These facts demonstrate that the reports of the Klondike gold diggings are not too highly colored. It is probably nearer the truth that more gold came out of the country in 1897 than there is any report of, for the reason that many of the lucky miners are very reticent about giving an account of their successes.

From English reports recently printed it is evident that there is much anxiety felt in London as to the future of the Golden Northwest, lest it should in some unforeseen manner fall under the jurisdiction of the United States government. This leads us to a few words of history.

It was a happy day, or will prove such for perhaps millions of souls, when, in 1867, Seward, backed by Sumner—acting for the government of the United

States—purchased Alaska from Russia for $7,200,000. The purchase was generally ridiculed at the time, and the price paid was characterized as extravagant. No one has yet given a true reason why, on the part of the United States or that of Russia, the purchase and sale were made. Many explanations have been made, but this is the true one:

England and Russia were the only nations on earth possessing information as to the value of the resources of the great north. The former received its knowledge through the officers, traders and factors of the Hudson's Bay Company. When Beaconsfield realized the situation, he determined on the consolidations of the British possessions in North America. The late Sir John A. Macdonald, of Canada, was his chief lieutenant in the work. First came the confederation of the four eastern Canadian provinces. Then British Columbia was added, and the whole Northwest territory was purchased from the Hudson's Bay Company.

Meanwhile Beaconsfield was reaching out for Alaska, but the relations between Russia and England were sufficiently strained in 1867 to enable Seward, who was watching the deal closely, to step in and make the purchase. In this way the United States obtained a foothold in the north. The wisdom of this piece of statecraft is only beginning to be understood. In the years to come it will be seen that the absorption of the whole Dominion of Canada by the United States, which must come as a legitimate result of development on this continent, will be accomplished largely through the good offices of Alaska.

It is impossible to obtain a proper conception of the great north by confining one's studies to Alaska proper. The gold diggers on the upper Yukon find themselves on both sides of the 141st degree, which is the international boundary line. The Northwest Territory, and indeed the whole north of this continent, is one and inseparable. Political divisions cut but little figure, after all, in the development of natural resources in a vast country which nature has not been pleased to divide.

It is a fact that the greater part of the Klondike gold fields are in British territory. So are Dawson City and Fort Cudahy. So are the rich, illimitable areas of park country—lying as low as 400 to 600 feet above the level of the sea—which stretch out from Lake Athabasca, westward along the Peace and Athabasca rivers to the foothills of the Rockies; northward to and along the upper waters of the mighty Mackenzie, to the 64th parallel; eastward to the head waters of the great Churchill; and southward, including the whole valley of the Peace River, stretching away to the north branch of the Saskatchewan.

This vast basin, many times greater than that of the Mississippi, in which all the states northwest of the Ohio and southeast of the Missouri could be duplicated, is sufficiently broad and productive to furnish the world's population with bread and meat for many centuries to come.

What then of political boundary lines? Canadian enterprise is too feeble and British push too slow to populate and develop such a country. It is left to the people of the United States to go in and possess the land, and as soon as they become informed of the boundless wealth there—awaiting the pick and the pan, the crusher and the stamp-mill, the rancher and the husbandman—they will go; and they will carry the stars and stripes with them. This will seal the political destiny of the great far Northwest.

Before another generation has risen, it is possible that the flag of the United States will be flying not only from Sitka and St. Michaels, not only from Juneau and Circle City, but above all the mining camps and trading posts from Rampart House to the valley of the Peace River and the western shores of Hudson's Bay.

It is significant that the national government has determined to establish an experimental farm to test the productive qualities of the soil in the valleys of

Alaska. This is the beginning of the end. There can be but one result of such an undertaking. The great value and productiveness of the soil of the north is already known to Great Britain, and will soon become equally well understood and appreciated by the people of the United States. Who can foretell the outcome? It may be a quarrel over the sealing grounds; and it is safe to say that nothing could familiarize the people of this country with the resources of the great north so effectively as marching an army of a few hundred thousand people across the 49th parallel over the branches of the Saskatchewan, through the illimitable park country of the Peace River valley, across the head waters of the Mackenzie and the summit of the Rockies, and thence to the Klondike.

Secretary Sherman has already sounded the keynote, and the British press is talking back impudently. These mutterings may ultimately culminate in a storm over the possession of the great northwest which, whatever other result might follow, would, more than anything else, tend to populate it and develop its vast resources. If we are ever going to have a war with England, as a solution of the hard times problem, or otherwise, by all means let it be a war for the possession of the great north; for that would advertise the country to the world, and send hundreds and thousands from the overcrowded cities of this country to find happy homes of peace and plenty in that region.

But it is more agreeable and, of course, much more reasonable to think of the colonization and development of the Golden North by peaceful methods. International difficulties likely to be met with will doubtless be solved peacefully, and the vast resources of the north land appropriated to the profit of both the countries immediately interested.

In a recent newspaper cablegram from London it is stated: "The Marquis of Lorne, in a signed statement, expresses the confidence of British statesmen in the ability of the Canadian government to retain their supremacy and maintain their hold of Klondike." At the same time there is no denying that a feeling of uneasiness begins to be felt in London over the liability of conflict between Canadian and American interests. Englishmen believe Canada should control the Klondike and would support Canada in any restrictions upon American enterprise, no matter how severe. The opinion is commonly expressed that Canadians should do precisely what the Boers did at Johannesburg, hold the mines and tax the Uitlanders, not seeing that this would give the Americans justification for a Jameson raid. But the inherent weakness of Canada is felt in the remoteness of the diggings and the necessity of reaching them through American territory."

The last sentence of the above is absolutely ridiculous. There is no necessity for the British or the Canadians reaching the country through American territory. They have a far shorter and better route by way of the Canadian Pacific Railway to Edmonton, thence overland through the Peace River country and across the head waters of the Mackenzie, as before stated. The report continues:

"Englishmen admit the Klondike is now controlled by Americans, but these are described in papers here as plunderers, ruffians and outlaws. The attempts of the Canadian authorities to enforce the new and special taxes upon Americans going to the Klondike are described as maintaining order and enforcing law. Fears are expressed that Canadian customs officers attempting to collect taxes at Skaguay will be wiped out by the Americans, and that the few Canadian officers at Dawson will be laughed at and defied and the stars and stripes raised by mob over the Klondike region.

"In that event it is said a strong force will be sent at once to the diggings, for England wants gold and hates to see it go to the United States. Any conflict or bloodshed between Americans and Canadian officers would at once raise the most serious complications.

"Many Englishmen fear the proximity of the Klondike to the Alaskan boundary, the sensational wealth of the mines, and the mad rush now being made, will end in war between England and the United States. One London paper has already announced that American politicians and journalists are now scheming to bring on war through the Klondike with a view of annexing Canada, and warns readers to be prepared for violent exhibitions of ill feeling.

"Shrewd observers here, however, say England would put up with almost anything rather than incur the risks of such a conflict, with the inevitable loss of Canada. London speculators are looking enviously toward the Klondike, but think Wall street will have the first picking and that England will get left in the rake-off. Nevertheless, many Klondike schemes are being floated and the newspapers are printing full accounts of the new diggings."

Chicago, more than any other city in the world, is deeply interested in this continuation of the northwestward march of civilization and material progress. This city must reach the Klondike by rail, not only for the tons of yellow metal which lie hidden in the sands and rocks along the gulches and hills bordering the tributaries of the upper Yukon, but also for the measureless bread and meat resources of the boundless country which lie between, and which spreads out in rich, broad valleys.

There should be no delay in this undertaking. Nature has already provided a highway for our British competitor. London and Chicago are the natural competitors for the boundless wealth of the great north. At first sight it may appear that London is so much farther from the Klondike than Chicago that competition is out of the question. Not so. The Hudson's Bay route is not new to the world of enterprise. It is only 1,500 miles from Churchill on the west shore of Hudson's Bay to the upper Yukon, and the highest elevation of the Rockies to be crossed is scarcely over 2,000 feet. Compare this with the Rocky Mountain grades of the Canadian Pacific, the Northern Pacific, the Union Pacific and the Southern Pacific, and the advantages of the more northern route are wonderful to contemplate.

A railroad from Churchill to the Klondike would pass through the great valleys of the Peace River to the upper Mackenzie, and might diverge to the north, from the neighborhood of Lake Athabaska, reaching the head waters of the Yukon with even a less elevation than 2,000 feet.

The distance from Churchill—where there is one of the finest harbors in the world, open the year round—to Liverpool, by way of Hudson's Bay and Strait, is only 2,960, and as transportation by water is so much cheaper than that by rail, it will be seen that, for seven months in the year at least, England could tap the resources of the great Northwest almost as effectively as could Chicago by rail across the plains.

At this point a suggestion to the capitalists of Chicago may be ventured. While companies are being incorporated for the purposes of carrying supplies to the Klondike gold fields, and of developing the gold mines located there, this question of a railroad from Chicago to the head waters of the Yukon through American and Canadian territory should not be left without solution. Capital and push will build a railway from Chicago to Bering Sea, over a route passing through the richest country on the face of the earth. There are not more than 500 miles of territory in the whole distance that is not either habitable and productive, or rich in gold fields. Congress would no doubt respond by assisting such an enterprise both with money and an Alaskan land grant. Such an enterprise would necessarily be of an international character. However, Chicago has vast interests at stake in the solution of this problem, and those who become the pioneers in such an undertaking will not only reap material rewards but write their names in history as founders of a new empire, besides opening the way to relief for the hundreds of thousands of the unemployed and suffering of our own population.

The international boundary question in the far Northwest is practically settled. General Duffield, of the coast and geodetic survey of the United States government, recently said:

"I do not believe that when the matter of the boundary line between the two countries is definitely settled there will be any appreciable change from what is down on the map at present. There certainly will not be as far as regards the Klondike region, which is beyond all manner of dispute in the British Northwest territory.

"Dawson City is a hundred miles or more east of the 141st meridian, which is the boundary line. Mount St. Elias is near the intersection of the ten marine league line with the 141st meridian. To be exact, the summit is 140 degrees and 55 minutes, or 5 minutes, on the Canadian side, which in that latitude represents two and one-half miles. But on the southern side it is only twenty-eight and one half-miles from the coast, which brings it inside of the ten league line, or thirty mile limit, and one and one-half miles on American soil.

"At Forty Mile Creek our survey agrees with that of the Canadian survey under Ogilvie within fourteen hundredths of a second, which in that latitude represents six and a half feet. The Canadian line steals the six and a half feet from us. Crossing the Yukon River the difference in the two surveys is fourteen seconds, which in that latitude represents 300 feet. According to the line of Ogilvie, the Canadian government surveyor, we gain 300 feet on the British side.

"We are anxious to compare the two lines at the Porcupine River crossing, which is several miles further north, but the Canadian government has given us no notice of where it has fixed its line there. I do not suppose that the difference will be worthy of note."

General Duffield added that if there is any dispute between the two countries over the boundary line it will be in regard to the ten league coast line in the southern portion of Alaska, as that is a question which admits of considerable diversity of opinion.

CHAPTER XVI.

THE GREAT FERTILE NORTH.

A boundless territory of inexhaustible bread, meat and dairy capabilities—Coal and other resources—How the lower levels are sheltered from storms and cold.

We now come to make some observations on that vast portion of the far northwest lying east of the Rocky Mountains and north of the 60th parallel, and between it and the Arctic Circle. This area, including the upper Klondike country, contains nearly 1,000,000 square miles, rich in timber, furs, fish, gold and minerals generally, with vast areas of good coal.

To the south of this district, and on the west, lies British Columbia, bounded on the north by the 60th parallel. While further east, and to the south, are the provisional territories of Athabasca, in the Peace River region, with 104,500 square miles; Alberta, with 106,100 square miles; Saskatchewan, with 107,092 square miles; Assiniboia, with 90,000 square miles; and to the east of this, the district of Keewatin, with 282,000 square miles; and to the south of the latter is the province of Manitoba, with 73,956 square miles. British Columbia has an area of 383,300 square miles.

The territory east of Keewatin and south of Hudson's Bay, known as the Eastern District, contains 196,800 square miles. The Hudson's Bay territory proper contains 358,000 square miles. The river basins which compose this great north country have already been quite fully described. These areas including the older provinces of Canada are equally as large as the whole of Europe and about 500,000 square miles larger than the United States without Alaska, and of about equal extent to the United States including Alaska.

In order to complete our observations on the entire north country, we must look with some care upon the several divisions above named, commencing with Manitoba, which, however, is so well known that it will not be necessary to dwell at any length on that part of the country. Manitoba is situated in the very center of the continent, being midway between the Atlantic and Pacific oceans on the east and west, and the Arctic Ocean and the Gulf of Mexico on the north and south. This province is now well settled and enjoys a high grade of schools, colleges, churches and a well developed social life. The climate is warm in summer and cold in winter. The summer mean is 65 to 70 degrees, about the same as that of the state of New York, but in winter the thermometer falls below zero, frequently from 30 to 40 degrees. However, the atmosphere is bright and dry, and the cold is not so unpleasant as that of less cold temperatures in the humid districts farther to the south. It may be noticed here that the isothermal line running from Winnipeg, the capital of Manitoba, bears duly northwest until Fort Simpson, on the Mackenzie River, is reached. Indeed, it may be said that there are higher temperatures, in the cold season, farther to the northwest than at Winnipeg. The country is one of the healthiest on the globe, and is exceedingly pleasant to live in. There are no diseases whatever arising out of the climate. Occasionally there are summer frosts, but these do not prove severe oftener than once in seven years.

Very little snow falls on the prairies—and this is all a prairie country for thousands of miles in every direction where the soil has been developed—the depth of the snow ranging from six to twelve and eighteen inches. Native horses can graze out of doors all winter, which they do by pawing the snow off the grass. The snow disappears and plowing begins about the middle of April, sometimes earlier. The Red River, which flows from the interior of Minnesota northward to Lake Winnipeg, opens about the same time. There is practically no spring. Winter bursts into summer during the month of April. The summer months include May, June, July, August and September. Autumn lasts until the end of November, when the regular frosts set in. Harvest work is always completed by the middle of September.

The soil is a rich, deep black mold or loam resting on a thick, very tenacious subsoil of clay. It is held to be, together with that of the vast regions northwest of it, the richest soil in the world, and is especially adapted to the growth of wheat. This wheat brings a higher price in the world's markets than that grown in any other portion of North America. Water is almost everywhere found by digging wells of moderate depth. The rivers and coulees are also available for water supply during the spring and early summer. Rain falls freely during the spring, but the summer and autumn are generally dry.

Agricultural pursuits are highly developed in Manitoba, there being in the present season about 2,500,000 acres of land devoted to the production of wheat, oats, barley, flax, rye, pease, corn, potatoes and roots. The yield for the present year is not yet known, but it is estimated to be: Wheat, 40,000,000 bushels; oats, 25,000,000 bushels; barley, 6,000,000 bushels; flax, 1,300,000 bushels; rye, 70,000,000 bushels; pease, 30,000,000 bushels. The potato and root crops have also been very successful. The inhabitants of that province are confident of a great future for their country from an agricultural point of view. Small fruits, such as strawberries, raspberries, currants, gooseberries, cranberries, plums, etc., are plentiful, and wild grapes are very common. Stock raising has been carried on in Manitoba very successfully, but is conducted on a much larger scale in the districts farther to the west. This province has railway communication with the Atlantic and Pacific oceans and all parts of the country to the south of it.

Very much that has been said respecting the soil,

climate and productions of Manitoba apply equally to almost all the northwest country east of the Rocky Mountains. To the north and west of that province extends the region known as the North-West Territories of Canada. It is bounded on the south by the 49th parallel, which divides central Canada from the United States. A remarkable feature of this great area is its division into three distinct prairie plains or plateaus, as they are generally called. The first of these is known as the Red River Valley and Lake Winnipeg Plateau. The average height above the level of the sea of this district is about 800 feet. At the boundary line it is 1,000 feet. The second plateau or steppe has an average altitude of 1,600 feet, and a width of about 250 miles. It is a rich, undulating, park-like country. It includes the Assiniboine and Qu'Appelle valleys. The third plateau, or steppe, begins on the boundary line at the 104th degree, where it has an elevation of about 2,000 feet, and extends west for 465 miles, to the foot of the Rocky Mountains, where it has an altitude of 4,200 feet, making an average height above the sea of 3,000 feet. A fourth vast prairie steppe, larger than the other three together, lies north and northwest of the last two named and includes the Peace River and upper Mackenzie basins. This region is still more fertile and better adapted to stock raising than that immediately to the south of it. This is because its surface does not rise above sea level more than from 400 to 800 feet.

It is an ascertained fact in meteorological phenomena that the cold storm-waves which rise in the arctic pass over the lower levels to burst in tempestuous fury and low temperatures on approaching the watershed near the 49th parallel, or the foothills of the Rockies.

CHAPTER XVII.

CANADIAN NORTHWEST.

Districts of Assiniboia, Saskatchewan, Alberta and Athabaska—The vast fertile plains to the north—Greatest agricultural and stock raising region on earth.

In this connection we continue our observations on the prairie and plain regions of the Canadian Northwest lying east of the Rockies, before covering the overland routes through the mountains to the Klondike country, north of the 60th parallel, before referred to.

The District of Assiniboia comprises an area, as already stated, of 90,000 square miles. The valley of the Qu'Appelle is in the district of Assiniboia, being on the second plateau or steppe of the continent, reaching from the Red River to the Rocky Mountains. This valley is a favored part of the Northwest, and settlement in it is proceeding with surprising rapidity. The transcontinental road traverses the whole breadth of the district, entering it a few miles east of Moosomin, about 200 miles west of Winnipeg. This rapidly rising town lies in the center of a highly favored district where mixed farming vies with wheat growing for the place of first interest. The railroad affords opportunity for the location of numerous market towns, advantage of which has already been taken at many points. In districts at some distance from the railroad, the ranching industry is less impeded by the pursuits of agriculture, and a large number of Assiniboia-fed animals now find their way each season to the English market. The Manitoba and Northwestern road enters the territories in the northern part of Assiniboia and runs through a prosperous district, the principal points in which are the towns of Saltcoats and Yorkton. Railroad communication is also provided for the settlers in the southern part of the district by the Souris branch of the Canadian Pacific, which joins the northern and southern extensions—more familiarly known as the "Soo" line—at Estevan. This latter road gives a direct means of communication with many of the large centers of the United States. At several points on this latter road coal is mined, which, though it is not of high quality, effectually settles the fuel problem, as it gives excellent satisfaction—both for cooking and heating purposes—when used with suitable appliances, while the low cost of production keeps its price within reasonable limits. In common with other places in the Northwest Territories, the dairy industry is taking a leading part in the up-building of Assiniboia, there being but few settled localities that are not within easy reach of a creamery or cheese factory. At present the principal market for these products is found in the mountains of British Columbia, but not a little is shipped to points across the Pacific, Japan, especially, being a large consumer of prairie-made butter.

At present Moose Jaw, the northern terminus of the "Soo" line, may be described as being the western limit of the purely agricultural area of Assiniboia, the whole country west of this point being, in the main, devoted to pastoral pursuits. The western part of Assiniboia, like the southern part of Alberta, bordering on the arid regions of the continent, is but sub-humid, and its rainfall, though admirably suited to a grazing country, is not at all times sufficient to produce cereal and root crops in such abundance as is done elsewhere in the territories where the natural conditions are more favorable. But the cattle of these western plains fully demonstrate that the ability of the country to sustain animal life has not departed with the buffalo that, not many years ago, roamed these regions. The district is everywhere covered with a short, thick, rich grass, which is unusually nutritious. Towards the middle of summer the grass presents to the eye a dried and burned appearance, but is in reality only cured, and retains all its natural sustenance. In this condition it is devoured by animals with avidity, and they fatten upon it to a surprising degree. The principal points in the western part of Assiniboia open for grazing leases lie in the hills to the south of the railroad, and are to be reached from all points between Swift Current and Medicine Hat.

The Dominion Experimental Farm for the Northwest Territories is located at Indian Head in Eastern Assiniboia, where extensive experiments in the selection of horned cattle, horses, sheep, pigs, grains, roots, trees and grasses, suitable to the climate are continually being made, and much of the improvement to be noticed in the methods of agriculture in the Territories may be directly traced to the experimental work done at this noteworthy institution.

The seat of the Territorial Government is established at Regina, where the Lieutenant-Governor and members of the local administration reside. This place is also the headquarters of the Indian Department for Manitoba and the Northwest, and also of the Northwest Mounted Police. From Regina a railway runs north to Prince Albert on the Saskatchewan, which at present forms the only means of rapid communication between this district and the markets of the world.

The district of the Saskatchewan lies to the north of Assiniboia and the province of Manitoba, and comprises about 107,000 square miles. But a small portion of the district has, as yet, been opened up by settlement, which has mainly sought the banks of both branches of the river from which the district takes its name. The oldest settlements in the Northwest are to be found on the Saskatchewan, which for many years formed the highway along which the furs exported by the Hudson's Bay Company from the districts to the far northwest were carried. Notable among these are the settlements of Prince Albert and Battleford, which latter place was for a number of years the seat of the Territorial Government, but, on the construction of the Canadian Pacific Railroad, it was deemed advisable to remove the departmental officials to a point nearer the railroad.

On account of its present difficulties of access, this district is not filling up so rapidly as the neighboring districts of Assiniboia and Alberta, but its immense resources are not altogether overlooked by new settlers, and a steady growth of population is reported. The Manitoba and Northwestern road is chartered to build to Prince Albert, and other roads are projected to various points on the Saskatchewan River, which, when completed, will open up a district of marvelous fertility. At present the only means of access to this district by railway is by the Qu'Appelle, Long Lake and Saskatchewan road, which runs into Prince Albert from Regina, but other parts of the district are easily reached by means of well-equipped stage lines. Settlement in this district preceded railroad construction in the Northwest by a number of years, and there are to-day probably no more prosperous and satisfied people in the country than those who thus braved the vicissitudes and trials of frontier life. These, however, are now almost altogether obviated, and the newcomer who takes up land in any portion of this district will find himself within reach of all the comforts and most of the luxuries of life.

In addition to the older towns of Battleford and Prince Albert, bright settlements are springing up at Jackfish Lake, Turtle Lake, Duck Lake, Shell River, Rosthern, Stony Creek, Carlton, Carrot River, Kinistino, Birch Hills, The Forks, St. Laurent, St. Louis DeLangevin and other places. In all these neighborhoods there are still large tracts open to the homeseeker on the usual government terms of 160 acres free to any settler who takes up the land to live on it and cultivate it.

The principal crops are wheat, oats, barley and roots, which are raised successfully and in abundance. The average yield of wheat (red fyfe) is about 30 bushels to the acre in ordinary seasons, from the sowing of one to one and a half bushels. Oats give a twenty-five fold increase. Though the district has proved an admirable one for the cultivation of barley, yet the small demand for this cereal has hitherto kept its production in the background. It being necessary at times to provide food and shelter for stock in winter, animals succeed better in the hands of the farmer than of the rancher. For herds of from 200 to 400 head no portion of the Territories offers better openings, but the farmer who has his 160-acre farm well stocked succeeds equally well with his ambitious neighbor.

The Saskatchewan district answers all the requirements of a good dairy district, pure water, cool nights and rich grasses. Every few miles there are streams fed by living springs, all tributary to the main river; while large lakes of fresh water are to be found in all directions. The whole of the district is well wooded, and the park-like character of the scenery has been spoken of in appreciative terms by travelers of all classes.

The climate of the Saskatchewan district is pleasant during nearly every portion of the year. Occasional storms occur in winter, but, speaking generally, the weather, even during the coldest periods of winter, is pleasant. The summer temperature averages about 60 degrees, the numberless lakes and vast water stretches probably accounting for this equability of temperature. The tenderest of garden produce, such as melons, cucumbers, pumpkins, squash, corn, tomatoes and beans are grown every year in the open air successfully, which is sufficient proof of the immunity of the district from summer frosts.

The sportsman will find this whole region a continual charm. Fish are caught in nearly all the lakes and rivers, while the prairie and woods teem with feathered game and deer of all descriptions.

The District of Alberta comprises an area of about

106,000 square miles. It is bounded on the south by the international boundary; on the east by the districts of Assiniboia and Saskatchewan; on the west by the province of British Columbia, at the summits of the Rocky Mountains; and on the north by the eighteenth correction line, which is near the fifty-fifth parallel of latitude.

Nature has been lavish in its gifts to Alberta. A great portion of the district, being immediately related to the Rocky Mountains, has scenery of magnificent beauty, and the numerous cold rivers and streams which flow into it from the mountains are as clear and blue as the sky above them, and abound with magnificent trout.

The great natural beauties of Alberta suggest that these foothills and spurs of the Rocky Mountains will be the favorite resort of tourists and health-seekers, when the eastern plains shall have received their population of millions. This district may also be said to be pre-eminently the dairy region of America. Its cold, clear streams and rich and luxuriant grasses make it a very paradise for cattle. This is at present the ranch country. Numerous ranches have been started in the southern half of Alberta, both for horses and neat cattle, which have already been developed into great importance. Experience has proved that with good management the cattle thrive well in the winter, the percentage of loss being much less than was estimated when the ranches were undertaken. There is in these enterprises the commencement of great industries, and they are now sending cattle to the eastern markets, and to those of Europe, by the ten thousand head. Sheep thrive exceptionally well in this district, as they do, in fact, all over the northwest.

The census returns of 1891 showed that horses over three years old numbered 20,704; colts and fillies, 11,-266; milk cows, 10,785; other horned cattle, 134,064; sheep, 16,057; and swine, 5,103. In the three provisional districts of Alberta, Assiniboia and Saskatchewan the increase of live stock in 1891 was 220,400 over 1885. It is not only in agricultural resources that the district of Alberta is rich. There are in it the greatest extent of coal fields known in the world. The Rocky Mountains and their foothills contain a world of minerals yet to be explored, comprising iron, gold, silver, galena, and copper. Large petroleum deposits are known to exist. Immense supplies of timber may also be mentioned among the riches of Alberta, and these are found in such positions as to be easily workable in the valleys of the numerous streams flowing through the foothills of the Rocky Mountains into the great Saskatchewan.

The climate of Alberta has features peculiarly its own. In winter it is liable to remarkable alterations. When the wind blows from the Pacific Ocean, and this is the prevailing wind, the weather becomes mild and the snow rapidly disappears. When, however, it blows from the north over the plains, the weather becomes very cold, the thermometer sometimes going down to 30 degrees below zero. In summer there is liability to frosts, but they are generally local, and do not discourage the settlers. Calgary, the chief town in Alberta, is advancing with very rapid strides. Many substantial and really fine buildings have been and are being erected. It is beautifully situated at the confluence of the Bow and Elbow rivers. It is very thriving, does a large business, and commands a beautiful view of the Rocky Mountains. The other towns are Lethbridge, connected by railway with the Canadian Pacific line, where coal mines are being worked; Macleod, a ranching center; Banff, in the recently formed National Park, near which anthracite coal is being mined, and where the famous sulphur springs are found; and Edmonton, which is the center of the oldest settlement in the district.

The District of Athabaska comprises an area of 105,000 square miles, and is bounded on the south by the district of Alberta; on the east by the line between the 10th and 11th ranges—west of the 4th meridian—of the Dominion lands system of survey, until, in proceeding northwards, that line intersects the Athabasca River; then by that river and Athabasca Lake and Slave River to the intersection of this line by the northern boundary of the district, which is to be the thirty-second correction line of the Dominion lands township system, and is very near the sixtieth parallel of north latitude; and on the west by the province of British Columbia.

This district also has vast resources, but, being yet, from its northern position, out of the range of immediate settlement, its riches in agricultural and stock-raising capabilities, and its excellent climate are known only to explorers and surveyors.

But even to the north of this provisional district, in the broad Peace River Valley, and alluvial plains of the upper Mackenzie, is a still greater country in extent and resources.

Two new provisional districts or territories have recently been erected in the far northwest by the Canadian government. The first is that called Mackenzie, lying to the north of Athabasca, and extending westward to the summit of the Rockies. The second is called Yukon, and extends westward from the summit of the Rockies to the 141st degree of longitude, and northward from the northern boundary of British Columbia.

CHAPTER XVIII.

RESOURCES OF BRITISH COLUMBIA.

Excellent climate—Abundance of coal—Gold in inexhaustible quantities—Iron, copper, galena, mercury, platinum, plumbago, mica, salt and many other valuable deposits—Progress of the mines.

And now a few words as to British Columbia. This province extends about 700 miles from south to north and nearly 500 from west to east—an area of more than 350,000 square miles. It is separated from the rest of Canada by the Rocky Mountains, while the Pacific Ocean bounds it on the west, except for nearly 300 miles on the extreme north, where the Alaskan possessions of the United States interpose between it and the sea. The southern limit is the forty-ninth parallel, which forms the international boundary between the province and the United States. The northern boundary is the sixtieth parallel. Vancouver Island is separated from the state of Washington by the Strait of San Juan de Fuca. It is oblong in shape, extending northwesterly parallel with the mainland, from which it is divided by the Strait of the Gulf of Georgia, a distance of 300 miles, with a varying width of from twenty to sixty miles.

The climate varies considerably, as the province is naturally divided into two sections, insular and continental. It is much more moderate and equable than that of any other province of the Dominion. In the southeastern portion of the mainland, and particularly on the southeastern part of Vancouver Island, the climate is much superior to that of southern England or central France. In this section of the province snow seldom falls, and then lies but a few hours or days. Vegetation remains green and the flowers are bright through the greater part of nearly every winter; while in spring and summer disagreeable east winds, excessively heavy rains and long-continued fogs are unknown. Generally speaking, spring commences in February in all parts of the province west of the Cascade Mountains. East of these mountains the winters are short, but sharp, continuing from six to ten or twelve weeks, with a temperature down sometimes as low as twenty or even thirty degrees below zero. Summers in this region are correspondingly warm. In the northern portions of the province the cold of winter is severe; but everywhere the climate is salubrious and healthy. In proportion to the area of the province, the extent of land suitable for agricultural purposes is small; but in the aggregate there are many thousands of square miles of arable soil, so diverse in character, location and climatic conditions as to be suited to the production of every fruit, cereal, vegetable, plant and flower known to the temperate zone. West of the Cascade Mountains spring and early summer rains are quite sufficient to bring crops to maturity; but further east, in the great stock-raising interior, irrigation is generally required for mixed farming purposes. In this part of the province there are immense areas of open bunch grass country admirably adapted to grazing; while the coast of the mainland and Vancouver Island are much better suited to mixed farming. Unoccupied land in these sections is all more or less timbered, but with a considerable acreage almost everywhere that can be easily cleared and brought under cultivation. Alder bottoms and small grassy swamps are to be found in nearly all the numerous valleys; and this is the description of land that settlers are looking after and locating on.

In mineral resources British Columbia is by far the richest of all the Canadian provinces. Coal is abundant, while gold, silver, iron, copper, galena, mercury, platinum, plumbago, mica, slate, salt and many others are widely distributed. With the exception of coal nearly all the mining industries are in their infancy and awaiting development.

The coal output from Vancouver's Island during 1894 was 1,012,953 tons, which is the second best year on record. It was disposed of as follows: Exported, 827,642 tons; home consumption, 165,776 tons; leaving less than two weeks' product on hand at the end of the year. On Graham Island, the northern of the Queen Charlotte group, three beds of bituminous coal have been discovered, varying from 7 1-2 to 16 feet in thickness, and of superior quality; also, two large seams of anthracite have been found near Yakom Lake, but neither have been developed. Near Crow's Neat Pass beds of excellent quality and immense thickness (one seam being thirty feet) extend a distance of about thirty miles. This coal is manufactured into coke. At the Kootenay mines, coke now costs $14 per ton, but when the projected British Columbia Southern Railway is built it is expected that better coke, from the Crow's Nest collieries, can be supplied in the Kootenay mining district at about one-half of the present prices. The smelters at work now in the Kootenay are greatly hampered on account of the high price of coke, one at Pilot Bay is using thirty tons per day. From this smelter, which only commenced its operations March 9, 1895, the bullion shipped to the United States, up to the 30th of June, amounted to 1,301 tons. In the Cariboo district great activity prevails in hydraulic mining. The success which attended the short runs made by the companies excited great interest. In June, 1895, a "clean up," after a run of 172 hours, gave sixty-six pounds, three ounces of gold, valued at $14,400. Several joint stock companies have been formed to prosecute gold mining on a large scale in the Cariboo district. In West Kootenay, near the boundary line, profitable investments have been made. The first cost and development work of the "War Eagle" mine amounted to

$32,500. Shipments of ore commenced January 1, 1895, and up to June 1, 1895, $82,500 were paid on dividends. During June the shipments of ore averaged 420 tons per week, at an average value of $37 per ton. The ore is mined at a cost of $9.50 per ton, freight and smaller charges amount to $14 additional per ton. In the Kootenay district 1,215 mineral claims were recorded, 797 transfers, and 962 certificates of work issued in 1894. There were ninety-seven placer claims recorded in the district of West Kootenay during 1896, and there were thirty-six mining leases in force in the Yale district during 1894, 140 mineral claims were recorded, seventy-seven transfers made, and 125 certificates of work issued. Reports from Alberni district, Vancouver Island, are encouraging. Assays of quartz found not far from Alberni town site gave from $103 to $135 value of gold per ton, with traces of silver. A large number of claims have recently been located in that district. For the year ended June 30, 1895, forty mining and smelting companies were incorporated in British Columbia to operate in precious metals, with nominal capital aggregating $24,344,000. The total output of gold in British Columbia during 1894 is officially stated at $456,066; estimated yield of silver, $8,500; with $784,965 in gold, silver, copper and lead ore shipped from Nelson to the United States, not included. Number of miners employed in 1894 is given at 1,610. Rich deposits of iron ore are found on Vancouver and the smaller islands, as well as on the coast and mainland. Those deposits are extensive and accessible, being situated mostly near good harbors, with the necessary fluxes for smelting conveniently at hand. The ore averages from sixty to seventy per cent of iron. There is an abundance of timber for charcoal, also coal and limestone in the vicinity of the various deposits of ore. Latest reports from Cariboo mining district state: "The Cariboo Gold Fields Company are progressing very well with their work. A large number of men are employed on the pipe line ditch. Several hundred Chinamen are at work on the big ditch, which will be nearly eleven miles long, three feet deep, and seven feet wide. They have already commenced the trestle work to carry the pipe past the town, which will take about 2,000 feet of trestling. The pay roll for whites alone is about $5,000 per month. The contract for the ditch was let to a Chinese firm, their tender being considerably lower than any other. The price is somewhere near $30,000. Taken as a whole, Cariboo will turn out double the quantity of gold this year that it did last."

The timber resources of British Columbia are practically inexhaustible. The immense value of this industry, also comparatively new, is beginning to interest eastern lumbermen both in Canada and the States. Large tracts of valuable timber lands have already been purchased or leased by eastern capitalists, and extensive mills erected here and there, while many others are to be built in the near future. The 524,573 acres of forest lands leased to lumbermen are estimated to contain at least twenty million feet of timber per acre.

Second to none of the above mentioned resources is that of the fisheries. The land-locked and quiet bays, inlets, and fjords, together with rivers and small streams, teem with valuable food fish of almost every variety known in the north temperate zone. Among them are salmon and cod, several species each; halibut, sturgeon, herring, oulachan and many other varieties, besides small fish. One of the most delicious of deep water fish is the skil, or black cod, as it is sometimes called. This is considered far superior to the cod of Newfoundland, and has only to be introduced into the markets of the world to create an almost unlimited demand.

CHAPTER XIX.

COUNTRY OF THE SKEENA.

Trip from Port Simpson on the Pacific to the summit of Pine River Pass—Wonderful mountain and valley scenery—Resources of the mighty valleys in the mountain slopes.

Let us make three distinct trips across the Rockies, first from the Pacific Ocean, at Port Simpson, eastward by way of the Skeena, the Pine River Pass, and thence down the Pine to Peace River and to Lake Athabasca; second, up the Lewis, from its junction with the Pelly to form the Yukon, in the Klondike region, to its head waters in the Rockies, thence across the low range of mountains at this point, to the headwaters of the Peace River, and down that stream to Lake Athabasca; and third, up the Pelly River, from the same point of departure, to Dease Lake, thence across the watershed by a chain of lakes, to the headwaters of the Liard River, and down the Liard to the Mackenzie. The latter will include a description of the wonderful Pelly River basin.

These journeys on the printed page will familiarize the reader with the best routes by which to reach the Klondike, and the entire gold regions of the far northwest, as well as with the districts in which future great gold discoveries are sure to be made.

And now as to the first route—from Port Simpson via the Pine River Pass to Lake Athabasca, and thence to the west shore of Hudson's Bay. This will carry us through a country unsurpassed in the beauty of its natural scenery, the value of its resources and its lessons in possible transcontinental communication.

The coast of Northern British Columbia, from which we are to select our starting point for this journey, dissected as it is with inlets, has by no means an abundance of good harbors. The inlets are, however, for the most part, deep, with bold, rocky shores, and traversed by strong tidal currents. The heads almost always receive rivers, each of which has formed shoal banks about its mouth, owing to which shallowness of the water they are unsafe anchorages. Take, for instance, the mouth and estuary of the Skeena. It is shallow and encumbered with bars and banks, and is unsuited for a harbor.

Not far to the north, however, and easily accessible from the valley of the Skeena, lies Port Simpson, one of the safest anchorages on the Pacific coast, and one of the finest harbors in the world. It is over three miles in length, with an average breadth of over one mile, is well sheltered, and very easy of access. Moreover, it lies at the eastern end of Dixon's Entrance, through which vessels lying in that port have direct connection with the Pacific Ocean between Cape Knox, the northern extremity of the Queen Charlotte Islands, and Cape Muzon, the southwestern extremity of Prince of Wales Island. Passing out of Port Simpson, through Chatham Sound, the Dundas Islands are on the left and Fort Tongus on the right. There are no obstructions of any kind to interfere with navigation.

The physical features of the coast in this neighborhood are full of interest. Professor Dawson, who has made a geological examination of this section, says: "The Coast or Cascade Range of British Columbia is that forming the high western border of the continent, but beyond it lies another half-submerged range, which appears in Vancouver and the Queen Charlotte Islands, and is represented in the south by the Olympian Mountains of Washington Territory, and northward by the large islands of the coast archipelago of Alaska. In this outer range there are three remarkable gaps, the most southern occupied by the Strait of Fuca, the central being the wide opening between Vancouver and the Queen Charlotte Islands, and the northern, Dixon's entrance. To the south of these, the lower part of the valley of the Columbia appears to occupy a similar depression, through which, and by Puget Sound, a moderate subsidence of the land would enable the sea to flow, forming of the Olympian Mountain region an additional large island. Whatever the ultimate origin of the gaps holding the Strait of Fuca and Dixon's entrance, they are features of great structural importance, and are continued eastward in both cases by depressions more or less marked in the coast range proper."

These observations are borne out by the fact that Fraser River, carrying the greater part of the drainage between the coast range and the Rockies, after flowing southward for several hundred miles, reaches the sea opposite the end of the Strait of Fuca; while the Skeena, the river we shall ascend, whose tributaries interlock with those of the Fraser, and derive their waters from the same plateau, falls into the Pacific near the head of Dixon's Entrance. We have but little to do with the Fraser, however, as our route leads us to its head waters only. The Skeena, to which we desire to direct attention more especially, falls into the ocean near the head of Dixon's Inlet, not far south of Port Simpson. The tributaries of this stream interlock with those of the Fraser. It is a wonderful volume of water, not so much for its greatness as for the beauty of its scenery and the magnificent valley through which it flows. Another large river, the Nasse, flows into the Pacific north of the Skeena, drawing its waters from the far north.

The country in the immediate neighborhood of Port Simpson is not of great agricultural value. There are patches of good soil; but for the most part the covering of soil is nearly everywhere scanty. There is, however, an abundance of good timber, except on the mountain sides, which are nearly all too steep for vegetation to cling to. This is considerably below the sixtieth parallel.

Port Simpson, as you may judge, is an old seat of the Hudson's Bay Company. The post wears a decidedly military appearance, notwithstanding that its defences have long ago fallen into disuse. Besides the company's officers and employes, there are quite a number of traders in the neighborhood, as well as Indians; and, like almost all the other important posts of the ancient company, its mission church is one of the most attractive features.

There is a large colony of Indians about sixteen miles south of Port Simpson, called Metlah-Catlah, where a station of the Church Missionary Society is in a flourishing condition. Still farther to the south, at the mouth of the Skeena, is a third Indian establishment, with one or two traders. These, with the exception of canning establishments, are all the settlements between the mouth of the Skeena and Port Simpson.

The fisheries here are fast becoming important industries. The salmon are of excellent quality, and are very abundant in both the Skeena and the Nasse to the north of it. These fish are chiefly taken in nets in the estuaries of the rivers, and a large number of Indians and Chinamen are employed in connection with the canning business. The sea fisheries of the coast also promise to afford a very profitable industry.

The climate of Port Simpson and neighborhood is not subject to great extremes of temperature. There is much rain at all seasons, and occasionally, in winter heavy falls of snow. We have at hand no meteorological data with regard to Port Simpson proper, but have what speaks volumes in support of its excellent climate in the records of Sitka, two and a half degrees north of that place. However, the latitude of Sitka is but 57.3 N., or only about a degree north of Glasgow in Scotland, while Port Simpson is about 54.33 N. At Sitka the temperature observations, extending over a period of sixty years, show that the mean temperature of spring is 41.2; of summer 54.6; of autumn 44.9; of winter 32.5; and for the entire year, 43.3F. The extremes of temperature for sixty years are 87.8 and—4.0. However, the mercury has fallen below zero in only four years out of the sixty, and has risen to about 80 degrees in but seven years of that period. The coldest month is January, the warmest August; June is slightly warmer than September. The mean of the minima for seven years of the above period is 38.6, and that of the maxima for seven years, 48.9, showing a remarkably equable climate.

Fogs do not occur in the neighborhood of Fort Simpson as on the southern part of the coast. In proof of this we may quote the adventurous La Perouse, the mariner who subdued Fort Prince of Wales, on Hudson's Bay, in 1782. He speaks of fogs in this locality as of rare occurrence, and records obtained subsequently to his fully justify his observations. Professor Dawson, who has made extended observations around Port Simpson, says that the cause of the exceptional mildness of the climate of that district is to be found not alone in the fact of the proximity of the sea, but in the abnormal warmth of the water due to the Kuro-Siwo or Japanese Current. The average temperature of the surface of the sea, during the summer months, in the vicinity of the Queen Charlotte Islands, as deduced from a number of observations in 1878, is 53.8. Between Victoria and Milbanke Sound, by the inner channels, from May 28th to June 9th, the average temperature of the sea surface was 54.1. In the inner channels between Port Simpson and Milbanke Sound, between August 29th and September 12th, 54.5; and from the last mentioned date to October 18th, about the north end of Vancouver Island, and thence to Victoria by the inner channels, 50.7. Observations by the United States Coast Survey in the latter part of July and early in August, 1867, gave a mean temperature of 52.1, for the surface of the sea between Victoria and Port Simpson, and outside of the Prince of Wales archipelago, from Port Simpson to Sitka. In the narrower inlets of the coast, the temperature of the sea falls, owing to the quantity of cold water mingled with it by the entering of the rivers.

Our journey is from Port Simpson to Churchill. We travel first to the mouth of the Skeena, where is situated the village of Port Essington, or Spuksute, a native hamlet. The surface of the country here is low, level and swampy, and rough with stumps and logs, the remains of an originally dense forest growth. Behind the little flat on which the village stands is a ridge, rising in one place to a remarkable peak.

As we are going over this route with a view to judge of its practicability for railway location, we must observe that, from the Skeena, Port Simpson may be easily reached by the iron horse. Mr. Crombie, C. E., in his report in 1877, says: "The distance to Port Simpson (from the Skeena) is probably eight miles greater than to a point on the mainland opposite Cardena Bay; but the obstacles to the construction of a railway line are not so great, and the cost of building it would probably be less."

The mouth or entrance to the Skeena was first explored by Mr. Whidbey, of Vancouver's staff, in July, 1793. He appears to have gone no further up than the mouth of the Ecstall, and to have been too easily convinced that the inlet was of no particular importance. To Vancouver the name of Port Essington is due, and was by him originally applied to the whole estuary. It is singular that, notwithstanding the diligence and skill of Vancouver in his exploration of the west coast, he passed the mouths of the three largest rivers—the Fraser, the Skeena, and the Nasse, without specially noting them.

The mouth of the river has become pretty much filled with debris brought down by the current, so that notwithstanding the banks are bold, the water is shallow. The mountains on either side, as you ascend the river, are steep, and mostly covered with a dense forest. Their summits, though scarcely ever over 4,000 feet high, are generally covered with snow until early in July, and at any season large patches of perpetual white will always greet the beholder. In a few cases wide areas of bushes and swampy meadows seem to occupy the higher slopes, but numerous large and bare surfaces of solid rock are visible, from which snowslides and landslips have removed whatever covering of soil may have originally clung there. The tide flows up the Skeena for a distance of eighteen or twenty miles above Port Essington. At this point the river valley narrows somewhat, and a mass of bare and rocky mountains appear on the north bank, whose slopes are exceptionally steep, and end at the river bank in bluffs and cliffs of considerable height. Between the head of tide-water and the mouth of Lakelse River, a distance of thirty-six miles, the Skeena receives several streams of some importance. The valley has an average width in the bottom of from 1 1-2 to 2 miles, the mountains bordering it everywhere, reaching 3,000 to 4,000 feet at a short distance from the river. At about half way between the two points mentioned, however, the height of the mountains appears often to exceed 4,000 feet, and they probably reach 5,000 feet on both sides of the river, west of the Lakelse. Near the Lakelse, with a decreasing altitude, they assume more rounded forms and show less bare rock, being covered with trees nearly up to their summits. The quantity of snow which accumulates on the higher mountains is evidently very great.

Through the greater part of the Skeena the dull, brownish water flows at the rate of four to six miles an hour, sweeping round its many islands, and pouring through the accumulated piles of drift logs with a steady rushing sound. No reaches of slack water occur. The river is evidently quite shallow, although it is navigable for steamboats for a distance of at least five miles above the Kitsumgalum, where the Sipkiaw Rapid is met with. Islands are exceedingly numerous, and so divide the stream as to cause it to occupy in many places a great portion of the valley. Above the rapid mentioned, there are but few islands. About four miles above the Sipkiaw, the Zymoetz River, from the southeast, joins the Skeena. It is a stream of considerable size. The mountains among which it rises are over 6,000 feet high.

About five miles above the Zymoetz, or seventy-seven from the Pacific, is Kitsalas Canyon. The mountains at this point crowd closely on the river, especially on the north side, and though the cliffs and precipices are seldom over 100 feet in height, they are rugged, and the hillsides above them are steep and rough. The channel of the river is also broken by several small islands. At the lower end of the canyon the river greatly expands. In foaming torrents, or dashing eddies of the canyon are the favorite salmon fishing stations of the Indians. It is difficult to ascend the river through this canyon, but the task may be accomplished by skillful canoe-men, who make two short portages; the rapids may be descended safely without portaging.

There is a small Indian settlement on the north side of the river at the lower end of the canyon. The huts are mostly rude, and in front of them are planted strangely carved totem-posts, having figures of birds, beasts, etc., at the top. At the upper end of the canyon on the south bank is another small Indian settlement with about a dozen huts, some in a state of great dilapidation. This canyon is in latitude 54, 37, 6 N. Not far to the north of the canyon, the mountains are over 6,000 feet high.

From Kitsalas Canyon to Kwatsalix, a distance of about twenty-four miles, the general course of the river is nearly north and south. Here the highest range of the coast mountains appears to be crossed; but the river has appropriated a natural valley, and not cut through the range. The river in this part of its course has several swift rapids, but when the water is not too high, these are not hard to overcome. The valley continues to be about a mile and a half wide—in places two miles—between the steep slopes of its bordering mountains. It winds considerably, but makes no abrupt turns. On either side of the stream there is a flat, sometimes more extensive on one side than on the other, about thirty feet above the water, well wooded, and containing a good soil. These spaces are, in season, mostly covered with wild peas, vetches, and other plants, growing luxuriantly, especially where the timber has been burned away. Speaking of the scenery along this part of the river, Professor Dawson says: "From various points a few miles above Kitsalas Canyon, fine glimpses of the higher peaks are obtained, but a better view, including the whole snow-clad Sierra, some tent-like peaks of which surpass a height of 8,000 feet, is gained on looking back on this region from the hills above the Forks. In several places small valleys in the upper parts of the range are filled with blue glacier ice, and one glacier, which appears to be of some size, is situated a few miles below Kwatsalix on the right bank. The semi-circular valley containing this, surrounded by peaks estimated at 7,000 feet in height and abundantly covered with snow, is probably the finest piece of mountain scenery on the river. The glacier occupies the bottom of a narrow V-shaped valley and is probably about a quarter of a mile in width, rising up between the slopes like a broad wagon-road. The ice appears from a distance to be completely covered with fallen stones and debris, and though the slope of the valley is considerable, the motion of the glacier must be slow, as the stream flowing from it was, at the date of our visit, nearly without earthy impurity. The end of this glacier is about four miles back from the river, and was estimated to be about 600 feet above it."

Kwatsalix Canyon is a part of the river less than half a mile in length, where steep rocks and low cliffs come down to the water's edge; but, although the water runs swiftly, there is scarcely a true rapid, and canoes may be worked up it without great difficulty. There are a few Indian huts at Kwatsalix, but the larger Indian village, Kitwanga, is situated on the right bank of the river some twenty-four miles above it. It consists of about fifteen or twenty huts, located on a flat of considerable extent, and at a height of about twenty feet above the river. A trail leads from this place across to the Nasse River, which is three days' journey to the north. The huts are of the usual style, and the village is marked by several totem-posts curiously carved.

About seven miles above Kitwanga the mouth of the Kitseguecla River is met with, and some of the strongest rapids on the Skeena are situated near the confluence with this river. From a point above this to the Forks, the current is less powerful. There is a small Indian village near the mouth of the Kitseguecla, consisting of about ten houses of quite modern style. The Forks, or Hazelton, is situated on the left bank of the Skeena, a short distance above the junction of the Watsonkwa. It stands on an extensive flat ten or fifteen feet above the river, and at the base of a higher terrace, which rises very steeply to a height of 170 feet. Two or three traders live here, and there is an Indian village of about half a dozen barn-like buildings, each accommodating several families.

The Skeena country, or valley through which we have traveled so far, may to some extent be called an agricultural country. On the lower part of the river, with the exception of a few islands there is no good land. At about twenty-five miles below the Forks, however, the higher terraces at the sides of the river, and a few hundred feet above its level, extend in many places some miles back from it. These plains contain excellent soil, consisting of a sandy loam with a considerable proportion of vegetable matter. Eastward from the Forks the valleys and plateaus present the same characteristics, only that the fertile areas are more extensive. Most of the rivers flowing into the Skeena have more or less extensive valleys all well suited to agriculture.

The climate of the Skeena country, especially in the neighborhood of the Forks, is similar to that of Montreal, except that the winters are colder. Snow generally falls first in October but melts again, the winter snow not coming until the middle of December. The winter is, in general, steadily cold, similar in all respects to that of Winnipeg except that there is always a thaw in February. Spring comes even earlier than in Manitoba. Grass begins to grow, and many varieties of trees to bud, the first week in April. Some little cultivation has been carried on. Potatoes are annually grown; they are usually fit for use by the first of July, and are harvested before the end of September. Wheat has been tried and found to do well. Oats do exceptionally well, and in 1878 two successive crops ripened before the frosts came. The second of course was a "volunteer crop." Squashes, cucumbers, and other tender vegetables can be grown successfully. Cattle and horses are wintered with ease in this section; but, as in Manitoba, they require to be stabled and fed during the winter months.

The Skeena opens during the last week in April, and ice forms over it during the last week in December. It is generally highest in July, and is lowest immediately after the ice goes out. Its vast volume of water is supplied from the melting snow on the mountains. The snow-fall is from five to ten feet on the lower Skeena, but in the neighborhood of the Forks it does not exceed an average depth of three feet. Above the Forks it is less than two feet, being less throughout than in any location for a long distance south of it. Upon the whole, the general characteristics of the climate are much the same as those of Manitoba.

The Watsonkwa River, which joins the Skeena from the south-eastward at the Forks, has a magnificent valley throughout its entire length. It is partly prairie, and produces a magnificent growth of grass.

From the Forks eastward to the summit of Pine River Pass, there are many routes which the traveler may take; but it is impossible to state, until further exploratory surveys are made, which is most suitable for a railway line. It is sufficient to say that there is a choice of some three or four, any of which offer good facilities for railway construction. Owing to the facts that the Skeena River, above the Forks, is very rapid, and that the Babine River which flows into it is quite impassable in its canyons for canoes, and that it makes a long detour to the north, we will leave the Skeena at the Forks for the north end of Babine Lake. The distance is about forty miles in a straight line; by the trail it is nearly fifty, and the direction is almost due east.

The Skeena Forks, or Kitma, is the site of an Indian village where about two hundred and fifty Tshimsians reside. Here the waters of the Bulkley River, flowing from the southeast, mingle with those of the Skeena, which, at, and above this point, flow from the north. The waters of the Bulkley come from the same series of small lakes in which the Nechaco River takes its rise, flowing easterly to Fort George, beyond which it is lost in the Fraser.

Our present route from the Forks to the north end of Babine Lake is on a trail known as the Old Indian route. It was cut out and improved by the Government of British Columbia a number of years ago, so as to afford easy access to the Omenica mining district. It is still used to a great extent by the Indians, who make a regular business of carrying goods and provisions across. After leaving the somewhat flat country at the Forks, the trail passes over nearly level country for several miles. It is wooded with poplar, cottonwood and birch mixed with evergreen trees, and seems to have a good soil, and to be well fitted for cultivation. Grass, with wild peas and vetches, grow in great luxuriance; and, traveling through this beautiful district in the spring or early summer months, one will find all the thickets fragrant with wild roses. A great variety of wholesome berries abound beyond the limit of description, and strawberries, in their season, might be gathered by the ton. It is indeed a wonderful country.

Not far from the Forks the trail reaches the gently sloping hill sides on the right bank of the Watsonkwa, which it continues to follow for seven or eight miles, till a stream called the Suskwa is reached, just above its junction with the Watsonkwa. In following the hill sides, the valleys of several small streams flowing in courses of greater or less depth, are crossed. The valley of the main stream, from the bases of the mountains to the river side is wide; but the immediate valley of the river is steep-sided, and its waters flow onward with great force between rocky banks. The Indians in this part of the country construct bridges across such streams as are too rapid to be crossed in canoes with safety, when they are not too wide for the means at disposal. These have been called suspension bridges, and are ingenious in plan.

About six miles from its mouth the Suskwa is joined by the Skil-o-kis, from the north, a very rapid stream, fifty-seven feet wide and two feet deep. This is crossed by a newly constructed Indian bridge like those previously mentioned. Five miles further on, in a general eastward direction, the main valley of the Suskwa turns to the south southeast, while the trail continues eastward by that of a large tributary. The sources of this stream, known as the Oo-ats-anli, are reached in about fourteen miles, and the summit is passed at a distance of seven miles from the north end of Babine Lake.

The summit of the range separating the valleys of the Watsonkwa and Skeena from the basin of Babine Lake is passed in a low altitude where mountain sheep and mountain goats are to be seen in considerable numbers. From this summit, looking eastward, Babine Lake is seen stretching far to the southeastward like a silver ribbon, its banks generally low, with flats or rounded hills of moderate elevation bordering them. Before reaching the lake the trail crosses a small stream called the Tzes-a-tza-kwa, or canoe-making river. It is about fifty feet wide by one foot deep at low water.

The group of lakes, says Prof. Dawson, of which Babine is one, may be regarded as occupying two parallel valleys, which conform to the general northwesterly and southeasterly bearings which govern the main features of the whole country lying between the Rocky Mountains proper and the coast. Babine Lake for the greater part of its length, lies nearly parallel to the Watsonkwa Valley, but at its southern end bends abruptly eastward, a wide valley running through from its extremity to the head of Stewart Lake. The watershed between the Skeena and Fraser River systems is situated in this valley:—Babine Lake discharging northward by the Babine River, which, after following the general direction of the valley occupied by the lake for some distance, cuts across the line of the Babine Mountains and reaches the Skeena; Stewart Lake discharging by the Stewart River into the Nechaco, and thence to the Fraser. The valley of Stewart Lake opens widely at the southeastern extremity of the low country of Nechaco and Chilacco. Stewart Lake occupies the southeastern part of the second or northeastern of the great valleys above referred to; and to the northwest of it, in the same line, lie Trembleur, Tacla, and Bear lakes. Stewart Lake is about forty miles in extreme length, Tacla forty-six miles, and Bear Lake about twelve miles; the dimensions of Trembleur and Traverse or Cross Lake are not known. Trembleur and Tacla lakes discharge southeastward into Stewart Lake, while Bear Lake forms the source of the Skeena. With the increasingly mountainous character of the country to the north the height of the water surface in the lakes increases, being approximately as follows: Stewart Lake, 2,200, Tacla Lake 2,271, Bear Lake 2,604.

The route from Fort Babine, on the northern portion of Lake Babine to Fort St. James, at the southern extremity of Stewart Lake, is by the lakes above described. It is a six days' journey with a pack train from Fort St. James to Fort McLeod, on the north end of McLeod Lake, which is in latitude 55 north, or the same as Fort Babine. From Fort McLeod to the summit of Pine River Pass the distance is short, and the direction northeasterly. From Stewart Lake to McLeod Lake the region, as a whole, is flat, and characterized rather by low ridges and terraces than by hills. Its eastern part drains towards Stewart Lake, but the greatest area is drained by Salmon River and its tributaries, which, flowing southward, join the Fraser near Fort George. East of the Salmon River lies the Pacific and Arctic watershed, beyond which the Long Lake River, a small stream, is found flowing toward McLeod's Lake. On leaving Stewart Lake the ground rises gradually till a height of 400 feet is gained at eight or nine miles from the lake. The surface is generally undulating, has been frequently burned over, and shows fine grassy meadows, suitable for cultivation. From this place to the crossing of Salmon River the country consists of undulating uplands, the highest point of which is about 700 feet above Stewart Lake.

We may travel from the Hudson's Bay post, Fort McLeod, at the northern end of McLeod Lake, to the summit of the Pine River Pass, by way of the Misinchinca River. The Pack River, issuing from McLeod Lake, is about two hundred feet wide, and has an average depth of about two feet in July. It flows northward about fifteen miles to its junction with the Parsnip River, which joins it from the southeast. At the mouth of the Misinchinca, the Parsnip, according to comparative barometer readings, is 2,170 feet above the sea. It has a width of five hundred feet, and is generally quite deep. The current is rapid, averaging probably three or four miles an hour, the waters being brownish and muddy, and evidently in great part derived from melting snow.

But we are nearing the Pine River Pass. The valley which is occupied by the lower part of the Misinchinca may be said to come to an end at the mouth of the Atunatche, inosculating with a second, which runs in a north northwest by south southeast course parallel to the main direction of flexure and elevation in this part of the Rocky Mountains. In the opposite direction this depression becomes the Atunatche Valley, and further on that of the upper part of the Pine River, which, after flowing north northwestward for eleven miles, turns abruptly to the eastward and finds its way to the Peace River below Fort St. John. Here on this summit, in latitude 55, 24, 17, the height is but 2,440 feet above the sea, or, according to all authorities, less than 2,500 feet.

From this point we are to descend to the great agricultural plains of the Pine and Athabasca rivers, and the vast fertile regions of the Peace River and its tributaries. We have hurriedly sketched the distance from Port Simpson on the Pacific to this Pass, in view of its fitness for the location of a railway line to connect the Pacific Ocean with the Atlantic, via Hudson's Bay.

The land in the Pine River Valley for fifty miles above its junction with the Peace is of excellent quality, and well suited for agricultural and grazing purposes. It should be observed that this fertile strip of land, lying nearly in the heart of the Rocky Mountains, is an extension of the Beaver Plains which connect with the great fertile belt stretching from Manitoba to and beyond the Peace River.

Finally, the following may be noted as the salient facts ascertained from this exploration, viz: That a depression occurs in the Rocky Mountain range, extending from 55.15 to 55.45, north latitude: That a pass exists in this depression which, together with its approaches from east and west is, with respect to railway construction, of a generally favorable character: That the summit of this pass is 2,440 feet above the level of the sea, which summit, for the sake of convenient comparison, it may be observed, is 1,293 feet lower than that of the Yellowhead Pass; 1,065 feet lower than the watershed between the Fraser and Homathco rivers; 660 feet lower than the summit to Dean Channel; and, to carry the comparison a little farther, 5,802 feet lower than the highest point on the Union Pacific Railway.

We have now to examine the country from the Pine River to Churchill on Hudson's Bay, and see what its advantages are, and to note some of its requirements from the standpoint of cheap transportation. This will complete our observations of the country to be traversed by the proposed transcontinental Short Line from the Pacific Coast to Europe, via the Pine River Pass and the Hudson's Bay route. We will then turn our attention to the other two before-named passes to the north, which lead from the great plains of the far northwest to the Klondike regions.

CHAPTER XX.

FROM THE ROCKIES TO CHURCHILL.

A transcontinental route from Atlantic to Pacific through Hudson's Bay and Strait—Across the rich, fertile prairies, through the Pine River Pass—Vast areas of rich lands.

We have traveled in the forgoing chapter from the Pacific to and through the Pine River Pass of the Rockies, and we will now complete the journey eastward to Hudson's Bay, and will travel more than a thousand miles through the finest agricultural country in the world. The descent from the summit is gradual towards the level plains. The great fertile valley or lower plain with its mighty rivers, its extensive, pure lakes and innumerable small streams, stretches away eastward to Hudson's Bay, northward, to our left, to the head waters of the Mackenzie, and southeastward for more than two thousand miles. The prospect to one descending from this pass is inspiring. The fertile area before the traveler comprises over 300,000,000 acres. Down to our left on the broad plains of the Peace River there is the climate of the most favored portions of British Columbia, with the finest soil in the world. There countless herds of cattle may roam and fatten upon the rich grasses that everywhere abound, without the shelter of barn or stable, and without being exposed to the severity of an ordinary winter climate. There all kinds of orchard and garden fruits may be cultivated and grown in plenty, and the best cereals of the northern temperate zone harvested in yields unequaled anywhere.

Down before us to the eastward, beyond the Smoky River, are spread out the limitless alluvial plains of the Athabaska and its tributaries, an expanse of fertile territory that must soon become thickly populated with a prosperous agricultural community; while away to the southeast, in the country of the North Saskatchewan, the heart of the wheat belt is reached.

Mr. Sanford Fleming, C. M. G., in a paper read by him in 1878 before the Royal Colonial Institute, London, England, gives the following description of the prairie region. He said: "It has been found convenient in describing the general characteristics of Canada to divide it into three great regions. Its leading botanical, geological and topographical features suggest this division. One region, except where cleared of its timber by artificial means, is densely wooded, another is wooded and mountainous, the third is a vast lowland plain of prairie character. The mountain region is on the western side; the prairie regions in the middle; the remainder, which embraces the settled Provinces on the St. Lawrence, originally covered with a growth of timber, may, for the sake of simplicity of description, be considered the woodland region.

"The prairie region of Canada lies in the northern drainage basin; it may be considered to extend from south to north more than a thousand miles, and nearly the same distance from east to west. It is not a treeless prairie; a considerable portion is thinly wooded; yet the whole is considered as more or less partaking of a prairie character. The prairie region, so called, is somewhat triangular in form. One side coincides with the International Boundary Line, and extends from the 95th to the 113th meridian; another side follows the eastern slope of the Rocky Mountains from the 49th to about the 64th parallel of latitude. The third side, about 1,500 miles in length, skirts a remarkable series of lakes, rivalling in size Lakes Erie and Ontario. These great water-filled depressions lie in a generally straight northwesterly and southeasterly direction. They embrace Great Slave Lake, Lake Athabaska, Lake Wollaston, Deer Lake, and Lake of the Woods, and they appear to occur geologically, on the separating line, between a broad band of Laurentian or metamorphic rocks and the softer Silurian formations. This great triangular-shaped region is estimated to measure about 300,000,000 acres. Its base, running along the series of lakes mentioned, will probably average less than 1,000 feet above the sea; and its apex, near where the International Boundary Line enters the Rocky Mountains, will probably be about 4,000 feet above sea level. This region may generally be described as a great plane sloping from its apex in a northeastery direction downwards to its base, but the inclination is not uniform and unbroken. Several terraces and well-defined escarpments stretching across the country are met with at intervals. A great proportion of the surface is gently rolling, and hills of no great height occur here and there. The rivers of this division of the country flow for a great part of their course in deeply-eroded channels, frequently of considerable width, and as the superficial formations are for the most part drift or soft rock, the channels which have been furrowed out are but little obstructed by falls or steep rapids. They generally present a uniform descent, and the long stretches of some of the rivers, although the current be swift, are capable of being navigated. A wide expanse of the region to the south of the main Saskatchewan is a prairie, without trees or shrubs of any kind; the treeless prairie passes by easy gradations into copse-woodland with prairie intervening. To the north of the Saskatchewan, woodland appears in various localities. On Peace River there are extensive prairies; there is also an agreeable mixture of woodland and prairie; and this character of country appears to prevail for a considerable distance still further north.

"It is scarcely to be supposed that a region so extensive would be found all fertile land. The great American desert, which covers a wide area in the center of the United States, was at one time thought to extend north for a considerable distance into Canada. The Boundary Commission's reports, however, appear to show that the arid and unproductive tract is more limited on the Canadian side than was previously supposed; and that a great breadth of the country previously considered valueless may be used for pastoral purposes, and some of it ultimately brought under cultivation. There are other places within the territory described as the prairie region which are favorable for farming pursuits; and although certain drawbacks claim recognition, there can no longer be any doubt respecting the salubrity of the climate and the existence of vast plains of rare fertility. Information on this head has been obtained year by year. Professor Macoun, a well known botanist, has recently been commissioned specially to investigate this subject. He estimates that there are no less than 260,000,000 acres of land available in this region alone for farming and grazing purposes.

"The mineral riches of this great division of Canada are but imperfectly known. It has, however, been established that immense deposits of coal exist in many parts, chiefly along the western side. The examinations of Mr. Selwyn, Director of the Geological Survey, carry the impression that the coal-bearing rocks pass, with their associated coal seams, and iron ores, beneath the clays farthest east, and it may be that shafts would reveal workable seams of coal at such limited depths beneath the surface as would render them available for fuel and for industrial purposes in the heart of the prairies. Should these views of Mr. Selwyn prove correct, their realization will be of the greatest possible importance to the country. Besides coal and iron ore, petroleum, salt and gold have also been found. The Red River settlers, exposed to many vicissitudes during a space of half a century, did not greatly prosper. But since the incorporation with Canada of the whole country formerly under the sway of the Hudson's Bay Company, marvelous progress has been made. The Province of Manitoba has been created around the place which was once the Selkirk settlement; its population has increased from a mere handful to many thousands, and it has to all appearance entered on a career of unexampled progress.

"Manitoba, although a province with prospect so brilliant, occupies but a small corner of the fertile lands in the interior of Canada. The prairie region, as set forth in the foregoing, is alone ten times the area of England, reckoning every description of land. Such being the case, it may be no vain dream to imagine that in due time many provinces will be carved out of it, and that many millions of the human family may find happy and prosperous homes on these rich alluvial plains of Canada."

Since the above was written by Mr. Fleming, much that he predicted has been realized. Extensive coal mines have been opened in the Saskatchewan Valley and are proving of vast utility. Petroleum has been discovered in large quantities, and arrangements are now being made to bring it into market; and the agricultural capabilities of the region are proving to be much greater than the estimate then placed upon them. The whole prairie region has been divided into five sections, viz: The Province of Manitoba, extending from the western boundary of Ontario westward to the 102d meridian, and northward to the 53d parallel; the District of Assiniboia and Saskatchewan, extending from the western boundary of the Province of Manitoba to the 111th meridian, and northward from the International Boundary Line to the 55th parallel, the former comprising the south half of the territory described, and the latter the north half; the District of Alberta extending from the western limits of Assiniboia and Saskatchewan to the eastern limit of British Columbia, and northward from the International Boundary to the 55th parallel; the District of Athabaska, extending northward from the northern limits of Alberta to the 60th parallel, and eastward from the eastern boundary of British Columbia to the 111th meridian. The last four will, in due time, be erected into provinces, with responsible governments, with about their present boundaries.

The carrying trade of that commerce will find its principal channel through the waters of Hudson's Bay; and the proposed railway line we are describing, from Port Simpson to Churchill, will not only bring Japan and Europe closer together by thousands of miles than by any other possible route, but must become the chief avenue of transportation for the whole District of Athabaska and the greater portion of Alberta to the south of it, as well as for the illimitable region to the north and northwest.

CHAPTER XXI.

METROPOLIS OF THE KLONDIKE.

Description of the immediate Klondike country—Life at Dawson City—Boom in real estate—Trading and the high prices of supplies—Saloons and gambling—The future of Dawson City.

But to return to the Klondike, from which point, or rather from the junction of the Pelly and Lewis rivers, we are to make two journeys up the western slopes of the Rockies, across their summits, and down to the great valleys to the eastward. As promised, one of these will be by the Lewis, through the pass between Fort Mumford and the mountains, bordering the southern portion of Lake Dease, thence to the head waters of the Peace River and down that stream to Lake Athabasca; the other, and more northern, will be by the Pelly River to Lake Frances, and through the pass between the Blue Mountains and the range to the southwest of Lake Frances, to the head waters of the Liard River, thence down the Liard or Mountain River, to Fort Simpson, where it joins the mighty Mackenzie in a magnificent prairie region less than 400 feet above the level of the sea.

Before following these routes on the printed page, it will be interesting to take a look at Dawson City, the metropolis of the mining camps of the far northwest, and of the country immediately surrounding it. A little above Dawson City, which is on the northeastern bank of the Yukon, Klondike River is met, flowing from the east or a little north of east. Thirty miles above Dawson City, for which distance the Yukon flows almost directly from the south, Indian River is met with, flowing from the east. Between Klondike and Indian rivers there is a net-work of creeks flowing into the former from the south, and into the latter from the north, and into the Yukon from the east, the banks of all being gold-bearing. An unexplored spur of the Rocky Mountains projects westward to the head waters of the Klondike and Indian rivers, and separates between them for a considerable distance. It is probably from this spur, in which it is believed rich quartz mines will be discovered, that the coarse gold has been washed down to the creeks and rivers of the immediate Klondike region. As before noted, the principal creeks flowing into the Klondike from the south are, commencing on the east, Too-Much-Gold Creek, Hunker Creek, Soda Creek, Last Chance Creek, Bear Creek and its branches, Boulder, Adams, Eldorado and French creeks. The principal streams flowing into the Indian River to the south are, commencing on the east, Dominion Creek, No-Name Creek and Quartz Creek. An equal number of streams flow southward into Klondike River from the north, and northward into Indian River from the south. On the west side of the Yukon, a number of rivers flow from the west into that river which have already been enumerated and described, the principal of which are the Forty and Sixty Mile rivers.

This is the Klondike country proper, and Dawson City is its metropolis. The place contains at the present time a population of about 4,000, and during the coming winter, when a large number of miners will take shelter there to await the warm weather of spring to begin mining operations, it will probably reach 6,000 or 7,000. It is believed that before the close of 1898, Dawson City will have a population of 20,000. However, as mining operations appear to be moving higher up the slopes to the eastward, there is a good prospect for towns of considerable size being developed somewhere on the upper waters of the Lewis and Pelly rivers. But the fact that Stewart River, which flows into the Yukon to the west, contains a vast area of pay gold, together with the rich quartz mines which are sure to be developed in the neighborhood of Dawson City, point to that place as the greatest commercial center of the gold regions west of the Rocky Mountains for a long period to come. More than this, it is near the head of navigation of the Yukon River for steamers of any considerable size, and is a convenient point to be reached by those going into the country, not only by the way of St. Michaels to the Yukon, but from Dyea and Skaguay through the mountain passes to the north of these places, and by way of the Lewis River.

It may be noted in this connection that border settlements of considerable size will no doubt grow up at St. Michaels, at the mouth of the Yukon, at Dyea, and at Skaguay. In the expectation that a large number of miners and prospectors will winter at St. Michaels during the coming season, the North American Trading and Transportation Company has asked the government at Washington that one of the Revenue Cutters, now in the Bering Sea, be stationed at St. Michaels this winter instead of going to Seattle or San Francisco, as usual. It is believed that the presence of a government gun boat, with a crew well armed, would have a good effect in showing the government's determination to preserve order and prevent robbery and other forms of outlawry which might otherwise occur there. At the time this is being written, our government has not decided what action will be taken in this respect. It is expected that a considerable population will be more or less permanently settled at St. Michaels, for which reason immense warehouses are about to be built there; besides, it is evident that a considerable trans-shipping business will be carried on at that place. At Dyea and Skaguay, both of which places have already a considerable population, permanent towns of considerable size will no doubt grow up in the near future, and it may be expected that the government which has jurisdiction over these places will amply provide for the enforcement of law and order. Although access to the Klondike country through the passes to the north of these places is not impossible, it is not likely that these routes will be abandoned, for their passes are being improved, and will no doubt continue to be traveled, especially by a large proportion of those who leave the Pacific Coast to go into the north country light.

There is another point at which a large border mining town will no doubt start up with good prospects next summer. We refer to some point on the Peace River near its head waters. Vast gold deposits have already been discovered in this region, both in northern British Columbia, and along the eastern slopes of the Rockies on the banks of the brooks and creeks which flow into the upper Peace and Liard rivers.

But to return to Dawson City, which is a typical mining town. It is laid out in rectangular shape into town lots. The streets are sixty-six feet wide and the whole plat has been regularly entered with the Dominion government, by Joseph Laduc, its proprietor, as a town site. It is situated on a stretch of low ground on the northwest bank of the Yukon, a short distance below the mouth of the Klondike. During the present summer a vast majority of its inhabitants lived in tents, but a great many houses were built during the season, preparatory to the requirements of winter. Some of these are quite substantial buildings. It is unfortunately true that the best and most commodious buildings in the town, aside from the somewhat extensive and imposing warehouses of the North American Trading and Transportation Company, are occupied by saloons and gambling houses; and these places, as is the case with all mining centers of population, are excessively patronized. Town lots in Dawson City are being sold at a high figure, some of them bringing as much as $5,000 each. Of course Dawson City is having a boom, and a real estate boom at that. But it is having a boom in trade also; for all kinds of supplies and provisions that have been taken into the country are being sold to miners at almost fabulous prices, and, of course, yielding immense profits. So far as the real estate boom is concerned, it will no doubt turn out like that of Winnipeg, Manitoba, which continued at high water mark from 1880 to 1883, when it collapsed with a precipitancy that stranded the entire population of that city. But the boom at Dawson City is on, and it will continue for two or three years at least, probably until the town has reached a population, during certain seasons of the year, of 25,000. During the present year the lowest standard of value in actual use there, has been the fifty-cent piece, or, in the parlance of the town, "four bits." This is the price of the smallest article, and takes the place, in small transactions, of the penny in our American cities. During 1897 the ruling prices at Dawson City have been about as follows:

Flour, per 100 pounds............$	12.00
Moose hams, per pound..........	1.00
Caribou meat, per pound........	.65
Beans, per pound................	.10
Rice, per pound..................	.25
Sugar, per pound................	.25
Bacon, per pound................	.40
Butter, per roll..................	1.50
Eggs, per dozen.................	1.50
Better eggs, per dozen...........	2.00
Salmon, each......................	1.00@ 1.50
Potatoes, per pound............	.25
Turnips, per pound.............	.15
Tea, per pound..................	1.00
Coffee, per pound..............	.50
Dried fruits, per pound..........	.35
Canned fruits, per pound.........	.50
Canned meats.....................	.75
Lemons, each.....................	.20
Oranges, each.....................	.50
Tobacco, per pound..............	1.50

Liquors, per drink...............	.50
Shovels	2.50
Picks	5.00
Coal oil, per gallon.............	1.00
Overalls	1.50
Underwear, per suit..............	5.00@ 7.50
Shoes	5.00
Rubber boots.....................	10.00@15.00

Lumber has been selling for $150 per thousand feet, rough, and $250 dressed. Wages for unskilled labor have run from $10 to $15 per day. This includes carpentering, for most of the joiners that have gone to that country up to the present time are called "saw and hammer men." Those who have been employed in the mines have received from $10 to $15 a day, but labor of this kind has been exceedingly scarce. Nearly every man who has gone into the country has either staked a claim for himself, or insisted upon working on shares. There are two or three saw-mills in the neighborhood of considerable capacity, but that at Dawson City is not very large. However, three or four more will be in running order early next spring.

Dawson City is of course a lively mining town. The population which has gone in there is of an exceedingly heterogeneous character, including a large variety of nationalities and men of nearly every phase of human experience. Notwithstanding this, up to the early fall of the present year (1897) no serious breaches of the peace have taken place. One shooting event is recorded, but the victim soon recovered, and at last reports the offender was in the grasp of the Canadian Mounted Police. This force is at Dawson City in considerable strength, and acting under and by virtue of Canadian laws, exercises a most salutary influence upon the conduct of the inhabitants. At Dawson City men are not what they appear. Everywhere characters are hidden beneath a rough exterior. One will often meet with a polished college graduate under an exceedingly rough garb. In Dawson City one may sit down and discuss almost any subject, including the widest range of science, literature and religion, with one having the general appearance of a highway tramp, and who, if casually met with in the state of Illinois, would be regarded as the veriest hobo. There is nothing in the way of what we call style in Dawson City. Bar-keepers do not wear boiled shirts, nor are those who preside at the piano or manipulate other musical instruments in the coarse dance-houses dressed in the garb of dudes.

Gold scales are found in every trading place in Dawson City, and the greater proportion of local retail traffic is carried on with gold dust as a medium of exchange. Dance-halls may be found in the rear of almost every saloon. There is also an apartment connected with almost every drinking place devoted to gambling, where the miner parts with his money or gold dust to satisfy his thirst for speculation. The liquors sold in these drinking places are of a vile character, much of them being compounded with drugs on the spot, and containing very small proportions of real whisky, gin or brandy.

It will not be a surprise to the reader that a large proportion of the inhabitants of the mining towns are addicted to drinking and gambling. Those who go into such a country are of a venturesome, speculating spirit, and the time not occupied in actual mining hangs heavily on their hands. Such restless spirits are always sure to engage in any excesses for which there are opportunities. But of course not all those who face the hardships of that country are addicted to the liquor habit or the game of chance. There are many sober, industrious people in the Golden North, and many more will follow them, who devote their time and energies to delving in the mines both winter and summer, or to grappling with other tasks, and who frequent neither the dance hall, the card room, nor the drinking bar. These are the men who succeed best, and who bring most gold out of the country.

There are many excellent women at Dawson City, notably Mrs. Capt. J. J. Healy, who has a quartz mine known as the Four Leaf Clover, on the west side of the Yukon opposite the mouth of the Klondike, which promises to yield enormous riches. Most of the women at this town are with their husbands, whose fortunes they are sharing bravely. Some of them, however, are working in various independent ways to improve their own circumstances. It is notable that several of the most fortunate men now struggling for wealth in the gulches of the Klondike region are accompanied by their wives. In this connection, it is noted with regret that the Canadian laws do not recognize a married woman's property rights, hence she cannot locate a claim in addition to that of her husband; but she can otherwise aid and assist him in ways of incalculable value. It was observable in the gold mining camp region, throughout the present year, that married men became very desirous of having their wives join them, while the unmarried men were sending letters to their sweethearts whom they had left behind, at considerable pains and expense.

There is a class of women at Dawson City, however, who constitute the worst element of the town. Fortunately the number is not large. These characters frequent the dance halls, and, as in all the years of the past, follow the miners through every danger and hardship. To his great credit, Inspector Constantine, who is at the head of the Mounted Police force at Dawson City, manages to keep the disreputable element under very strict control.

As before stated, the currency of Dawson City is for the greater part gold dust. One entering a place to trade, or a saloon to drink, has a quantity of gold dust weighed out, which he exchanges for chips of various denominations. These chips he, in turn, exchanges at the place where they were obtained for whatever he chooses to purchase.

Dawson City is a most delightful place during the short summer season. Daylight is continuous, and one fortunate enough to possess a book or newspaper may read without artificial light every hour out of the twenty-four. Of course the mosquito and little black fly keep up an unceasing annoyance, but this is really the only drawback to one's happiness while in the town. The climate is excellent and there are no diseases of any sort arising from climatic conditions. In the winter season it is very cold, but with proper supplies one will not suffer from the extremes of winter temperature. The atmosphere is exceedingly dry, and a person can endure with much less suffering twenty degrees more cold than in the more humid districts of our own northwest.

A newspaper is about to be established at Dawson City, and in a short time the place will be in telegraphic communication with the outside world. Steamers already arrive frequently by way of the Yukon during the summer season, but the winters will be greatly enlivened and improved when telegraphic communication shall have been established between it and the regions of civilization. At present the only exciting news in the town, aside from the arrival of steamboats, consists in fresh gold discoveries. When the latter are authenticated, they always result in a stampede for the locality in which the important finds have been made, and in the staking out of new claims. It may be mentioned in this connection that during 1897 the policy of the miners in the Klondike region has shown too much vacillation. Men have gone from one location to another whenever reports indicated that there were deposits further on, richer than those which they were working. In this way many good claims have been abandoned, which, in the future, will no doubt be taken up by others and successfully worked. A part of this constant changing of location has been due to the preference for coarse gold. Miners will always forsake the work of washing fine gold dust from gravel or sand for the prospect of locating a placer claim where coarse gold is known to exist.

During 1897 (as will no doubt be the case during 1898), the frequent discoveries of rich gold deposits have kept Dawson City up to fever heat of excitement. It is almost impossible for one located in the great cities of civilization to realize the high pitch of excitement which almost constantly prevails in a border mining town. Old experienced miners are frequently disgusted with themselves when they hear of the rich "strikes" which "green-horns" are constantly making. A party of the latter will sometimes start out for a point which has been prospected by veteran miners and adjudged to be worthless, and will return with the most sensational reports, bringing with them ample evidence, in virgin gold, of the truthfulness of the stories they tell. Then the "old time miners" look into one another's faces with expressions of the deepest mortification. It is a fact that during the present year more rich "strikes" were made in the Klondike country by "green-horns" and "tenderfeet" than by the most grizzled and weather-beaten miners of the experienced type. The latter have to a great extent followed in the footsteps of the former, and in this way have located and staked out their best claims. Nevertheless, while they have not been the discoverers of the richest gold deposits, they have proven themselves to be the most successful miners when a profitable location has been made. Then it is that the value of experience comes into play; for, one who has been trained to operate with the pan, the rocker and the sluice, no matter how crude the apparatus may be, can wash out more gold in a single day than can the inexperienced miner in a whole week.

At present dogs do most of the hauling in that country, but horses may be successfully and not very expensively kept there, so that in another year the distribution of supplies will no doubt be carried on from Dawson City to the mining camps not only by boat along the rivers, but also by means of horses. Arrangements for sending a vast number of these useful animals to that region are already being made. The country around Dawson City is also pretty well adapted to the maintenance of cattle, and beef may be produced in districts not far distant at but little expense. There is room for at least a dozen more saw-mills in the Klondike country, and a greater degree of competition in trade and transportation will prove of value not only to those engaged in these lines, but to the miners and settlers generally.

Mission churches have been established at Dawson City by both Protestants and Roman Catholics, and the condition of society is rapidly improving. New business enterprises are starting up and the place is rapidly taking on the air of an important commercial center. The only competition of any importance in that country is between the North American Trading and Transportation Company and the Alaska Commercial Company, but this is of considerable advantage, and is likely to prove more beneficial next year than it has during the present one. The business of the first named corporation at Dawson City is in charge of Capt. John J. Healy. He was the originator of the company, and it was through his personal efforts that John Cudahy and P. B. Weare of Chicago were induced to make large investments in the enterprise. Out in the far north, Capt. Healy, who is well known in Chicago, and in Grand Army circles almost everywhere, is a very important individual. Down in Chicago, one might speak of the organization as "Cudahy's Company" or "Weare's Company," but in the Klondike it is "Capt. Healy's Company." The Alaska Commercial Company's business at Dawson City is in charge of Capt. J. E. Hansen, who is an energetic, liberal minded and public spirited young man.

Capt. Healy and his wife have a comfortable home at Dawson City. He moved there from Fort Cudahy some time ago. He was one of the first to prospect for gold in that vicinity, and five years ago located a valuable quartz mine, which is now owned by his wife, who has named it the "Four Leaf Clover" mine, to which reference has already been made. The blacksmith shops at Dawson City are doing well, and there is room for one or two more. The same remarks will apply to barber shops, bakeries and laundries. A very large lodging house has been put up at Dawson City during the present season, where board and lodgings are provided, and where the price of a meal is $1.50 for the regulation fare, which includes nothing in the way of luxuries. There are several other restaurants in the city, all in a flourishing condition.

The facilities in the Klondike for sending money to and from the United States are about to be very much improved. Wells, Fargo & Co. are establishing a branch of their business in Dawson, and this will furnish the opportunity for miners to send gold to their friends and families in this country at a reasonable cost for transportation and with almost perfect security.

Among the more notable women at Dawson City, aside from Mrs. Capt. Healy, are Mrs. Clarence J. Berry and Mrs. E. F. Gage, wife of the son of Lyman J. Gage, Secretary of the United States Treasury. The latter was in the country when the first Klondike discoveries were made, and soon after returned to Chicago. She embarked again for the Klondike in the early autumn of the present year. Her husband is auditor of the North American Transportation and Trading Company.

On the return of Mrs. Gage to Chicago in July, 1897, she made the following statement concerning her experiences in the far north:

"It is wonderful how fascinating the life on the frontier becomes. The man or woman who gets a taste of it and succeeds and thrives by it, rarely gets to like anything else. It may be a barbarous confession, but it seems to me that the kindest, most considerate and most practically honest people that I ever met are the miners who are risking all at one throw in the work on the Klondike. It was here that I saw a code of honor which made all men honest—a life in which each man must live a fair part or get a forcible and roughly polite invitation to move.

"It takes men of sturdy character to get into the valley, and the virtues which they cling to are ones from which they want no man to part. I do not think that I heard of a single case in my summer's stay in upper Alaska where prospectors and diggers had been guilty of dishonesty. It may be that honesty is a trait which thrives because it is backed by the point of a gun, but it is there nevertheless. Explorers going to the field or miners coming out, frequently undertake greater loads than the teams can pull through. It is the custom at such times to put the surplus at the roadside and go on with half. The part left behind is perfectly safe until it shall be called for. I doubt that this rule would work in Chicago or other civilized places."

CHAPTER XXII.

NORTHWEST ROUTES TO GOLD FIELDS.

Description of trail by the Lewis and Peace rivers—Short and cheap cut to the Klondike—Route by the Pelly and Liard rivers.

The route from and to the Klondike country by way of the Lewis and Peace rivers, and across the mountains between them, is already being traveled and is likely to become a popular one during the latter part of the approaching winter and early spring. A party recently organized in Chicago has started out over this route, in charge of Lambertus Warmolts. Concerning the trip he made the following statement before leaving:

"We estimate we will make the trip from Edmonton to Peel River in twenty-three days. I have traveled the same route before, having been in that country all winter three years ago on a hunting expedition.

"There is only one portage to make, of sixteen miles, near the foot of Lake Athabasca, and there is a horse tramway there, built by the Hudson's Bay Company, that makes it easy. In fact the whole trip to the Peel River is dotted with the company's posts. Their steamers will take us down Great Silver Lake, and the trip will not be a hard one until we reach the Peel.

"There we will knock our boats to pieces and build sledges. We are going to haul our stuff the rest of the way. We go up the Peel about 250 miles, and will use sails, the wind being almost always from the north in winter. We will have to make a trip across about fifty miles of snow fields from the head of the Peel to the head of the Beaver. We have not decided yet which to strike. We will work between the head waters of those two streams."

The Beaver above referred to is of course the Peace River.

From the junction of the Pelly and Lewis rivers, at Fort Selkirk, this route is by the Lewis River, which has already been fully described. Considerably above Vatchee Lake this river divides, the two branches finding their source in lakes of considerable size not far west of Dease Lake. The latter lies southwest of the Blue Mountains, a part of the Rocky Mountain chain. On the southwestern shore of this lake is Dease House, a Hudson's Bay trading station. South of the lake and between the mountain ranges which lie along, in an east and west direction, north of Fort Mumford on the one hand, and to the south of Dease Lake on the other, is a very convenient pass extending to the head waters of the Peace River. There are no records at hand which give the height above sea level of this pass, but it is between 2,000 and 2,500 feet, and is one of the easiest passes for pack travel through the northern Rocky Mountain range, and is convenient throughout its whole distance, during a greater part of the year, for bob-sled or buck-board travel. The Lewis River is left at about the 131st degree of longitude and the head waters of the Peace River are reached at about the 128th degree, which, in that latitude, is not more than one hundred and twenty-five miles. Stretches of the head waters of the Peace River may be navigated, with slight interruptions, to "Old Fort," and below it to Fort Dunvegan, and below it Fort au Tremble, and still below that to Fort Vermilion at the Falls, and from the Falls at Red River Fort, where the Red joins the Peace River, to Lake Athabasca at Fort Chippewyan. This is one of the most convenient routes of travel that can be adopted for reaching the Klondike country. It may be used successfully during any portion of the year except in the springtime, when, for about forty days, when excessive freshets prevail in the mountain streams, covering the lowlands with much water.

The distance from Lake Athabasca to Edmonton, which is on the north branch of the Saskatchewan River, is not great, and may be traveled almost entirely by water during the summer months, and in winter by sleds. At Edmonton the Canadian Pacific Railway is reached, which will carry the traveler to Pacific or southwestern points of civilization.

This whole route may be covered from Edmonton in the Canadian Northwest to Fort Selkirk at the junction of the Lewis and Pelly rivers, or to the Klondike country in about three months. It may be traveled from Edmonton to the rich gold fields on the upper Peace and Liard river systems in about two months or less, and by water and land to those points or to the Klondike regions beyond the mountains. Any quantity of horses and supplies may be transported overland, in winter or summer, by the use of boats, sleds and wagons, and at little cost. There is an abundance of wild fowl and game of all kinds throughout this whole country, and in season grasses of most luxuriant growth abound everywhere. In the winter season native horses will paw the snow from the ground in the lower levels and subsist in excellent condition with one feed of oats daily; but in the mountain section the snow is too deep to permit of this method of subsistence. Everywhere along the route there is excellent timber, and one will not travel more than one hundred miles in any direction without finding a hospitable stopping place at or near some thriving Hudson's Bay trading post.

The more northern route is by the Pelly River to Lake Frances, which finds its bed well into the Rocky Mountain region; on the western shore of this lake is Fort Francis, an old Hudson's Bay trading station. Near this fort to the south, and exactly on the 130th degree of longitude, is the entrance to one of the most accessible passes in the Rocky Mountains. Fort

Francis and Lake Frances are upon the highest elevation of the Rockies in this region, and as one enters the pass north of the Blue Mountain range he immediately meets with the head waters of the Liard River, and begins to descend the mountains towards the alluvial plains of the upper Mackenzie system. The Liard River is descended to Fort Halkepp, a Hudson's Bay trading post, on its banks. A considerable distance below this post the river turns abruptly northward and flows down to the Mackenzie, joining it at Fort Simpson. The Liard River may be left at the turn where one of its branches flows due south; this may be followed to a point where the traveler can proceed overland, traversing a beautiful park or prairie country, until Fort au Tremble, another Hudson's Bay trading post, on the Peace River, is reached. From that point the route is southeastward over the same line that would be traversed in coming out of the Peace River Valley.

The head waters of the Liard and Peace rivers, which reach far up into the Rocky Mountains, are reenforced everywhere by innumerable smaller streams flowing into them and connecting with still smaller currents. Here and there are unexplored creeks and brooks draining one of the richest auriferous mountain-slope districts to be found anywhere in North America. It is because of the gold discoveries already reported from this region, and of those that are sure to be made known hereafter, that the two routes last mentioned are certain to become popular and much traveled by those who will go from these fields of civilization into the higher latitudes in search of gold.

There is not a great deal of difference between the distances or the time occupied in making the journey over these natural lines of travel. The Peace River trail is the shortest, but passes over greater altitudes, while that by way of the Liard River is of course the longest, being farther to the north; but the mountain paths leading from its upper waters to Lake Francis, which is the chief source of the Pelly River, is considerable lower than that from the source of the Peace River to the lakes at the head of the Lewis.

In addition to this the overland route to be traveled on the summit of the Rockies between the two points last named is much greater than that of the more northern line of travel; the head of Liard River is not more than ten miles from Lake Francis, which is the principal source of Pelly River.

One feature common to both of these routes is not enjoyed by any other line of travel leading to the Klondike country; it consists in the fact that during the winter months very high temperatures, comparatively speaking, are recorded in the passes named. This is due to low altitudes and to the northern Chinook winds which blow from the Pacific through all the mountain passes of that region, constantly pouring a mighty volume of warm atmosphere upon the alluvial park and prairie plains of the Peace and Mackenzie River basins. The snowfall is less than in any of the mountain ranges either to the south of it or on the western coast, and one may travel throughout all this region during the coldest winter months without suffering to any extent, if properly clad. We do not hesitate to state from the authenticated information in our possession that these are by all odds the best routes for reaching the gold fields of the far north; and, what is more, they are pre-eminently winter routes and may be traveled quite as successfully during the cold season as during the warm months of summer, and vastly more so than in the springtime, when the country is somewhat flooded for a little over a month.

CHAPTER XXIII.

YUKON AND JUNEAU ROUTES.

Description of St. Michaels—Temperature and ice—Season of navigation on the Yukon—"Fort Get There"—The Dyea and Skaguay passes.

The gold seeker who reaches the Klondike country by the St. Michaels route will occupy a longer time from the start to the finish of his journey than by any other line of travel open. From Pacific ports he may take his choice, if traveling by St. Michaels and the Yukon, of the North American Trading and Transportation Company or Alaska Commercial Company steamers. The town of St. Michaels, at the mouth of the Yukon, is a carelessly built collection of old Russian structures, the principal features of which are the warehouses of the companies doing business on the river. A number of independent traders also have warehouses there of considerable extent.

At the close of the present summer St. Michaels had a white population of about 500, mostly transient, although it was expected that a still larger number would winter there. The place includes about 300 Eskimos or Innuits, who are going and coming to and fro in the fur and fish trade. There are no trees on the island upon which St. Michaels is located, but it is well covered with grass during the summer season. Its surface is quite undulating and presents a pleasing aspect. Of course it is not as cold at St. Michaels as in the interior. The average temperature for the twelve months in the year 1896 is recorded as follows:

January	—5	April	22.1
February	—6	May	32.8
March	9.5	June	45.2

July	53.1	October	28.0
August	52.1	November	18.3
September	43.3	December	8.9

The season of snowfall begins about the first of October, and by the middle of the month ice has formed at the mouth of the Yukon. Navigation closes about the middle of September, however, for the upper part of the river freezes much sooner than its mouth. When the ice once forms, it remains fast until the end of the first week in June, when it breaks up and flows into the sea. The river is cleared in about ten days.

Near to the town proper is a station of the North American Transportation and Trading Company, to which the name of "Fort Get There" has been given. All merchandise, supplies and passengers are transshipped at St. Michals and "Fort Get There" by the respective transportation companies. This is done because a class of steamers of lighter draught than those which traverse the ocean are required for the river traffic. Then the trip is made up the river, through the country which we have already described, for about 1,750 miles to Dawson City. Different authorities give us different lengths of this route, ranging from 1,650 to 1,800 miles. It is probably about the latter distance from St. Michaels to the junction of the Lewis and Pelly rivers at old Fort Selkirk.

Fresh salmon is almost a constant diet on board the river steamers until one becomes tired of it. The route by which one travels does not make much difference as to the kind of clothing and character of supplies he should take with him into the Klondike country, for these necessaries are for his use after he arrives rather than during the journey.

Perhaps next in importance to the Yukon is the Juneau route, the starting point of which may be reached from any of the Pacific ports. Juneau is the largest city in Alaska, and will probably continue to be such. Dawson City, which has already passed it in population and commercial importance, is located in the Canadian Northwest. Juneau is situated on the mainland on level ground between the sea and lofty mountains which rise nearly 4,000 feet above the sea level. These mountains are capped with perpetual snow and ice. The town was founded by Joseph Juneau and Richard Harris in 1880. This Joseph Juneau is a nephew of the Juneau of history, who founded the city of Milwaukee, Wis. The city has a population at the present time of about 3,000, five or six hundred of which are constantly going and coming. It has a pretty good waterworks system, an electric light plant, and two flourishing newspapers.

From Juneau the traveler proceeds by Lynn Channel, which has two sources or inlets, called Chilcat and Chilkoot. These inlets lead respectively up to the passes of the same names. The former is not very well known and has not been extensively traveled up to the present time. It has been called the "Dalton Trail." The White Pass is being greatly improved and has been recently much used from Skaguay. There is some talk of the Canadian Government constructing a wagon-road through this pass in order to ascertain its advantages as a railway route. It is now generally believed that this pass will prove superior to that of the Chilkoot, which has heretofore been much more generally traveled. To reach either the Chilkoot or White passes, the route from Juneau is by Dyea or Skaguay, which is only eight miles. Dyea has become quite a town. It had for many years been a thriving Indian village and trading post.

From Dyea, through the Chilkoot Pass, the route leads to Lake Lindemann. The distance is a little less than thirty miles. The ascent and descent through this pass from Dyea to Lake Lindemann are very steep, but the highest elevation reached is not more than 3,000 feet above sea level, although the snow-crowned mountains on either side of the traveler reach thousands of feet into the clouds. We have already fully described the routes of travel from Lake Lindemann and Lake Bennett, at the northern termini of these passes, to the Lewis River, which is the first objective point of all travelers through them.

Near Dyea and to the east of it is Skaguay, where there is a considerable town of delayed miners, and from which many depart to scale the mountain passes for the Klondike country. It will be some time before travel in these regions will demonstrate which is the preferable pass over the mountains, but, as before stated, it is likely that a considerable volume of travel and transportation will continue to seek these routes.

CHAPTER XXIV.

ALASKAN BOUNDARY QUESTION.

Alaskan boundary controversy and correspondence between the United States and Dominion of Canada—Population of Alaska—Increase owing to gold discoveries.

Returning to Alaska proper we take a farewell survey of that territory, considering very briefly the boundary question, the population, the towns and trading posts, the fur trade, the seal and other fisheries, the commerce and transportation facilities, institutions, etc. In the treaty of session of March 30, 1867, by which the United States acquired Alaska, the boundaries between the territory and the British possessions were defined as:

"Commencing from the southermost point of the island called Prince of Wales Island, which point lies in the parallel of 54 degrees 40 minutes north latitude, and between the 131st and 133d degree of west longitude (meridian of Greenwich), the said line shall ascend to the north along the channel called Portland Channel as far as the point of the continent where it strikes the 56th degree of north latitude; from this last-mentioned point, the line of demarcation shall follow the summit of the mountains situated parallel to the coast as far as the point of intersection of the 141st degree of west longitude (of the same meridian); and finally, from the said point of intersection, the said meridian line of the 141st degree, in its prolongation as far as the Frozen Ocean."

"With reference to the line of demarcation laid down in the preceding article, it is understood—

"1st. That the island called Prince of Wales Island

shall belong wholly to Rússia (now, by this cession, to the United States).

"2d. That whenever the summit of the mountains which extend in a direction parallel to the coast from the 56th degree of north latitude to the point of intersection of the 141st degree of west longitude shall prove to be at the distance of more than ten marine leagues from the ocean, the limit between the British possessions and the line of coast which is to belong to Russia as above mentioned (that is to say, the limit to the possessions ceded by this convention) shall be formed by a line parallel to the winding of the coast, and which shall never exceed the distance of ten marine leagues therefrom."

The treaty of cession was concluded March 30, 1867, and the consideration first agreed upon was $7,000,000, but when it was learned that there was a fur company and also an ice company enjoying monopolies under the Russian government, it was thought best that these should be extinguished; hence the United States added $200,000 to the original amount agreed upon, in consideration of which the Russian government handed the territory over free of all incumbrances.

Not long after the territory was annexed the eastern boundary line of Alaska became a subject of some controversy between the United States and the British governments. In 1872, President Grant recommended a commission to deal with the matter, but Congress took no action. In 1886, President Cleveland asked Congress for an appropriation of $100,000 for a preliminary survey of the frontier territory.

During the winter of 1887-88 informal conferences were held in Washington between Prof. W. H. Dall, of the United States Geological Survey, and Dr. George M. Dawson, of Canada, both authorities on the Territory of Alaska, but the conferences led to no result. On August 20, 1895, Lord Gough inquired of Secretary Olney if a joint surveyor could not be appointed to act with Mr. William Ogilvie, who was then about to survey the intersection of the 141st degree and the Yukon River. The acting Secretary of State asked if the proposed survey could not be delayed until Congress had had an opportunity to consider the question. This suggestion was transmitted to the Canadian government, which answered that the season was so far advanced that it would not be possible to communicate with Mr. Ogilvie before the next summer, when a considerable portion of the 141st degree would already be marked on the ground. An extract from a letter by Secretary Olney, dated March 11, 1896, was as follows:

"So far as the recent and existing surveys on either side have progressed they exhibit a close coincidence of results. At one point, as I am informed, the difference between Mr. Ogilvie's location and that made by the United States Coast and Geodetic Survey is only about 6 feet 7 inches. In another point the difference is in the neighborhood of 500 or 600 feet, and at other points even closer coincidence than this latter is expected when the comparison of calculations shall have been worked out."

Mr. Olney proposed that the two governments should agree upon certain points of the 141st degree at the intersection of the principal streams, locating the same at a point midway between the determinations of the Coast and Geodetic Survey and of Mr. Ogilvie, and providing for the junction of the points so located by convenient joint surveys, as occasion should require, until the entire line should be established. This would supply a permanent line which for international purposes would be coincident with the 145th degree, stipulated under existing treaties, and would require no further immediate arrangement than the dispatch of a joint surveying party to set up monuments at the points defined, with perhaps the survey of a traverse line connecting the monuments on the Yukon and Forty Mile Creek, and farther south if necessary. The Canadian government agreed to this proposition, and the convention is now pending before the Senate of the United States.

No accurate estimate of the population of Alaska was made until the census of 1890. In 1868, in a report by Major General Halleck, the number given was 82,400. In the same year, the Rev. Vincent Collyer, in his report to the Commissioner of Indian Affairs, added 11,900 Thlinket Indians to the number given by General Halleck, making 94,300, while Ivan Petroff, special agent for the tenth census (1880), states the population as 33,426. The census of 1890, which is the first detailed statement, fixes the number at 32,052, which is made up of 4,298 white, 23,531 Indians, 2,288 Mongolians, and 1,935 mixed blood. The gold discoveries of the Klondike region during the present year have had the effect of increasing the population of Alaska by about 10,000.

CHAPTER XXV.

TOWNS AND TRADING POSTS OF ALASKA.

Sitka and Juneau—St. Michaels and the trading posts of the Aleutian Islands—Douglas City and the great Treadwell gold mine—Trade and traffic.

Sitka is the capital of Alaska. It is located in 57 degrees north and 135 degrees 17 minutes west, on a low strip of land on the west of Baranof Island. The population at the present time is about 3,000. An industrial school is conducted in the city and is in a flourishing condition. Of course salmon fishing and canning is the chief industry. Steamers ply quite frequently between Sitka and Portland, Oregon. The harbor is small but safe.

The January temperature for Sitka for more than forty years averages 31.4 above zero. The rainfall for thirty years averages 84.06 inches annually. The winters at this place are much milder than those of many European cities. By the inner passage, between the archipelago and the coast of British Columbia and Alaska, the distance from Portland, Oregon, to Sitka is 1,647 miles; large sailing vessels have to go outside. Juneau is located near the Lynn Channel, by which there are trails to the Yukon. Mr. Wilson says that the year 1895 witnessed a great improvement in the town, and Juneau is to-day a progressive city, with fine buildings, wharves, electric lights, waterworks, hotels, etc. Wrangell, on the northern part of the island of the same name, is about ten miles from the mouth of the Stikine, and is the point of departure for traders and miners penetrating into the interior by way of that river. Douglas City, on Douglas Island, near Juneau, has a population of about 600. Here the celebrated Treadwell gold mine is located with the largest quartz mill in the world. The mine has proved a great success financially.

Joseph P. Smith, director of the Bureau of American Republics, in a document recently issued, speaks of the principal towns and trading posts of Alaska as follows:

"Yakutat (population 308) is on Yakutat Bay. Nuchek is situated on Hinchinbrook Island, 432 miles by sea from Sitka, and 50 miles from the mouth of the Copper River. It was formerly an important trading post, but much of the commerce has been transferred. St. Paul, on the northern part of Kadiak Island, does a large fur trade. There are a number of salmon canneries on the island, employing in 1890, according to Longman's Gazetteer, 1,100 hands. Karluk (population 1,123) is said to have the largest cannery in the world. Kadiak (495), Alitak (420), and Afognak (409) are other villages on the island.

"On the Aleutian Islands there are many settlements. The one on Ounga Island has a population of about 200, according to Mr. Petroff. Belkowsky, on the southern end of the Aliasla Peninsula, has 300 inhabitants. Near Protassof (100 inhabitants) there are warm sulphur springs and ponds. Iliuliuk, on Unalaska Island, is a point of considerable commercial importance, having a church, custom house, trading establishments, wharves, etc. Nikolsky, on the south of Unimak Island, has 127 inhabitants: it was formerly much larger. Nazan, on Athka Island, has a population of 230, described by Mr. Petroff as thrifty and prosperous. St. Paul, on the Pribilof Islands, has a population of 398. The Amukhta and the Unimak are the two safe passes between the islands.

"St. Michaels, on Norton Sound, is one of the most important localities on the coast. It is a trading post, says Mr. Petroff, where rival firms have established their depots for the Yukon River and Arctic trade. The station keepers come down from the interior to the coast at the end of June or first of July, and each receives his allotment of goods to take back with him in sailboats and bidars during the few months when navigation on the river is not impeded by ice. The vessels supplying this depot can seldom approach the post before the end of June, on account of large bodies of drifting ice that beset the waters of Norton Sound and the straits between St. Lawrence Island and the Yukon delta.

"Port Clarence, on the bay of the same name, is the place where whalers wait for their tenders before proceeding through the straits. The harbor is excellent. There is a reindeer farm here. The population numbers 485. Point Hope (population 301), Cape Lisburne, Icy Cape, and Point Barrow are the most important points on the northern coast.

"Nulato and Nuklakayet are trading posts on the Yukon River, the former being 467 miles from the sea, according to Lieutenant Allen, and Nuklakayer, 201 miles farther. Fort Yukon (about 300 miles distant from Nuklakayer) was formerly a trading post. Lieutenant Schwatka says it was abandoned about 1880 as not remunerative, and Fort Reliance and Belle Isle were established. Both of these have since been abandoned. At Fort Yukon the river is said to be seven miles wide."

Circle City, on the Yukon, near the international boundary line, has become quite a trading center, but when gold was discovered on the Klondike most of its inhabitants moved to Dawson City, in Canadian territory.

CHAPTER XXVI.

THE FUR-SEAL CONTROVERSY.

Account of the fur-sealing grounds, and their great value—The annual catch—Pelagic sealing—History of the great controversy—Solution of all difficulties practically accomplished.

We are indebted to the argument made by James C. Carter, on behalf of the United States, before the Tribunal of Arbitration in Paris in 1893, for the following instructive observations on the Alaskan fur-seal resources and controversy: During most of the eighteenth century, as all are aware, the efforts and ambitions of various European powers were directed toward the taking possession, the settlement, and the colonization of the temperate and tropical parts of the American continent. In those efforts Russia seems to have taken a comparatively small part, if any part at all. Her enterprise and ambitions were attracted to these northern seas, seas which border upon the coasts which in part she already possessed, the Siberian coast of Bering Sea. From that, coast explorations were made by enterprising navigators belonging to that nation, until the whole of Bering Sea was discovered, and the coasts on all its sides explored. The Aleutian Islands, forming its southern boundary, were discovered and explored, and a part of what is called the Northwest Coast of the American Continent, south of the Alaskan Peninsula and reaching south as far as the 54th or 50th degree of north latitude, was also explored by Russian navigators, and establishments were formed upon it in certain places. The great object of Russia in these enterprises and explorations was to reap for herself the sole profit and the sole benefit which could be derived from these remote and ice-bound regions, namely, that of the fur-bearing animals which inhabited them, and which were gathered by the native inhabitants. To obtain for herself the benefit of those animals and of the trade with the natives who were engaged in gathering them constituted the main object of the original enterprises prosecuted by Russian navigators. They had at a very early period discovered what we call the Commander Islands on the western side of Bering Sea, which were then, as they are now, one of the principal resorts and breeding places of the fur seals. They were carrying on a very large, or a considerable, industry in connection with those animals upon those islands.

Prior to the year 1787, one of their navigators, Captain Pribilof, had observed very numerous bodies of fur seals making their way northward through the Aleutian chain. Whither they were going, he knew not, but, from his knowledge of the habits of the seals in the region of the Commander Islands, he could not but suppose that there was, somewhere north of the Aleutian chain in the Bering Sea, another great breeding place and resort for these animals. He therefore expended much labor in endeavoring to discover these resorts, and in the year 1786, on one of his voyages, he suddenly found himself in the presence of that tremendous roar, a roar almost like that of Niagara, it is said, which proceeds from the countless multitudes of animals upon the islands. He knew then that the object for which he was seeking had been obtained; and waiting until the fog had lifted, he discovered before him the islands to which his name was afterwards given. That was in 1786. Immediately following that discovery many Russians, sometimes individually and sometimes associated in companies, resorted to those islands, which were uninhabited, and made large captures of seals from them. The mode of taking them was by an indiscriminate slaughter of males and females; and of course it was not long before the disastrous effects of that method became apparent. They were greatly reduced in numbers, and at one or more times seemed to be upon the point almost of commercial extermination. By degrees, those engaged in this pursuit learned what the laws of nature were in respect to the preservation of such a race of animals. They learned that they were highly polygamous in their nature, and that a certain draft could be taken from the superfluous males without sensibly depreciating the enormous numbers of the herd. Learning those facts, they gradually established an industry upon the islands, removed a considerable number of the population of one or more of the Aleutian Islands, and kept them permanently there for the purpose of guarding the seals upon the islands and taking, at the suitable time for that purpose, such a number of superfluous males as the knowledge they had acquired taught them could be safely taken.

Finally the system which they established grew step by step more regular and precise; and sometime in the neighborhood of 1845 they had adopted a regular system which absolutely forbade the slaughter of females and confined the taking to young males under certain ages and to a certain annual number. Under that reasonable system, conforming to natural laws, the existence of the herd was perpetuated and its numbers even largely increased; so that at a time when it passed into the possession of the United States, it was true that the numbers of the herd were then equal to, if not greater, than ever had been known since the islands were first discovered. A similar system had been pursued by the Russians with similar effect upon the Commander Islands, possessions of their own on the western side of the Bering Sea.

That was the condition of things when these islands passed into the possession of the United States under the treaty between that government and Russia, in 1867. At first, upon the acquisition by the United States government, its authority was not immediately established, and consequently this herd of seals was exposed to the indiscriminate ravages of individuals who might be tempted hither by their hope of gain-ing a profit; and the result was that in the first year something like 240,000 seals were taken, and although some discrimination was attempted, and an effort was made to confine the taking, as far as possible, to males only, yet those efforts were not in every respect successful. That great draft thus irregularly and indiscriminately made upon them had undoubtedly a very unfavorable effect; but the following year the United States succeeded in establishing its authority and at once readopted the system which had been up to that time pursued by Russia, and which had been followed by such advantageous results.

In addition to that, and for the purpose of further insuring the preservation of the herd, the United States Government resorted to national legislation. Laws were passed, the first of them as early as the year 1870, designed to protect the seal and other fur-bearing animals in Bering Sea and the other possessions recently acquired from Russia. At a later period, this statute, with others that had been subsequently passed, was revised in the year 1873, when a general revision of the statutes of the United States was made. They were revised and made more stringent. It was made a criminal offense to kill any female seal; and the taking of any seals at all, except in pursuance of the authority of the United States and under such regulations as it might adopt, was made a criminal offense. Any vessel engaged in the taking of female seals in the waters of Alaska, according to the phrase used in the statute, was made liable to seizure and confiscation; and in this way it was hoped and expected that the fur seals would be preserved in the future as completely as they had been in the past, and that this herd would continue to be still as productive as before, and if possible made more productive. That system thus initiated by the United States in the year 1870 produced the same result as had followed the regulations established by Russia. The United States Government was enabled even to take a larger draft than

Russia had, prior to that time, made upon the herd. Russia had limited herself at an early period to the taking of somewhere between 30,000 and 40,000 seals annually, not solely, perhaps, for the reason that no more could be safely taken from the herd, but also for the reason that at that time the demand for seals was not so great as to justify the putting of a larger number of skins upon the market.

At a later period of the occupation by Russia, her drafts were increased. At the time when the occupation was transferred to the United States they amounted to somewhere between 50,000 and 70,000 annually. The United States took 100,000 from the beginning, and continued to make those annual drafts of 100,000 down to the year 1890. That is a period of something like nineteen years. The taking of this number of 100,000 did not at first appear to lead to any diminution in the numbers of the herd; and it was only in the year 1890, or a few years prior to that time, that a diminution in the numbers of the herd was first observed.

Such was the industry established by the United States. It was a very beneficial industry, beneficial, in the first instance, to herself. She had adopted the practice of leasing these islands upon long terms, twenty years, to a private corporation; and those leases contained an obligation to pay a large annual sum in the shape of a revenue tax and a gross sum of some $60,000 as rent. In addition to that, the lessees were required by the terms of the lease to pay to the United States Government a certain sum upon every seal captured by them, which, of course, resulted in the enjoyment by the United States of a still larger revenue. It was beneficial to the lessees, for it is to be supposed, and such is the fact, that they were enabled to make a profit, notwithstanding the large sums they were compelled to pay to the United States Government upon the seal skins secured by them. The whole product of the herd was contributed at once to commerce, and through the instrumentality of commerce was carried all over the world to those who desired the sealskins, and those who desired sealskins, wherever they might be on the face of the globe, and whatever nation they might inhabit, got them upon the same terms upon which the citizens of the United States enjoyed them. This contribution of the annual product to the purposes of commerce, to be dealt with as commerce deals with one of its subjects, of course amounted substantially to a putting it up at auction, and it was awarded to the highest bidder, wherever he might dwell.

The effect of this was, also, to build up and maintain an important industry in Great Britain. It was there that the sealskins were manufactured and prepared for sale in the market, and thousands of people were engaged in that industry, many more, indeed, than were engaged in the industry of gathering the seals upon the Pribilof Islands. That particular benefit was secured to Great Britain in consequence of this industry.

In the few years preceding 1890, the government of the United States was made aware of a peril to the industry which had thus been established and which it was in the enjoyment of, a peril to the preservation of this race of seals, a peril not proceeding from what may be called natural causes, such as the killing by whales and other animals which prey upon the seals in the water, but a peril proceeding from the hand of man. It was found that the practice of pelagic sealing, which had for many years, and, indeed, from the earliest knowledge of these regions, been carried on to a very limited extent by the Indians who inhabited the coasts, for the purpose of obtaining food for themselves and skins for their clothing, and which had made a limited draft upon the herds in that way—it was found that this practice was beginning to be extended so as to be carried on by whites, and in large vessels capable of proceeding long distances from the shore, of encountering the roughest weather, and of carrying boats and boatmen and hunters, armed with every appliance for taking and slaughtering the seals upon their passage through the seas. That practice began in the year 1876, but at first its extent was small. The vessels were fitted out mostly from a port in British Columbia, and confined their enterprise to the North Pacific Ocean, not entering Bering Sea at all; and their drafts upon the seals even in the North Pacific Ocean were at first extremely small, only a few thousands each year. But the business was found to be a profitable one, and, of course, as its profit was perceived, more and more were tempted to engage in it, and a larger and larger investment of capital was made in it. More and more vessels prosecuted the fishery in the North Pacific Ocean, and in 1883, for the first time, a vessel ventured to enter Bering Sea.

Up to this time, during the whole of the Russian and the whole of the American occupation of these islands, there had been no such thing as pelagic sealing, except in the insignificant way already mentioned by the Indians. Those two nations had enjoyed the full benefit of this property, the full benefit of these herds of seals, in as complete a degree as if they had been organized as the sole proprietors of them, and as if a title in them, not only while they were ashore and upon the breeding islands, but while they were absent upon their migrations, had been recognized in them during that whole period, or as if there had been some regulation among the nations absolutely prohibiting all pelagic sealing. Up to the period when pelagic sealing began to be extended, those advantages were exclusively enjoyed by Russia and the United States; and at first, this pelagic sealing did not extend into Bering Sea, but was carried on in the North Pacific Ocean and south and east of the Aleutian chain.

Why Bering Sea was thus carefully abstained from it may, perhaps, be difficult to say. It may be for the reason that it was farther off, more difficult to reach. It may be for the reason that the pelagic sealers did not at first suppose that they had a right to enter Bering Sea and take the seals there, for it was well known that during the whole of the Russian occupation Russia did assert for herself an exclusive right to all the products of that region of the globe; and it was also, of course, well known to all governments, and to these pelagic sealers, that the United States had, when they acceded to the sovereignty over these islands, asserted a similar right, and made the practice of pelagic sealing, in Bering Sea at least—perhaps farther, but in Bering Sea, at least—a criminal offense under their law. But from whatever cause, it was not until the year 1883 that any pelagic sealers ventured into Bering Sea. During that year a single vessel did enter there, took a large catch, was very successful and was not called to any account; and this successful experiment was, of course, followed during the succeeding years by many repetitions of the same enterprise.

The extent to which pelagic sealing was thus carried on in Bering Sea, its probable consequences upon the herds which made their homes upon the Pribilof Islands, was not at first appreciated either by the United States or by the lessees of the islands. There was no means by which they could easily find out how many vessels made such excursions, and they did not at first seem to suppose that their interests were particularly threatened by it. Consequently, for the first two or three years, no notice seems to have been taken of these enterprises by the government of the United States, although it had laws made against them. But in 1886, this practice of taking seals at sea became so largely extended that it excited apprehensions for the safety of the herd, and it was perhaps thought at that time that there was already observable in the condition of the herd some damaging, destructive consequence of that pursuit of them by sea.

The attention of the United States having been called to the practice, that government determined to prevent it, and the first method to which it resorted was an enforcement of the laws upon her statute book which prohibited the practice, and subjected all vessels engaged in it to seizure and confiscation. Instructions were accordingly given to the cruisers of the United States to suppress the practice and to enforce its laws. The result was that in the year 1886, three British vessels and some American vessels were taken while engaged in the pursuit illegally under the laws of the United States. They were carried in and condemned.

These seizures, after much diplomatic correspondence, led to the final adoption of a treaty between the United States and Great Britain, which was signed at Washington, February 29, 1892.

The arbitrators under this treaty, Hon. John M. Harlan and Hon. John T. Morgan, representing the United States; Baron Alphonse de Courcel, arbitrator named by France; the Right Hon. Lord Hannen and Sir John Thompson, representing Great Britain; Marquis E. Visconti Venosta, arbitrator named by Italy, and Mr. Gregers Gram, arbitrator named by Sweden and Norway, met at Paris on February 23, 1893, and were in session until August 15, 1893. The public is familiar with the terms of their award, which were not only satisfactory to this country, but practically a final settlement of the controversy.

Since 1893, efforts have been made by the United States for the further prevention of pelagic sealing and the protection of the fur-seal fisheries. With this end in view, Hon. John W. Foster was sent as agent to England to secure the adoption of a modus vivendi prohibiting all sealing until a final disposition of the question can be had and a treaty can be entered into establishing further regulations for the government of the fisheries. At this writing no official data of the results of this mission can be had, the agent not having as yet submitted his report.

As a further result of the arbitration of 1893, a convention was concluded between the United States and Great Britain, February 8, 1896, for the settlement of the claims of British subjects growing out of the seizures of British vessels in Bering Sea from 1886 to 1892, which provided for the appointment of two commissioners, and, if necessary, an umpire. This commission was to sit at Victoria, British Columbia, and San Francisco, Cal. Sessions have been held in both places, but as yet the results of their labors have not been made public.

CHAPTER XXVII.

SALMON, WHALE, COD AND HERRING.

Extent of the Alaskan fisheries—Statistics of the salmon catch—Product of oil, bone and ivory—Cod and herring fisheries.

The products of the sea, the lakes and the rivers are the chief resources of Alaska. The native populations have always obtained much of their food supply from the waters, and in a less degree their clothing and many of the conveniences of life. Their winter supply of food is still largely made up of dried fish, seaweed, and fish eggs, while fresh fish are eaten at all seasons of the year, not only by the natives, but by all classes of people, and the abundance of this product insures the most thriftless of a ready means of subsistence.

*Salmon fishing is by far the largest and most important industry. Thirty-seven canneries and seven or more salting establishments were reported as in operation in 1890. The aggregate pack of the canneries was 688,332 cases of four dozen one-pound cans, falling a little short of the pack in 1889. The amount of salted salmon was about 7,300 barrels, a little more than the year previous. The salmon fisheries represent a capital of about $4,250,000, and they give employment to about 2,000 white laborers, 2,500 Chinamen, and 1,000 natives, and require in their business for transportation, and in their work, about 100 steam vessels and 500 fishing boats. The white and Chinese laborers do not usually remain in the territory after the season is over.

The report for 1895 of Mr. Joseph Murray, special agent to inspect the fisheries of Alaska, says that

---

* **Joseph P. Smith, Director Bureau American Republics.**

during the year nearly 7,000,000 cases, of 48 pounds to the case, were packed, and the total value of the salmon canned was over $2,000,000.

"The whaling business," says Mr. Lyman E. Knapp, governor of Alaska, in his report for 1892, "in which forty-eight vessels are engaged, resulted in a catch for 1891 of 12,228 barrels of oil, 186,250 pounds of bone, and 1,000 pounds of ivory. The total value was $1,218,293. Below is a comparative statement of the amount of oil, bone and ivory taken during the last eighteen years:

Year.	Oil. Barrels.	Bone. Pounds.	Ivory. Pounds.
1891	12,228	186,250	1,000
1890	14,890	231,232	4,150
1889	12,834	231,981	1,506
1888	15,774	303,587	1,550
1887	31,714	564,802	875
1886	37,260	304,530	2,850
1885	24,844	451,038	6,564
1884	20,373	295,700	5,421
1883	12,300	160,200	23,100
1882	21,100	316,600	17,800
1881	21,800	354,500	15,400
1880	23,200	339,000	15,300
1879	17,400	127,000	32,900
1878	9,000	73,300	30,000
1877	13,900	139,600	74,000
1876	2,800	8,800	7,000
1875	16,300	157,000	25,400
1874	10,000	86,000	7,000
Total, 18 years	318,917	4,931,950	272,410

The codfish business is next in importance in Alaska. It is carried on at the Shumagin Islands and in the Bering Sea. The catch of 1890 amounted to a total of 1,138,000 fish. Since the beginning of the codfishing industry in this territory in 1865 the total number of fish taken is 25,723,300, of the value of $12,861,650. The first four years, the business did not come near to its present proportions.

A hasty survey has given an idea of the extent of the banks, and there is much yet to be done to properly define their limits and determine their character. Portlock Bank, extending northeasterly from Kadiak, has an immense area; Shumagin Bank, south of the Shumagin group of islands, has an area of about 4,400 square miles; Albatross Bank, off the southeastern side of Kadiak, has an area of 2,900 square miles; Slime Bank, north of Unimak Island, in Bering Sea, covers an area of 1,445 square miles, embracing depths of twenty to fifty fathoms; Baird Bank stretches along the north coast of Alaska Peninsula 230 miles, with an average width of forty miles, covering an area of 9,200 square miles. The depths range from fifteen to fifty fathoms, with a bottom of fine gray sand.

The business of the Alaska Oil and Guano Company, at Killisnoo, gives employment to forty-five white men, fifty Indians, and a few Chinamen. Their principal business is fishing, and the manufacture of oil and fish fertilizer, though they also have a trading post. Their capital stock is $75,000. They have a fishing fleet of three steamers, four scows and two small boats. The product of their factory in 1891 was larger than in 1890, being 300,000 gallons of oil instead of 157,000 reported the previous year. They also put up 700 barrels of salt salmon, and manufactured 800 tons of guano. The value of the product was not less than $114,000. The oil is worth about thirty cents per gallon and the guano about $30 per ton.

The fish used for the manufacture of oil is the herring, which is very abundant, very rich in oil, and finely flavored. It is much used as a food-fish, and also as bait in taking halibut and other large fish. It is caught by the natives for their own use with a stick, toward the end of which are inserted several sharpened spikes. They dip the stick in the water, catch one or more herring, and with a single motion land the fish in the canoe, and then thrust the stick into the water again. In this way they take immense quantities in a short time. These fish frequent the still waters of bays and inlets by the million, at different places, and in varying seasons of the year, from August to February.

Halibut abounds throughout central, southern, and western Alaska, and can be taken at any time during the year. They vary in size from 15 to 250 pounds each, those weighing from fifty to seventy-five pounds being preferred. It is not uncommon, says Governor Knapp, of Alaska, for Sitka Indians to visit Silver Bay or the vicinity of Mount Edgecombe and return the following day with nearly a ton of these fish. White-fish, losh, and graylings are found in large quantities in the Yukon, and afford more food for the natives than the salmon. Black bass are abundant in south-eastern Alaska, and trout and pike inhabit almost all the rivers.

CHAPTER XXVIII.

COMMERCE, GOVERNMENT, TRANSPORTATION.

Transportation facilities—Exports and imports—Territorial government—The civil list of Alaska.

Correct statistics as to the trade of Alaska are not easily obtained, and this is largely due to the various and uncertain transportation facilities. *The large companies engaged in business in the territory usually employ their own ships. There were some eighty-seven trading houses reported in Alaska in 1891, located in not less than sixty towns and villages, and scattered from Point Barrow to the southern extremity, and from Loring to Attu. The number of stores for the sale of general merchandise in southeastern Alaska in 1892 was forty-seven. The imports consist of merchandise, machinery, powder, clothing, provisions, tools, furniture, etc. The exports are made up of fish, furs, whalebone, ivory, oils, gold and silver bullion and ores. The total imports in 1892, according to the report of Governor Knapp, of Alaska, amounted to the value of $2,164,238.

Exports.

Furs, curios, etc. from 13 stations, southeast Alaska	$ 351,000
1,220,000 codfish (7,500 tons)	375,000
789,294 cases of salmon	3,157,176
9,000 barrels of salted salmon	81,000
186,250 pounds of whalebone	1,210,625
1,000 pounds ivory	5,000
12,228 barrels whale oil	103,668

* Joseph P. Smith, Director Bureau American Republics.

Product of the Killisnoo manufactory, oil and guano	114,000
Gold bullion, Alaska Treadwell Gold Mining Company	707,017
Gold and silver ore and bullion by other companies	400,000
13,500 seal skins taken under the lease; 52,087 seal skins taken by sealing fleet; 10,000 seal skins taken by natives and others	755,587
Furs shipped by Alaska Commercial Company	348,991
Furs shipped by other parties, western Alaska	90,000
Other products not enumerated	60,000
Total	$7,759,064
Balance of exports above imports	$5,594,886

Among the furs may be mentioned those of the sea otter, the seal, the beaver, the silver and blue fox, the mink, and the marten.

Governor Knapp, in his report for 1892, says: "The mail contract with the Pacific Coast Steamship Company requires stoppage for receipt and delivery of mail by their regular passenger and freight steamers, two each month, at seven ports, viz: Kichkan, in Tongass Narrows, Loring, Wrangel, Douglas, Juneau, Killisnoo and Sitka. For this service they are paid the sum of $18,000 per year. When other trips are made and other places are visited by the steamers of the company, mails are carried and delivered wherever they call. By this more uncertain service, several mails have been delivered at Metlakahtla, Mary Island, Chilcat and Hoonah, and the mail has been carried weekly instead of semi-monthly to the first named places during the months of June, July and August. Another mail contract insures monthly mail service from Wrangel to Klawak and Howkan. A small steamer, or steam launch, plies between Wrangel and Howkan. Between Sitka and Unalaska, a distance of about 1,350 miles, a small steamer has made seven regular monthly trips, from April to October, stopping at six places.

In Special Consular Reports on "Highways of Commerce, 1895," it is stated that the fare from San Francisco to Wrangel, by the Pacific Coast Steamship Company, is $50; to Juneau or Sitka, $70. There is also steamship service from St. Michael's via Unalaska to Seattle and San Francisco.

The report of the Second Assistant Postmaster-General of the United States for 1896 says that a post-office was authorized at Circle City March 19, 1896. The carrier for the first trip started from Juneau June 11th, and reached Circle City July 14th, carrying 1,474 letters. He returned by way of St. Michael, reaching Seattle August 19th. On the second trip, the carrier left Juneau July 8th, reaching Circle City August 6th. Another trip was made in September, and four between November and May, 1897.

In 1886, in reply to an inquiry on the part of the United States Senate, the director of the United States Geological Survey, J. W. Powell, presented a report on the feasibility of constructing a railroad between the United States, Asiatic Russia, and Japan. Mr. Powell said that from all available information the proposed line appeared to present no greater obstacles than those already overcome in transcontinental railroad building. It was suggested that the line start from some point on the Northern Pacific Railroad in Montana, and run, via the head waters of the Peace River, to the head waters of the Yukon; and thence to some point on the shore of Bering Sea, the total distance covered being about 2,765 miles. A branch line of 375 miles from the head waters of the Peace River might run to the mouth of the Stikine River, so as to facilitate communication with Sitka.

There is not much of special interest in the government of Alaska. In 1884 a district government was created, with a governor and district court, which sits alternately at Sitka and Wrangel. The laws are principally those of Oregon. There is a land office at Sitka. Commissioner Hermann, of the United States General Land Office, on July 31, 1897, stated that the mineral-land laws of the United States, the town-site laws (providing for the incorporation of town sites and acquirement of title thereto from the government to the trustee), and the law giving each qualified person 160 acres of land in a square and compact form, are applicable to Alaska. The coal-land regulations and the public-land laws do not extend to Alaska, as the territory is expressly excluded by the laws themselves from their operation.

The following is a list of United States officers in Alaska, furnished by the Department of the Interior, August 7, 1897:

John G. Brady, governor, Sitka.

Albert D. Elliot, clerk of the court, and ex-officio secretary of Alaska, Sitka.

William L. Distin, surveyor-general, Sitka.

John W. Dudley, register of the land office, Sitka.

Russell Shelly, receiver of public moneys, Sitka.

Caldwell W. Tuttle, commissioner at Sitka.

Kenneth M. Jackson, commissioner at Wrangel.

Lycurgus R. Woodward, commissioner at Unalaska.

John Y. Ostrander, commissioner at Juneau City.

Phillip Gallaher, commissioner at Kadiak.

John E. Crane, commissioner at Circle City.

L. P. Shepard, commissioner at St. Michaels.

John U. Smith, commissioner at Dyea.

Charles H. Isham, commissioner at Unga.

The following is a list of the judicial officers of the United States in Alaska, furnished by the Department of Justice, August 7, 1897:

Charles S. Johnson, district judge, Sitka.

Burton E. Bennett, United States attorney, Sitka.

Alfred J. Daly, assistant United States attorney, Sitka.

James M. Shoup, United States marshal, Sitka.

CHAPTER XXIX.

RESOURCES OF HUDSON'S BAY.

Mountains of pure mica—The salmon fisheries of Ungava—The Eskimos and their language—Extracts from prayer and hymn books—On to Churchill.

The reader is invited to accompany the writer on a voyage from the Atlantic Coast through Hudson Strait and Bay, in order to study the natural features, resources and native populations of that wonderful region. These observations are based on the travels of the author during 1884, in his capacity as meteorological observer of the Canadian government expedition sent out to enquire into the practicability of the navigation of those waters in connection with a proposed transcontinental railway line from Churchill to Port Simpson through the Pine River Pass. The journey covering the country between the two points named had been previously made.

Our good steamship Neptune is "laying to" off Resolution Island, waiting for the fog to lift, so that her weatherbeaten commander, Commodore Sopp, of the Liverpool Job Brothers fleet, can see his way to round Cape Chidley and enter Hudson's strait.

We have passed through Belle Isle, and made the acquaintance of a score or more of mighty icebergs which are going down from the Arctic rock mountains to be dissolved in tropical seas. We have traversed 700 miles of rugged Labrador coast, paid a visit to Nain, the capital of the Moravian mission stations, called at Nachvak, the first of the Hudson's Bay trading posts, and are now ready to make the voyage through the strait and across the bay to Churchill harbor, which lies in the shadow of the big stone fortress abandoned by Hearne about 1782.

At Nain we were introduced to a village of 500 civilized and educated Eskimos. They live in neatly built thatched roof log houses. Nearly a century and a half ago, when these Moravian missions and trading stations were established, there was but little vegetation and no timber in the neighborhood, but both have come to them since. Now they "switch" down from the hillsides, by means of husky dogs, logs ten to twelve inches in diameter and from fifteen to twenty feet long. It was there that we got our first lesson on the phenomenon of the march of soil, vegetation and timber to the north, and we were able to enlarge on this at Nachvak.

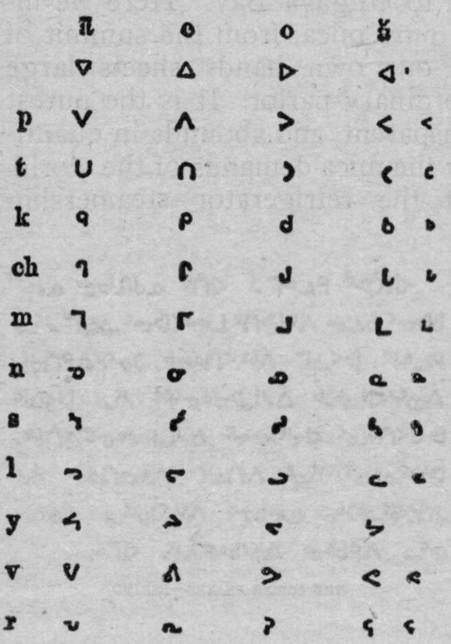

ESKIMO SYLLABARIUM.

At Nain we learned the rudiments of the Eskimo language, and now all we need is practice to make ourselves perfect in its oral and written use. These natives have the old and new testaments and numbers 1 and 2 of Sankey's Hymns, translated and printed in their own language. They have a church, and in it a harpischord, after the pattern of our old-style melodeon, which was brought from Germany nearly a century ago, but is yet in fair condition. They are fond of music and have a trained violin orchestra.

Do you ask why these people are not taught a language other than their own? That has been found an impossible thing to do. They consider the attempt to speak another language "the unpardonable sin." But we can only speak of these strange people as a memory now. Here is a leaf from one of their hymn books containing a portion of the familiar hymns, "Knocking, knocking," and "Safe in the arms of Jesus."

But we must hurry forward. The fog has lifted and our good ship has rounded the cape, entered Hudson's Strait, and paid a visit to Ungava Bay. Here we inspected a mountain of pure mica, from the summit of which were torn with our own hands sheets large enough to carpet an ordinary parlor. It is the purest of mica, faultlessly transparent, and abounds in quantities sufficient to supply the mica demands of the world.

In Ungava we met the refrigerator steamership Diana on her way from Ungava River to England with a full load of salmon, taken in one tide, by means of a trap. This incident, and the mountain of mica, constitute the two first hints on the resources of the north.

ᐊᑖᑖᕗᑦ ᑮᓚᓐᒥ! ᐊᑎᑦ ᓇᑯᕆᔭᓂ ᓇᓂ-
ᑲᐅᓂᑦ ᑳᓚᓂ ᐱᖁᔫᑎᑦ ᒪᓂᒃᑕᐅᓂᕐᓄᓇᒥ ᔪᕐᓗ
ᑭᓚᓐᒥ ᐅᐸᓗᒥ ᐱᒃᓴᐸᑎᓐᓂᒃ ᑐᓂᖅᓯᕕᑭᑎᒍᕐ.
ᐃᓄᖅᓯᐊᕐᓗᒃᑐᒃ ᐃᓱᒪᑭᔪᓐᓂᕐᑭᑦ ·ᔪᕐᓗ ᐅᕙᒍᑦ
ᐅᕙᐸᑎᓐᓄᑦ ᐊᔪᕌᓂᔪᑦ ᐃᓱᒪᑭᔪᓐᓂᖃᐸᑎᑭᒃ.
ᐅᒃᑐᕐᓗᓐᓇᕌᕌᕐᓄᑦ ᐱᑎᓇᑕ ᐱᓐᓂᑎᑯᓂ ᐃ-
ᓄᖅᓯᐊᕐᓗᒃᑐᒃ. ᓇᓂᑲᓂᒃ ᐱᕋᕌᓂᕐᓗ ᐊᓇᓇ-
ᓂᕐᓗ ᐱᑭᑲᓐᓂ ᐃᔅᓯᑲᓐᑭᑐᓗᕐ. ᐊᒥᓐ.

THE LORD'S PRAYER—ESKIMO

But we must be away. Not, however, until we have paid a short visit to the Eskimos on the south shore of Hudson's Strait. Here the natives have not been disturbed by civilization, and they do not meet with even Hudson's Bay traders oftener than once in three to five years. They are a greasy, dirty, happy-go-lucky set, living for the most part on the blubber of the seal, and on wild fowl, which abounds in great plenty, cooking all their food thoroughly, except the fat of the seal, thus giving contradiction to much that has been falsely written about them in this respect. Seal oil, with lichen moss for a wick, supplies their stone lamps, and they are seldom short of this fuel.

There is no soil on either side of Hudson's Strait. The rocks are bare except as covered by patches of lichen moss, upon which great droves of cariboo or reindeer feed to their heart's content. The natives dwell in reindeer skin tents, which are easily moved from place to place.

45. ᐃᖕᐃᕈᑎᓂᒃ ᓱᒍᕈᑎᖕ
ᕆᓂᒃ.

1. ᓈᓛᒋᑦ, ᓈᓛᒋᕝ,
ᕿᓪᓚᒃᑯᑦ ᑮᓇᐅᓈ
ᐋᐱᓗᒃᑖᒃᑯᑦ ᐅᒫᓘᑦ ᕈ
ᒋᓴᕓᐆᒡᒃ ᐃᓛ
ᐃᑎᕈᒫᕙᒃ ᐃᓪᓘᓅᑦ.
ᐆᐸᑰᐃᐆᑎᓚᐅᕈᒃ.

2. ᓈᓛᒋᑦ, ᕿᓪᓚᒃᐳᒃ,
ᑎᑯᐄᑦ! ᒫᓂᐳᒃ,
ᑭᒥᕐᔪᓪᓚᑭᑦ ᐋᒪᓇᒋᑦ
ᐳᕍᒫᕙᑦ ᐱᕙᓘᑎᑦ;
ᐃᓵᓪᓚᐆᓚᐅᕝ ᐃᓛ
ᐃᓪᓗᓂᑦ ᓅᑯᓈᒍ.

---

46. ᐃᖕᐃᕈᑎᓂᒃ ᓯᒍᕈᑎᖕ
ᕆᓂᒃ

1. ᑎᕝᓗᖕᓈᕋᒥᐤᓘᓂ
ᒋᓴᐸ ᕇᒃᐱᖕᐊᓂ,
ᕊᐸᔪᒫ ᑖᓪᓕᖕᓂ
ᑯᐱᐋᓈᐤᓛᖕᒥᒃ!

THE HYMN "KNOCKING, KNOCKING," ETC.—ESKIMO.

We enter Hudson's Bay from the straits at the sunrise of a bright, still morning, with the Diggs Islands on our right and the mighty Cape Wolstenholme on our left. From the former, Henry Hudson and his son were set adrift in a jolly boat by a mutinous crew, never to be heard from more; and from the summit of the latter, 3,000 feet above the water, streams are pouring down from a crown of perpetual snow and ice.

A few days and nights bring us to Fort Churchill; and now we must take time to go to the Rose Welcome whaling ground, to the north, and to visit York Factory far to the south, at the mouth of the Hayes and Nelson rivers.

CHAPTER XXX.

IN HUDSON'S STRAIT.

Its length, width and islands—Height of its tides, and velocity of its tidal currents—Talks with Eskimos.

Before going up to Rose Welcome, where we will enjoy the excitement of seeing a whale taken, let us make some observations on Hudson's Strait, through which we have passed. From Cape Chidley to Cape Best, on Resolution Island, at the entrance to the strait, the channel is forty-five miles wide. The narrowest channel of the strait is at its western extremity, where between Cape Wolstenholme and the south shore of Nottingham Island, the channel is not more than thirty-five miles wide. The tides in the strait rise and fall from fifteen to thirty-five feet, and the tide race runs at from four to ten miles an hour, at half tide, according to location.

Its principal islands are Resolution on the north of the entrance from the mouth of Davis' Strait; Big Island on the north side of the strait, close to the mainland, called North Bluff; Charles Island, about fifteen miles from its south shore, and about the same distance northwest of Cape Weggs; Salisbury, about forty miles from the north-main coast, with Mills Island twelve miles to the northwest of it, both at the mouth of Fox Channel; and Nottingham, near the center of the strait at the entrance to Hudson's Bay.

The smaller or group islands are the Buttons, about five miles north of Cape Chidley; Lower Savages, northwest of Resolution, and between it and the northmain shore; the Middle Savages and Saddle Backs, lying close to the north main coast, about sixty miles northwest of the Lower Savages, and a little to the east of the Upper Savages; Big Island at the entrance to North Bay; and the Digges, six miles west of Cape Wolstenholme, at the south side of the entrance to Hudson's Bay.

The water in the Strait is uniformly very deep; between Resolution and Cape Chidley it is three hundred fathoms. The center of the Strait to the west will average from two hundred to one hundred and fifty fathoms, getting shallower as the entrance to Hudson's Bay is neared. There are no shoals or dangerous reefs to render navigation precarious. The same may practically be said in regard to fogs and gales; fogs occur, but are usually of short duration, and heavy gales are of rare occurrence. In this respect the Strait is in happy contrast with the ever-squally waters of the Labrador Coast. The variation or error of the magnetic needle, in its application to the navigation of Hudson's Strait, is as regular and reliable as in any part of the world. It is about 50 degrees west at Cape Chidley, and at the entrance of Hudson's Bay, say at Nottingham Island, about 55 w. There is no local magnetic force to interfere with navigating the center of the Strait, and the compass, that is, the patent Sir William Thompson compass, may be depended upon; but the ordinary marine compass is practically worthless. This arises from the close proximity of the Strait to the magnetic pole, on account of which the directive force acting on the needle is greatly diminished.

The shores of the Strait are high, bold and barren, consisting of the Laurentian gneiss formation. The waters abound in whales, porpoise, walrus, seal, and many kinds of fish, while on the shores and the borders of the lakes and streams of the interior, fur-bearing animals, deer, white bears and a great variety of small game, are plentiful. The Eskimos inhabit both the north and south shores, and the borders of the rivers.

A visit to some of the Eskimo camps on the north shore of Hudson's Strait proved interesting. There we obtained some rare skins and talked to the natives, to a limited extent, in their own language. The author had, by that time, gained a slight knowledge of Eskimo. The following is from the author's book "North Land," printed some years ago:

"I had in my hands a Snyder rifle, which attracted the admiration of a young hunter. I allowed him to examine it, and remarked, 'oonla-ko-olik,' which means, 'It is a rifle.' He was greatly pleased with the idea that I could speak his tongue, and went into a rigmarole of gibberish, of which I understood nothing, and to which I responded: 'Ontuke,' which is, 'I do not understand.' Then his countenance dropped, but to revive him I said: 'Ki-chin-a-coma,' which is, 'I will give you tobacco.' His smiles returned, and extending one hand he waited anxiously, for all Eskimos love tobacco. Exhibiting the tobacco, I asked, 'kito-ma-shima-yuk?' This demand for deer skin brought another cloud to his face, but after a moment's pause he shouted out, 'ko-le-tuk,' meaning a woman's dress of deer skin. He exhibited two of these, made of beautifully dressed skins, with shoulder hoods for papoose, and the inevitable long tails, the only distinguishing mark between the dress of the men and that of the women. He laid them on the ground, and I placed four plugs of black tobacco near by and asked, 'Oonah, oomung de?' or 'will you take this for that?' He nodded assent and the trade was over, but not until his explanation of 'Match-a-mic,' had softened me to the extent of one card of matches.

"I then asked for 'poyea,' or seal skin. He brought from his bag of the same material four large skins, and the same performance was repeated. I obtained them for four mean little black plugs of tobacco, and felt that the native had been badly swindled; while, on the other hand, he seemed to think he had struck a bonanza, and grinned all over his great broad ugly face.

"With a disposition to continue the traffic, I inquired for 'Nannuk,' or white bear skin. He exhibited a piece about eighteen inches square, and I brought out some more tobacco, but he shook his head and wanted 'og-jik' (powder). I had none of this. Then he wanted 'in-nip-a-lowlite,' (gun caps); I had none; and then he shouted 'de-vine-looka,' all of which meant only 'shot,' but I had none. However, he was not to be easily discouraged and called for a 'shi-powit,' or a pipe. I had only one and could not part with that, so I said, turning away, 'ok-shan-i,' or good-bye. This was a good stroke, I mean a business stroke. He came to time without delay and called after me: 'Pish-shee-yon-ma-go-lova-too-goot,' or 'I want to trade.' I then exhibited two plugs of black-strap, and asked in a decided tone of voice, as if it were my last offer, 'oomungde?' He yielded and I became the happy owner of this small piece of valuable skin.

"Just then a new arrival advanced, and, extending my hand, I said carelessly, 'kan-we-kuk' (how are you). He took my hand and shook it heartily, and spreading out his skins, said 'pish-shee-yon-ma-go-lova.' I turned him over to a companion who relieved him of his peltries, giving in return therefor as little in value as I had done for the goods obtained from the first."

CHAPTER XXXI.

CAPTURING A WHALE.

Scenes and impressions of Marble Island—Visit to the Rose Welcome—The "crow's nest" and Lookout-man—Harpooning a whale—An exciting contest—A "flurry."

On our way to the Rose Welcome we stopped at Marble Island and were at once surprised at seeing so many indications of the dead at the old winter quarters of the New England whalers. On a high gravel ridge, near the harbor, there was a string of graves, some twenty in number, marked by large, well formed oak monuments.

The scene about us was singularly impressive. In the stillness of the morning, we viewed the little city of the dead from the quarter-deck of our good ship. The sun, yet low in the eastern sky, bathed in golden brightness the vast sea over which its refreshing rays greeted the little island. The breeze had not yet awakened, and there was no voice of beast or bird, nor breath of life to stir the atmosphere.

It was a place and an hour for contemplation, and one could not readily turn away from its opportunities. Standing there and looking back over the history of ancient and modern times, it seemed that, stretching from the land of the Norseman, and the waters of Archangel, to "India's coral strand," all peoples, and tribes, and tongues, from the earliest days of Chaldean power down to the history of Assyrian, Persian, Grecian, Roman, and Anglo-Saxon supremacy, have, in the progress of the arts and sciences, in the growth of political institutions of government and civil liberty, in the development of commerce and the advancement of industrial pursuits, and in the rise and glorious reign of Christianity, been moving forward northwesterly. The contemplation, visionary in one sense, was real in another, and history was the source of its inspiration. The general course of human progress, for thousands of years, has been to the northwest; it is still, in the flood tide of its strength, northwesterly.

> **Mankind, in all ages, in marching along**
> **The highway of commerce, by mighty and strong**
> **Impulse of progress, invariably throng**
> **A course that leads north-westerly.**

The first wooden monument met with on the far north grave-ridge bore the following inscription:

Sacred to the Memory

of

CAPTAIN WILLIAM MURPHY,

of

Schooner Abbie Bradford,

who died of consumption at Marble Island,

April 5, 1881, aged 48 years.

There were many others. The bodies occupying these had fallen victims to scurvy. Leaving Marble Island, we steam north into the whaling ground, called the Rose Welcome, to witness the capture of one of these monsters of the sea. This calls for some observations on whales. They live entirely in the water, and obtain their livelihood there; hence their whole structure is fitted for the seas only; and when they are unfortunately cast upon shoals, they cannot of their own power re-enter the water, but perish from starvation.

They are forced to rise to the surface of the water to breathe, which is called "spouting," because a column of mixed vapor and water is ejected from the "blow-holes," rising above the surface to a height of more than twenty feet. The fins are simply undeveloped legs, suited to aquatic locomotion; but their chief use seems to be to keep their immense bodies in position and in caring for their young, as the propelling power is located altogether in the tail.

The northern whale is, when fully grown, about seventy feet long, and in girth about thirty-five or forty feet. Its color is velvety-black on the upper half of its body, as also on its fins and tail, but its belly and the lower part of its jaw are nearly white. The sleek, shiny appearance of its body is due to the oil which is constantly emitted through the pores of the skin. The skin is threefold; the inner, or true skin is nothing more or less than the blubber, or fat. This blubber is generally about eighteen inches to two feet thick according to location on the body, and besides being of value as an article of commerce, it is of great use to the whale, offering an elastic resistance to the waves and pressure of the water. In a full-sized whale the blubber will weigh thirty or forty tons.

The head of the whale is of enormous size, being about one-third of the entire length. The jaws are very long—more than fifteen feet, and about eight feet wide, and ten to twelve feet from top to bottom when open. The most peculiar part of the mouth is the abundance of whalebone that it contains. It lies in a series of plates, thick and close where it is attached to the jaw, but running into hair-like fibers at the ends. On each side of the jaw there are over three hundred of these rows with the bone usually about ten or twelve feet long. A good sized whale will furnish about one ton of bone, which is very valuable as an article of commerce. The whalebone is of use to the whale in catching its food and in separating it from the water.

The whales suckle their young. When first born the young whale is without whalebone, and, therefore, its mouth is not equipped for supplying itself with food, so that it is wholly dependent upon the mother for subsistance. The maternal whale keeps close to her offspring, and does not forsake it until the whalebone is grown and it is able to support itself.

Whaling is one of the most exciting vocations known to man. It is not attended with as many dangers as writers have generally depicted, but it necessitates many hardships, great exposure, and, of course, some risk of life. Steam vessels have pretty much superseded sailing craft in this trade, and are found, for many reasons, to be very much more adapted to it; but in Hudson's Bay the sailing vessel is still used. When the ship, with her crew and hunting appliances, has reached the whaling waters, the "crow's nest," which consists of a barrel, supplied with furs and comfortables, without any top, and with its bottom arranged so as to open and shut on hinges, is arranged on the cross-tree of the foremast. The lookout-man ascends the rigging, passes up into this nest, closes the trap after him, and, with the aid of a telescope keeps a vigilant outlook for whales. Meanwhile all is gotten ready on deck for putting off in the boats whenever a monster is sighted. The lookout-man may have to endure many long, weary, tedious hours before his aching eyes are gladdened by a sight of the object of his watch, but as soon as he observes a whale, he carefully notes its location and the direction from the vessel to it. Then, opening the trap, he rapidly but quietly descends. Not a word is spoken, but the man on the bridge gives the sign and a boat is made ready. Six oarsmen and a helmsman are at their posts. The lookout-man jumps into the boat, takes his place at the swivel harpoon gun, and at once becomes the harpooneer. He gives the course, and the boat with muffled oars puts away toward the whale, and, after cruising about for several hours, it may be, the giant comes to the surface to blow, perhaps within a hundred yards of the hunters. He generally remains partly out of the water five or ten minutes, so that there is time to get the boat into position. The swivel gun is turned upon him and discharged, sending into his side a harpoon, some two feet, to which is attached a line six hundred and twenty fathoms long. The harpoon is about eighteen inches or two feet in length. The stock is inserted in the muzzle of the gun, and the line is fastened to a ring at one side. The barbed point of the deadly weapon projects from the gun some ten or twelve inches. Fourteen fathoms of the line are left loose, in a proper coil, so that the harpoon will be impeded as little as possible. If they have succeeded in making fast to the whale, which generally makes off under water, the line is payed out with the friction of two turns round the "bullet head," and a small flag, called the "boat's jack," is sent up as a signal indicating the situation of the ship.

Meanwhile the captain has taken up his position in the "crow's nest," and as soon as the signal is given he gives the word from the lookout, "a fall!" This is taken up by the cook or others on deck; and, for a minute, all are shouting "a fall!" "a fall!" and all are rushing for the boats. Should the men be in their berths, no time is allowed or needed for dressing. They sleep with their clothes on, and with such extra garments as they may require in a small bag attached to their persons by a rope, so that when the word is given they require only to jump for the boats. Each man knows his station in one of the six boats sent out on "a fall!" The helmsmen, the oarsmen, the lancers, and the harpooners, are each and all at their posts, while with muffled oars they speed away toward the struggling whalers in the first boat sent out, leaving on ship-board only the captain, the cook, and one or two sailors.

The great object of these assisting boats is to get as near the whale as possible when he comes to the surface, and to discharge the contents of their harpoon guns into his sides, so as to secure him by additional lines. A premium is placed upon this work to the extent of one dollar a man for each harpoon inserted. The assisting boats are equipped with swivel guns, the same as the first boat sent out. When the whale has been secured by four or five harpoons, and when he has "flurried," and not until then, the lancers approach him. The whale "flurries" soon after being harpooned, or by the time he has been fastened by two or three lines.

It is hard to describe a "flurry," but it is a flurry with a vengeance. The whale becomes alarmed, excited, and loses his head, and in this condition he blows and tears around in indescribable fury, lashing the water with his tail, and rendering approach to him exceedingly dangerous. All keep their distance during the "flurry;" but this exhibition of power is generally succeeded by a calm, in which the victim is said to be getting sick. He comes often to the surface, and remains partly out of the water for several minutes each time. The boats approach closer and closer, near the forward fin, so as to avoid his tail, and with hand-lances, lances on poles about ten feet long, pierce his sides. Sometimes he is fired into with "exploding bomb lances," which, after piercing his flesh some two feet, explode inside, making great havoc of his vital parts.

Under this treatment he soon begins to blow blood, which is a most wonderful spectacle. But there is no mercy for the whale. He is lanced and pierced and butchered until he turns himself over, in a sort of death act, and yields himself up to his captors. The men with knives make holes through his tail and lower lip, and fasten lines thereto, when another signal is given for the approach of the ship, which presses hurriedly towards them. No matter how long and arduously the men have worked, or how cold and exhausted they have become, they are all jolly now, and, holding on to their prize, they while away the minutes until the vessel arrives, by singing some of their favorite songs.

On the approach of the vessel, the whale is made fast to her side, tail forward, so that the large open mouth will not fill with water in case of the advance of the ship, and the work of sculping is begun. This is done under the superintendence of an official called "the Inspectioneer." Eight or ten men are lowered upon the body of the whale, with nails or brads in the soles of their boots, like creepers, in order that they may not slip off his round form; and with long knives well sharpened for the purpose, commence the work of removing the blubber, which is generally eighteen inches thick over the whole carcass.

The whale industry is in the hands of citizens of the United States from New England.

CHAPTER XXXII.

DAY AT FORT CHURCHILL.

Rev. Mr. Lofthouse—A curious courtship by photograph and letter—An intended bride starts from the old country for Hudson's Bay to become the wife of a missionary—The porpoise fishery.

It is about six hundred miles from the Rose Welcome whaling ground to Fort Churchill, or old Fort Prince of Wales, which is at the mouth of the Churchill River. The fort is a magnificent structure. One corner of it was shattered by an attempt made to blow it up when abandoned by Hearne in 1782; but it is otherwise in an excellent state of preservation, and will remain so, unless taken down, for centuries to come. It was built by the Hudson's Bay Company and occupied nearly half a century as payment for its construction. A little way up the river from the fort is the trading post, where Chief Factor Spencer resides in a well appointed cottage with his good wife and children. This cottage has been standing for nearly fifty years and is still sound in every part. Besides the other residents at this trading post, we meet with the Rev. J. Lofthouse, who at once becomes a person of peculiar interest. He is, as the reader will have supposed, the missionary stationed at this post by the Church of England, and is a pleasant looking, affable young person, well qualified to get along in a quiet way, without occupying any more space in the world of thought and action than the small duties of his limited sphere require. He came out from his Yorkshire home in 1882, and has been since located part of the time at York. He had, only a few days before, completed the journey from that place to Churchill along the coast on foot, a distance of over one hundred and fifty miles, in order to meet the outcoming Hudson's Bay Company's ship as soon as she reached her first anchorage on the west shore of the bay. Do you ask why he could not wait for her arrival at York? For the best of all reasons. His future wife came out with the vessel to join him in matrimony and the cares of married life in his adopted home on the shores of Hudson's Bay.

There is a good deal of romance connected with the story of the reverend gentleman's courtship. After becoming settled in his new northwestern charge, he bethought him of the necessities of his new position. Of course the comforts of homê could not be complete without a wife, and neither at York nor at Churchill was there to be found a person suitable. In fact there were no unmarried ladies at these places except Cree ladies; and although some of these are really beautiful and fairly well educated, they are not just suited to the necessities of the parsonage. Under these circumstances, the Rev. Mr. Lofthouse exchanged photographs, through friends in the old country, with a young lady whom he had never seen, but of whom he knew something by hearsay. The courtship, the proposal, the acceptance, and the whole business had been completed in the narrow scope of two letters; but let not the reader suppose it lacked sentiment and feeling on that account. Far from it. On the contrary, the intended bride and the intended bridegroom, were greatly overcome by the peculiarity of the circumstances. They were to meet as strangers, as lovers, betrothed, promised, engaged, and for the purpose of marriage. And they did meet, and were married.

There is neither an Eskimo nor yet a resident Indian population at Churchill. The inhabitants of the place number about forty. These are Chippewayan half-breeds, except the officers of the post and their families. There are, however, about two hundred natives in the neighborhood which visit the fort, off and on, during various seasons of the year. The Indians

(Chippewayans) come, in the early spring, to trade, bringing with them the valuable skins of the otter, the deer and the marten, the mink, the silver-gray fox, etc. The Eskimos visit the fort, generally during the winter, laden with white bear, deer, white fox, wolf and other fur-bearing skins. In this way a considerable traffic is carried on, to the great profit of the Hudson's Bay Company and to the many hardships and privations of the natives, who, however, appear most in their true element when half naked, half starved, and very dirty.

The half-breed population of Churchill, less than forty souls, dwell with a few exceptions, in a long low building owned by the company, in which they are a sort of tenants at will. In the best sense of the term they are nothing more nor less than slaves. They are called servants. That name, perhaps, suits their condition and circumstances best. There is generally a sort of engagement or agreement between the men and the company. They are engaged for periods of from three to five years, at stipends ranging from one pound to two pounds ten shillings a month, and are always paid in merchandise at Hudson's Bay Company's prices, prices that are never complained of, because there is not the slightest advantage in complaining, but which are large enough to make up for the infrequency of purchases. They live and die in the service of the company, enjoy but few privileges, few comforts, and have no opportunities of learning anything about the world in which they live.

From the large number of children among them, and their very healthy condition, it is plainly to be seen that they are on the increase. They are provided with all the absolute necessities of life in full supply. They are seldom in want of food, except occasionally when the supplies at the post run short, as the country is full of deer, wild geese in their season, and small game; and as the company's agents treat them honorably, their condition is one of comparative comfort.

In conversation and manners they are very simple, plain, dull and quiet people; and, in speaking with them, one is impressed with their dense ignorance of all things. Their knowledge of mechanics is confined to fire-arms and sailing craft.

Walrus hunting is an important industry at Churchill. Early every spring two large boats are sent up to the walrus grounds just to the northwest of Marble Island. Last season this enterprise was conducted by George MacTavish, chief clerk, who, with a crew of half-breeds and Indians, took twenty-two large walruses in a few days, and could have easily secured as many more, only that the blubber from the carcasses of those he captured more than loaded his boats. He experienced a very successful trip, with the exception that one of his Indians died suddenly of heart disease during the voyage up.

Aside from the walrus hunt, Mr. Spencer is developing a large porpoise, or white whale fishery, on the very shores of Churchill harbor, where, with his nets and traps, he took, last season, one hundred and ninety of these mammals, of immense size. By increasing his facilities, five hundred or a thousand might be taken annually. Two large blubber refineries have been opened at Churchill, where the fat of the porpoise and walruses is refined and placed in casks ready for shipment to Europe. This oil, together with the furs which are taken from the natives in exchange for merchandise, and the ivory from the walrus, make up an annual budget at Churchill of great value. These products are exported each year in the company's ships, and find a ready market in the old world, to the great advantage of the Company's treasury.

CHAPTER XXXIII.

OBSERVATIONS AT YORK FACTORY.

Buildings at the trading post—The Church and the School —An interesting murder trial.

York factory at the mouth of the Nelson and Hayes rivers, is not the splendid place it was half a century ago, but is in good condition and is yet an important Hudson's Bay Company trading post. The buildings, of which there are about fifty belonging to the post proper, many of them large and handsome, are clean and bright-looking, and must have been erected at great expense. The main factory building is a square, with a court-yard in the center, being over two hundred feet on each side. The front center is three stories high, the other portion two stories. It is of wood, as are all the buildings belonging to the place. It stands back about three hundred feet from the front palisade, which runs along parallel with the Hayes River, upon which it fronts.

Potatoes and turnips do pretty well in the gardens at York Factory.

Away to the north of the village, about three miles, are the ruins of old Fort York, which was captured and destroyed by La Perouse in 1782. Between this and the new fort, as it is generally called, and near to the latter, is the powder magazine, enclosed by a high palisade, and the grave-yard.

The little church within the palisade, where the white people attend service, is a neat structure, much like that at Churchill, but about double the size. It contains a melodeon, and is otherwise well appointed. Next to it is the school house, just outside of the palisade. It is a neat, clean, well kept building, where in the summer months school is kept up from eight o'clock in the morning until about five o'clock in the evening. There are, including white and Cree, about one hundred and twenty-five children. These have but one teacher, but are taught separately.

The white children attend school, and English branches are taught, from eight to half-past ten in the forenoon. From that hour until five in the evening the Indian children are taught in Cree, to read and write, and to apply the rudiments of arithmetic. Great progress has been made in the education of the Cree Indians. The same syllabic characters are used as in teaching Chippewayan. A number of useful text-books have been printed, and, through the indefatigable efforts of Mrs. Mason, the mother of Mrs. Fortesque, wife of Chief Factor Fortesque, the entire Old and New Testaments have been printed and published in the Cree language. It is a great credit to the efforts put forth at York factory, on behalf of education, that almost all the Indians there, who are of sufficient age, can read and write with ease in their own language.

ALPHABET.

INITIALS.	SYLLABLES				FINALS.
	ā	e	o	a	•
a	ᐁ	ᐃ	ᐅ	ᐊ	ᐤ ow
w	·ᐁ	·ᐃ	ᐅ	·ᐊ	X Christ
p	ᐯ	ᐱ	ᐳ	ᐸ	ᑊ p
t	ᑌ	ᑎ	ᑐ	ᑕ	ᐟ t
k	ᑫ	ᑭ	ᑯ	ᑲ	ᐠ k
ch	ᒉ	ᒋ	ᒍ	ᒐ	ᐦ h
m	ᒣ	ᒥ	ᒧ	ᒪ	ᒼ m
n	ᓀ	ᓂ	ᓄ	ᓇ	ᐣ n
s	ᓭ	ᓯ	ᓱ	ᓴ	ᐢ s
y	ᔦ	ᔨ	ᔪ	ᔭ	ᕑ r
					ᓬ l

The dot over any syllable lengthens the vowel sound

CREE INDIAN SYLLABARIUM.

A few years ago the quiet of York Factory was disturbed by a murder. In a brawl between two Indian women, named Nancy Natainew and Mary Quaqua, the former threw an ax at the latter, which she managed to avoid, but it struck her son John, a small boy, on the head. He died from the effects of the blow two days after. The woman, Natainew, was duly tried before Justice Fortesque in the school-house. Chief Factor Fortesque, besides exercising some judicial functions as the head officer at the post, is a Justice of the Peace for the Northwest Territories of Canada.

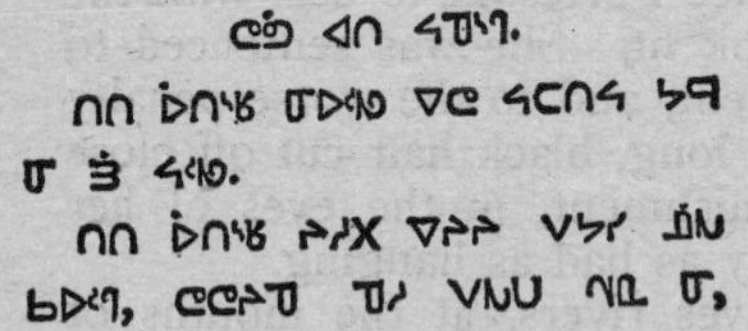

"APOSTLES' CREED"—CHIPPEWAYAN.

Dr. Matthews, acting as Clerk of the Court and Crown Prosecutor, interested himself in bringing the murderess to justice; but before the trial had proceeded far, he found himself surrounded by many and great difficulties. At the outset the natives were loud in their denunciations of the conduct of the hostile squaw, and manifested the greatest desire to see her brought under the penalties of British law, but as the trial proceeded, their manner became greatly changed. All the feelings of their race became aroused, and they looked upon the prosecution as a piece of tyranny or persecution on the part of the Hudson's Bay Company. Before the trial came on they had seen the whole affair, and related every phase of it with great exactness; but in the witness-box they knew nothing about it whatever. Indeed, they were dumb. As the examination progressed the feelings of the natives became more intense in favor of the prisoner; and finally the woman, Natainew, became a martyr to the fullest extent of their appreciation of the idea.

It was plain that anything like conviction by the testimony of Indian witnesses would be an impossibility, and Doctor Matthews gave the case up, leaving it to the discretion of Justice Fortesque to deal with the squaw as he might think fit. She was sentenced to one month's imprisonment, and to the worse penalty of having her beautiful, long, black hair cut off close to her head. This punishment, in the eyes of her sympathizers, was nearly as bad as hanging.

The Nelson and Hayes rivers, at the mouths of which York Factory is located, wind away to the southwest to Lake Winnipeg, a distance of about 425 miles. There are over 100 rapids on the Nelson, all of which have to be portaged.

CHAPTER XXXIV.

PORPOISE, WALRUS AND SEAL.

Character and value of these animals—The porpoise fisheries—The Walrus hunt—Peculiarities of Narwhal—Probabilities of a seal breeding ground in Hudson's Strait—Great possibilities of the oil industry.

Hudson's Bay and Strait are the dwellings of the porpoise, or white whale. There countless thousands may be seen tumbling about on the waves and performing all sorts of sportive exercises. They herd together in vast droves, often thousands and tens of thousands in one school. Sometimes these shoals will form in "Indian file" and shoot over the water, showing their backs like a long, black, winding, ever-changing streak on the surface of the sea. We met with them everywhere, and I am justified in saying that the waters are alive with them.

Their mouths are furnished with sharp teeth, which are so arranged that they interlock when the jaws are closed; thus they are well provided with the means of capturing and devouring food.

The porpoise is seldom seen in deep water, and generally keeps pretty close to the coast, frequenting bays, inlets and the mouths of rivers. They generally ascend the rivers with the tides and will never go further up than the tidal flow, but will always stop when it stops, and descend with it. They are very fat and contain blubber similar to that of the whale. A good sized porpoise is worth $75.

The walrus belongs to the seal family and presents a very grotesque appearance. Its head is its most conspicuous part. Its nose is covered with long bristles and its head with long wiry hair. Its ivory tusks, often eighteen inches long, project from the upper jaw. The tusks of the walrus are of a superior quality of ivory.

The walrus is an exceedingly valuable animal, both as an article of commerce and to the Eskimo of the north. The blubber, ivory, and skin are always in demand. The tusks furnish ivory of a peculiarly white hue, said to hold its color longer than that of the elephant's tusk. The oil produced from the blubber is very delicate, and always commands a high price. The skin is thick and extremely tough, and is valuable to the Eskimo for dog-harness, and to civilized man for many purposes. The Eskimos use the tusks for harpoons, spears, and fish-spears; the intestines for nets; its oil and flesh for food, and its bones for kayak frames and other purposes.

The narwhal, or sea unicorn, is valuable for its oil and ivory. Its horn, from five to seven feet long, is of the very finest ivory, and susceptible of an exceedingly high polish. A full sized horn is valued at from $60 to $80.

The oil seal, which abounds in countless millions in the North Atlantic and adjacent seas and bays, is richly coated with blubber, while the skins are of great value either when tanned into leather or prepared with the fur on, and used for garments. Cod and salmon abound in the inlets on the south shores of Hudson's Strait.

CHAPTER XXXV.

FUR BEARING ANIMALS.

The silver, blue, gray, red and white foxes—The ermine—The marten—The otter—The varying hare—The lynx—The wolf—The sable, musk ox, etc.—The fur trade.

Having spoken of the oil-bearing mammals of the Hudson's Bay region and the economic fishes, we will now briefly direct attention to the fur-bearing animals of that district. In the first place, should the traveler in that region depend upon the Hudson's Bay Company's employes for his information concerning these resources, he will remain in ignorance. These people, when being questioned concerning the furs or other products, can manage to talk and yet say the least of any persons to be met with.

Beaver are very scarce, but foxes are still plentiful. Of these there are many kinds, and the price of their skins ranges from one dollar to five hundred, so that the fur trader must be well versed in all these varieties in order to know the commercial value of the various skins brought to him for traffic. Foxes have so many names, and there are so many different names for the same kind of fox, that one meets with difficulty in attempting to describe them. We hear of the black, the blue, the silver, the gray, the cross, the red and the white fox.

Probably the most fashionable fur of to-day is that of the silver fox, which is found plentifully in the Hudson's Bay region. It is a rich, deep, glossy black, with a bluish tinge; so beautiful are they that $500 has been given for a single skin, and La Houtan states that, in his time, the skin of one of these foxes brought its weight in gold. Skins frequently bring $250. Of the two thousand caught yearly in different parts of North America, about one thousand are used in England, and a much smaller number in the United States. The choicest skins are taken on the northern shores of Hudson's Strait and on the rough coast of the extreme northwestern portions of Hudson's Bay. Some are caught in Russia, but the fur is of a poorer quality and not valued so highly.

The cross, red, blue, gray and white foxes are all of considerable importance, each having a certain commercial value. The best cross fox skins are worth $40 each, and over 10,000 are shot or trapped in the northern regions yearly. The blue fox skins are worth $20 apiece, and about 7,000 are captured annually, but some of these are secured on the borders of the White Sea and in Greenland. The other varieties bring from one to five dollars each. Of the ordinary red fox over 100,000 are secured every year by the Hudson's Bay Company's posts of the north.

The fur of the ermine, or stoat, has been esteemed from ancient times, when only the nobility were allowed to wear it; but the demand for it to-day is as great as when the use of it was confined to the upper classes. They are small animals, but when the fur is secured in very cold weather, from the snow-clad slopes, their skins are valued at $250 each.

There are many other varieties of valuable furs taken in the Hudson's Bay region, as will be seen by the following list showing the catch for one season in and about Cumberland House:

Bear	372	Beaver	4,684
Ermine	226	Fisher	50
Blue Fox......	4	Cross Fox....	30
Red Fox......	91	White Fox....	332
Silver Fox....	3	Lynx	442
Marten	2,157	Mink	7,790
Musk-rat	180,791	Otter	424
Skunk	6	Wolverine.....	175
Wolf	76	Weenisk	1
Musk-ox	1		

CHAPTER XXXVI.

OBSERVATIONS ON THE ESKIMOS.

Romance of the marriage of an Eskimo Princess—Habits of life—The Kayak.

Before quitting the Hudson's Bay country we must relate a little piece of romance and say something about the Kayak and the Eskimos generally. One day in wandering among the rock hills on the south shore of Hudson's Strait in the neighborhood of Prince of Wales Sound, we came to a little inlet, a narrow arm of the sound extending in among the rocks, entirely hid from view until the traveler approached the water's edge. There were natives residing on both sides of the cove. It was evident that something unusual was going on. An old chief, with his great red cap, stood upon a cliff near his tent on one side, while, upon the waters of the lake-like inlet, a boat and half a dozen kayaks were filled with Eskimos, apparently enjoying a holiday. Upon inquiry, we found that the chief's daughter, his only child and a native beauty, had just given her hand in marriage to a young Eskimo. The event was much out of the general order of marriages, as the newly-made husband was to succeed the old chief as head-man over this scattered population. A few questions revealed sufficient romance to make the wedding very interesting. The story is given in the following measure:

Nestled in rocks of gneiss,
Formed while chaos-gloom yet shrouded earth,
And sheltered by eternal snow-crowned cliffs,
The placid waters of the cove, by not
One ripple stirred, bore on their liquid breast
Kayaks, trimmed out with spears and gaffs and hooks,
A guard of honor due the pair made one
In bonds unsanctified by rite of church or creed.

The whale-boat had, by generous loan, or from
The loancr's wish to foster trade, contained,
Besides the tawny brave and blushing bride,
Seated aft on skins of Polar bear, four more
Strong bending to the oars. Her jacket was
Of seal, the tail bedecked with finer furs
Contrasting shades and colors gay—not wide,
But pennant-shaped, and further trimmed with strips
Of feathered skins of Arctic birds of white
And shades of every hue. Of raven black
Her hair in braids hung down upon her breast,
And falling back, trailed in the liquid blue.
Her head was bare; nor was the use of veil
Indulged, nor decorations grand, except
A neatly twisted wreath, extending from
Her forehead back, of Arctic poppies bright,
And freshly gathered from the rocky shore.
Her hands ungloved; her feet in boots of seal;
Her neck was girt about with ivory balls
And balls of Latrobite, strung on a thread
Of skin, and from it, on her throbbing breast,
Hung down a cross, hewn from a tusk,—
A cross without a meaning to the bride,
But patterned from the pictures left
By sailors, who for furs had traded them.

Her charms had famed her in a hundred camps,
And far and wide her name, on native tongues,
In words of praise and boast was spoken oft.
A princess of a royal line of chiefs,
An heir to idleness and ease, with right
To be attended by the common herd
And give command. Her home a ruler's hut,
And hence a palace grand. The only heir
And only child of Chief Utongkakum,
Whose rule of thirty years as native chief
Of Eskimos for many miles around
Had blessed his race, and made his name a word
For common use. The aged chief could not
Much longer wear his modern cap of red,
But soon his crown must rest on other's head.
To gain the princess-daughter's hand was much
To be desired for her natural charms,
But more because with that the winner gained
A crown. Princess Lu-killia-ke-a-kum
Utongkakuk, by many suitors wooed,
But won by none, until by test to find a man
As true, as brave, and worthy to be called
A chief, the conquest of her heart was made
By young Shemomamik.

The contest for her hand, the battle for
The crown, was brought on thus. The evening shades
Were falling, when, as four brave hunters sat
On skins about her royal father's hut,
Each waiting for the word, the answer to
A prayer that sweet Lu-killia-ke-a-kum
Would stoop to be his bride. Behold, a grim
Huge Polar bear approached, but turned
Away as yelping dogs disclosed to him
His peril. The princess answered, pointing to
The monster, king of Arctic seas: "To him
Who brings, unaided but by lance and nerve,
The soft, white pelt of that huge bear,
I give my hand and grant my father's crown."

The bear-skin on the whaler's stern-sheets spread,
As cushion for the beauty, princess-bride,
Was from the body of that bear. The groom,
Whose arm supported her, and on whose head
The ruling crown, a cap of reddish cloth,
Reposed, and at whose side a lance was slung,
Our hero! Brave Shemomamik had won!

Now, there is very little ceremony connected with an Eskimo marriage, even with the marriage of a chief's only daughter, and that little consists of the fortunate man conducting his wife from the tent of her people to the tent of his people. That is all there is to it. And, very often, the little romance that might be connected with this performance is annihilated by the fact that the bride is so conducted against her will; for the Eskimos are mated, so to speak, while they are yet children. That is to say, the parents of the girl and the parents of the boy agree that, when the proper time comes, their children shall live together as man and wife. This agreement, of course, comes to the knowledge of the boy and girl concerned while they are yet very young, and it may be that they grow up to think very much of each other, and become happily joined together; but it may also happen that the girl will take a hearty dislike of the choice made on her behalf, and grow up to thoroughly hate and despise him. All the same, when he becomes old enough to maintain her by the chase, he demands his property as it were, and she is compelled to submit. But we must not suppose the latter to have been the case with the marriage in question.

It is an error to state that the Eskimos have no chiefs, or "Uttericks," as they call them. They do not dwell in large settlements, but in every district the number of families dwelling there submit themselves, in many things, to the ruling voice and advice of their chief man, and generally contribute to his support. They are but little governed, and never go to war with each other, and seldom quarrel. However, they are not without courage. On the Coppermine and Mackenzie rivers, where they sometimes come into collision with the Indians, they fight fiercely, and are greatly dreaded.

We must correct most writers on the customs of these people in saying that polygamy is rare among them. All their head men maintain two or three wives, and it is a sign of importance that a man supports more than one wife. Moreover, they often separate, the man finding another wife and the woman another husband.

Their courtship and marriage are very simple. They have only to do a limited amount of courting, and at a very early age—say ten or eleven for the girl, and twelve or thirteen for the boy—before they dwell together as man and wife. There is neither marriage nor burial ceremony among the unchristianized Eskimos. All is simplicity, and very unromantic.

The whole Eskimo population of the world is put down at forty thousand. It is probably less. There are, perhaps, not more than ten thousand between Cape Chidley on the north Atlantic and Alaska; certainly not over fifteen thousand.

They remain for the most part pretty close to the shores. Even on hunting expeditions they follow some coast. On the eastern side of the continent they extend southward to the fiftieth parallel of latitude, while on the western side they are seldom found south of the sixtieth, on the eastern shore of Bering's Strait. On the shores of Hudson's Bay, 55 north latitude, is their southern limit.

Throughout this vast domain no other tribes intervene, except in two places on the western shore, where Kennayan and Uglange Indians come down to the sea for purposes of fishing. Rink divides them into the following groups:

1. The East Greenland Eskimos, few in number, every year advancing further south.

2. The West Greenland Eskimo, civilized, living under Danish rule, and extending from Cape Farewell to 74 north latitude.

3. The Arctic Eskimos, living in the neighborhood of Smith's, Whale, Murchison's and Wolstenholme sounds, not, within the memory of man, having any intercourse with those residing south of them. They are very isolated and have greatly diminished in numbers of late years. These Eskimos did not until very recently possess the kayak—skin-covered canoe—nor the uomiak, or open skin boat; nor the bow and arrow. They are bold hunters, pagans, and are thoroughly typical Eskimos. There are at present about 300 of these people, and one authority says that they have begun to increase in numbers again.

4. The Labrador Eskimos, mostly civilized.

5. The Eskimos of the interior, occupying the coasts of Hudson's Bay, Hudson's Strait, and westward to Barter Island, beyond the Mackenzie River, inhabiting a stretch of country 2,000 miles long and 800 miles wide.

6. The Western Eskimos, from Barter Island to the western shores of America. These differ somewhat from the others in their habits and style of dress, and they are allied to certain Indian tribes in Alaska.

7. The Asiatic Eskimos, different altogether from those of America, with whom they have no connection whatever.

First, as to their appearance. They are not a very small race. Their height is about five feet eight inches or five feet ten inches, sometimes six feet, but rarely; but their style of dress makes them look smaller than they are. Both men and women are muscular and active, having pleasant, good-natured faces. Sometimes they are handsome. They are sure to "grin" on the slightest provocation.

Their faces are oval, broad and flat, with fat cheeks. The forehead is not high, and quite retreating. Their teeth are good, but owing to the character of their food are worn down to the gums by the time they have reached old age. Their noses are flat, generally, but not always. Their eyes are small, black and bright. Their heads are large and covered with coarse, black hair, which the women generally keep in braids, or dress into a top-knot on their crowns; the men clip their hair in front and allow it to fly loose behind. The men have a slight mustache and insignificant whiskers. The skin, when cleaned of grease and smoke, is only so slightly brown that red shows readily in the cheeks, especially of the women and children.

They soon age, and seldom live to be over sixty. Their hands and feet are small and well-formed, and as a rule they are better looking than the best of the Indians. The men, women and children dress entirely in skins of the seal, reindeer, bear, dog, and even fox; but the first two greatly predominate. The men and women dress much the same. The jacket of the men has a hood which, in cold weather, is used to cover the head, leaving only the face exposed. This jacket must be drawn on over the head, as it has no opening either in front or behind. The women's jacket has a fur-lined "amowt," or large hood, for carrying a child, and a very absurd-looking tail behind, which is generally trimmed.

The trousers are usually fastened into the tops of boots well made from prepared sealskin. The women's trousers are nearly always ornamented with eider duck's necks or embroidery of beads, or other decorations. In the winter they wear two suits of clothes, boots, trousers, jacket and all, one with the fur out, and the other, that worn next the body, with the fur turned in. They also sometimes wear shirts of bird-skins, and stockings under their boots of dog or young reindeer skin, but this is noticeable only in the case of chiefs.

Their clothes, like all other articles of Eskimo manufacture, are very neatly made, fit perfectly, and are sewed with "sinew-thread" and a bone needle, if a steel one cannot be had. In person they are usually filthy, and never wash themselves. The children, when very young, are sometimes cleaned by being licked with their mother's tongue before being put into the bag of feathers, which serves them as bed, cradle and blankets, when they are lucky enough to have such bags, they being more generally consigned to the "amowt," without clothing of any kind.

In summer the Eskimos live in conical skin tents, and in winter in half underground huts (igloos) built of stone, turf, earth, etc., entered by a long tunnel-like passage which can only be traversed on all fours. Sometimes they erect neat dwellings from blocks of snow, with a sheet of ice for a window. These are comfortable only in cold weather. As soon as the soft weather of spring comes they begin to leak and are deserted.

In their dwellings one will always find a stone lamp, the flames of which, being fed by oil through a wick of moss, supply both heat and light. On one side of the tent is the bed or lounge where, on innumerable skins of all kinds, they sleep and lay around day and night. The floor is usually very filthy, being often defiled by a pool of blood or the carcass of a seal.

These tents or huts are always surrounded by a host of wolf-like dogs. These, in summer, sleep outside, but in winter in the huts, or in the passages leading to them. Sometimes one hut or tent accommodates two or three families, but more often each family will have a dwelling by itself.

They are exclusively hunters and fishers, and derive nearly the whole of their subsistence from the sea. They use no vegetables, and live exclusively upon the flesh of animals and fish. The seal and other oil-bearing animals, the reindeer, the polar bear, supply them with food, clothing, fuel and light, and frequently also, when driftwood is scarce, the material for various articles of domestic economy.

The shuttle-shaped kayak, covered with hairless seal-skin, usually stretched on a wooden frame, is sometimes made on a frame of bones from the walrus, or of horns from the reindeer.

One of the most attractive features of Eskimo life is the kayak. What the canoe is to the Indian, the kayak is to the husky denizen of the north. They are not the same in shape, nor in construction, nor in anything else, except in weight, and in the dangers to which a greenhorn is exposed in attempting to navigate them. In shape they are similar to an old-fashioned weaver's shuttle, and draw less water than the ordinary canoe. They are about thirty feet long, not more than two feet from top to bottom at the center, and about thirty inches wide at the same point. The top is straight from forward point to stern point, except that from the center to the ends each way they gradually become narrower, until at the points the width is not over two or three inches; and from the center, each way toward the ends, and toward the top as well, the bottom slants upwards and outwards, until at the points the thickness is about two inches. It is flat at the bottom, but much narrower than at the top. There is a round hole at the top, at the center, formed by a hoop, to which the sealskin is attached. The Eskimo sits in this hole, with his feet stretched out toward the forward end and his head and shoulders above it. The Eskimo in his kayak is generally covered with a waterproof entrail dress, tightly fastened around the mouth of the hole in which he sits; so that, should the craft overturn, which sometimes happens, not a drop of water will enter. A skillful kayaker can turn a complete somersault, kayak and all, through the water.

It is a sight to see an Eskimo fighting a walrus in one of these kayaks. The latter invariably attempts to pierce the kayak with his tusks; but when he makes the venture, in his foolhardy courage, he not only fails to succeed, the little craft being too nimble in the water to give him any chance, but receives a harpoon in his side, or is pierced to the heart with a deadly lance. With a buoy attached to the carcass to keep his prize from sinking, the hunter paddles it in tow to the shore.

The natives use but one paddle in the kayak; but it is not the same as that used by the Indians in the canoe. It is a double paddle; that is to say, both ends are flattened, and, in paddling, first one end is used and then the other, on one side and the other alternately. The central portion of the paddle is round, and the water is prevented from running down on the hands, as the instrument is used, by pieces of skin which are placed tightly around at the proper places. A new beginner will have some trouble in navigating the kayak, and it will be well for him, at first, to keep in shallow water. It tips over with the slightest provocation, and, as you cannot extricate yourself from the hole without some little difficulty, and are precipitated into the water head first, it becomes a matter of importance that you either know how to balance yourself properly, or are prepared for a plunge bath. One of our party, in making the attempt, went over head first into ten fathoms of water; but, as he was a good swimmer, he soon managed to kick himself loose and take refuge in a neighboring boat. It does not take long, however, to learn to handle one, and we would recommend kayak clubs as a means of healthy amusement for young Americans.

CHAPTER XXXVII.

NATURE'S NEWEST LAND.

Wonders of the new north—Product of natural laws for the last one thousand years—Specific work of glaciers—New areas for many millions—Probable gold and other products—Hard times to disappear as dew before an advancing sun.

We are nearing the completion of this work, and must now speak of the probable future of the Golden North Land. Gold mining is already the pioneer industry, and it must be through the excitements and push of this enterprise that the great resources of the far north will become known and developed. The thirst and search for gold will carry a vast population to parallels above the fifty-fifth and sixtieth, but when the rich deposits of the yellow metal have given up the bulk of their treasure, which will probably not be realized for more than two generations, those high latitudes will not be deserted. Other richer and possibly more permanent resources will hold a mighty population there for all time to come.

One of the most remarkable characteristics of the north—one pre-eminently for the solution of scientists—is that, with every succeeding century, the climate and soil become better adapted to the habitation and pursuits of man. It has been estimated that, on an average, soil and vegetation, forests, and in their train, cereal capabilities, are marching upward across the parallels of latitude at the rate of considerably over a hundred miles in a century.

The author has traveled across the continent, above and below the sixtieth parallel, from the Atlantic to the Rocky Mountains, touching the Hudson's Bay trading posts on the following chain, and at each point named, the same story was told by those in charge, to wit: That the soil is every year increasing in its depth and capabilities, the climate gradually improving, and forest resources rapidly developing. Starting at Nachvak, on the Upper Labrador, nearly up to the sixtieth parallel, we learn from the traders that while, 100 years ago the largest specimens of tamarac and spruce were not more than four feet high, and that these bushes were scarce at that, to-day Nachvak inlet, from the Hudson's Bay trading post, which is twenty miles from the coast, up the river for a long distance there is an abundance of forest trees from six to fifteen inches at the butt, and from twenty to fifty feet in height, some of them much higher. The garden at the trading post now produces quite a variety of vegetables, whereas, a century back, little or nothing in that line could be cultivated.

These remarks will apply with equal, and in most cases, far greater force, o Fort Chimo at the head of Ungava Bay; to Fort George, at the mouth of Big River on the east main coast of Hudson's Bay; to Moose Factory, at the mouth of Albany River, on James' Bay; to Fort Severn, at the mouth of the river of that name on the southwest shore of Hudson's Bay; to Fort York and Fort Churchill, on the western shores of the same bay; to Fort Chippewyan, on Lake Athabasca; to Fort Resolution on Great Slave Lake; to Fort Providence, on the western extreme of the same lake; to Fort Franklin, on Great Bear Lake; and to Fort Simpson, and even to Fort Norman, on the Mackenzie River.

The natural laws under which Providence is pushing back the cold of the north towards the pole, and extending the regions for man's profitable occupancy, do not yet appear to be fully understood. Many travelers of the far north, some of them men of scientific attainments, contend that there is a very slow and almost imperceptible revolution of the earth from north to south, but meteorological phenomena in the south, which, however, is not very fully understood, scarcely warrants such a theory. We leave this question to those better able to grapple with it. However, the facts are as we state them. Northern thermal limits are moving northward, and forests, vegetation and agricultural possibilities follow closely upon these advancing limits. Why and wherefore, we know not.

Many learned men talk strangely about "glacial periods." Much of this appears to be absurd to those who visit and commune with the glaciers of the far north. Far too much is charged up to glaciers. At any rate that is the belief of the author. It would seem that glaciers are simply river builders, and when they have accomplished this task, they depart for tropical seas where they are dissolved.

It must be a mistake to suppose that there was any soil or vegetation on the solid formation of the great North American plain, which now comprises the Mississippi basin, when monster glaciers chiseled out the channels of the Father of Waters, and its principal tributaries. Icebergs seldom, if ever—we think never—work in latitudes where they can be dissolved before reaching the ocean. Natural laws do not operate in such a futile way. Under such circumstances a glacier would sink into dissolution with its task but half done.

It is more reasonable to suppose that at some period in the past a line drawn due west from the site of New York City to that of San Francisco, traversed the most northern habitable limit of the continent. Existing prehistoric remains support this theory. Glaciers are drainage constructors. They prepare the natural drainage systems of the earth's surface, and make ready the barren areas, for the coming of soil and vegetation, and, if one will look at the great river systems of this continent, he will conclude that they do their work well, leaving it in such a state of perfection that the hand of man finds it quite easy to carry it forward to suit his necessities. When a mighty glacier has chiseled out a deep channel four or six or ten or fifty or 500 miles long, and enters the sea, the track left behind is called an inlet. When it has, later on, become bordered with soil and forests, it is called a river.

These hints give a new interest to the north land. It is a country of great resources already, and with each succeeding generation it will improve in this respect. There is wealth enough in its auriferous regions to make a million persons rich, and its greater alluvial areas will, in the not far distant future, support a vast population, who will become rich in supplying the world's markets with bread, and meat, and butter and cheese, and other soil products.

The gold deposits of the far north are nearly, if not quite, inexhaustible. Long before the rich placer gold regions have been gone over or even explored, quartz gold mines of great richness will be opened and profitably worked, and while the gold is being taken from the earth, during the next few years, many thousands will go to that country. Some will grow rich in the transportation business; others in mining and selling coal; thousands will gain wealth in silver and other minerals; forests which invite sawmills will yield up their treasures; the carpenter and builder and plumber and gasfitter will leave overcrowded industries in these older cities to find profitable employment in the north; merchandising will be a means of great gains in that land of high latitudes; the blacksmith and the machinist will thrive there; so will the baker and the barber; the hotel, restaurant and boardinghouse keeper will flourish; and, later on, horse and cattle ranchmen, with their herds on the plains to the east of the mountains, will enter upon an era of wonderful prosperity, to be closely followed by the agriculturist, who will enjoy even greater gains.

It will be from the development of these resources, more than from anything else, that general prosperity will return to the United States. That wonderfully rich north land will, it is believed by some, produce gold, most of which will be coined into money and put in circulation in the United States, in about the extent and ratio represented by the following diagram:

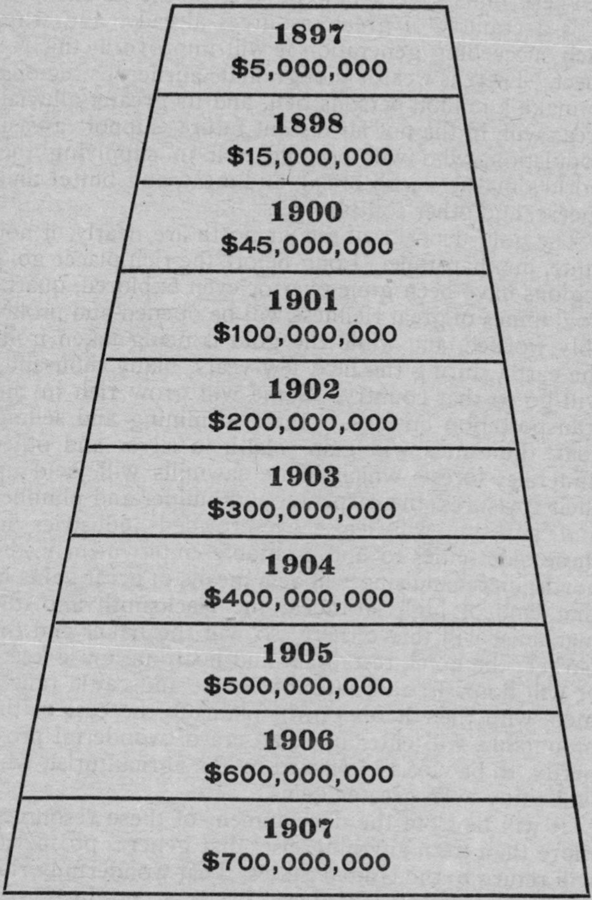

Possible Ten Year, $2,865,000,000 Product.

If this enthusiastic forecast is half realized, there will be no scarcity of money in this country, and millionaires will spring up among the common people everywhere. Hard times will disappear as dew before an ascending sun. The silver agitator will "lose his usefulness," and the days of the socialist crank and the anarchist will come to a close in this country.

It is within the bounds of solid facts to say that two good miners working together can produce $10,000 each in the gold regions of the far north annually. This may be regarded as a minimum average. Then why should people starve or suffer in these lower latitudes. Listen to the clanging of the Klondike bells! Buckle on the armor for battle with the snows and frosts and mosquitoes of the north; endure hardships for a season or two, and peace and plenty will probably be your lot thereafter.

CHAPTER XXXVIII.

GOLD OUTPUT OF THE WORLD.

Great increase of 1897 over 1896—Probable stability of the gold product of the Klondike—Influence of increased gold supply on silver—Gold monometallism likely to be continued—Views of Director Preston of the United States Mint.

We have at hand some valuable statistics from R. E. Preston, director of the United States Mint, at Washington, D. C. He gives the probable output of gold for 1897, and a very valuable contribution to gold statistics generally. His article which recently was printed in the New York Herald is as follows:

"That gold exists in large quantities in the newly discovered Klondike district is sufficiently proved by the large amount brought out by the steamship companies and miners returning to the United States who went into the district within the last eighteen months. So far $1,500,000 in gold from the Klondike district has been deposited at the mints and assay offices of the United States, and from information now at hand, there are substantial reasons for believing that from $3,000,000 to $4,000,000 additional will be brought out by the steamers and returning miners from St. Michael the last of September or early October (1897). One of the steamship companies states that it expects to bring out about $2,000,000 on its steamer sailing from St. Michael September 30 (1897), and has asked the government to have a revenue cutter act as a convoy through the Bering Sea. In view of the facts above stated I am justified in estimating that the Klondike district will augment the world's gold supply in 1897 nearly $6,000,000.

"The gold product for the Dominion of Canada for 1896, as estimated by Dr. G. M. Dawson, director of the geological survey of that country, was $2,810,000. Of this sum the Yukon placers, within British territory, were credited with a production of $355,000. The total product of that country for 1897 has, therefore, been estimated at $10,000,000, an increase over 1896 of $7,-200,000. From this the richness of the newly discovered gold fields of the Klondike is evident.

"In this connection it is important to know what will be the probable increase in the several countries of the world, and for the purpose of comparison, based upon information received, the following table of the gold product of the United States, Australia, Africa, Mexico, the Dominion of Canada, Russia and British India for 1896, and the estimated product of these countries for 1897 is here given:

	1896.	1897.	Increase.
United States ..	$53,000,000	$60,000,000	$7,000,000
Australia	46,250,000	52,000,000	5,750,000
Africa	44,000,000	56,000,000	12,000,000
Mexico	7,000,000	9,000,000	2,000,000
Dom. of Canada	2,810,000	10,000,000	7,200,000
Russia	22,000,000	25,000,000	3,000,000
British India ..	5,825,000	7,000,000	1,175,000
Totals	$180,885,000	$219,000,000	$38,125,000

"The world's gold product for 1896 is estimated to have been $205,000,000. In justification of the above estimate of the increase in the countries mentioned I may remark that of the United States is based upon the deposits at the mints and assay offices for the first six months of the year, which clearly indicate a largely increased production, and that the increase for the year will aggregate $7,000,000. The gold product of Africa for 1896 is estimated to have been $44,000,000. For the first six months of 1897 the output of the Witwatersrandt mines, as shown by official returns, was 1,338,431 ounces, an increase of 333,928 ounces, as compared with the first six months of 1896. There is no doubt that the rate of production in the Witwatersrandt mines will be maintained for the remainder of the year, and their output of gold for 1897 will be fully $12,000,000 greater than that of 1896.

"The deposits of gold at the Australian mints for the first five months of the year clearly indicate a substantial gain in 1897 over 1896. Upon the basis of the deposits for the first five months at the mints the Australian Insurance and Banking Record for the month of June estimates that the gold product for 1897 of the several colonies will aggregate 2,700,000 ounces, of the value of $52,550,000. This would be an increase of $5,750,000 over the product of 1896.

"The gold product of Mexico for 1896 is estimated to have been $7,000,000. The information received indicates that the product for 1897 will approximate $9,000,000, an increase of $2,000,000.

"The Russian product for 1896 was $22,000,000; for 1897 it is estimated at $25,000,000, an increase of $3,000,000.

"The gold product of British India for 1896, from official information received, is estimated at $5,825,000. The returns of the mines for the first six months of 1897 indicate an increased production over 1896 of $38,700,000, and that the world's product for 1897 can therefore be estimated at not less than $240,000,000. There is no doubt that the world's product of gold will continue to increase for a number of years to come, as new mines will be opened up in all parts of the world, and, with improved appliances for mining and methods of extracting the gold contained in the ores, I believe that by the close of the present century the world's gold product will closely approximate, if not exceed, $300,000,000.

"I have spoken above of the addition likely to be made in 1897 to the world's stock of gold by the Klondike district, by the Transvaal, by the United States, Australia, Russia, Mexico, India, etc. Of all these gold producing countries, of course, the Klondike is at present the one of most absorbing interest. It strikes the imagination to-day as California did the minds of the '49ers. It will add in 1897 possibly $6,-000,000 to the gold treasures of the world.

"Now as to the influence of such addition to the world's gold. The influence it will exert depends mainly on how many years the Klondike district shall continue a producer and how large its annual increment to the world's existing stock of gold shall be. There is every reason to believe that Alaska and the adjacent British territory are possibly as rich in gold as was California or Australia when first discovered. I have estimated that the Klondike district will in 1897 produce $6,000,000 worth of gold. It will add to this product from year to year probably for a minimum of one or two decades. And whether the gold comes from American or British territory is a matter of indifference, except to the owners, and, to some extent, to the countries producing it. The effect of the increase on the economic condition of mankind, on the rate of discount, the rate of interest, the rate of wages, on prices and on monetary policies, of a newly discovered gold field of wonderful richness is the same, whether the field be located in American, British or Chinese territory.

"Now, the first influence that the new addition to the world's existing stock of gold will have will be felt by silver. In fact, it has already been felt by it. Gold is the natural competitor—we might always say antagonist—of silver as a monetary medium, and every ounce of gold newly placed on the market deprives from 17 1-2 to 35 ounces of silver of a possible employment as money that it might have. I say this because gold, weight for weight, is now worth thirty-six and six tenths times as much silver, and because, at most, half of the gold discovered finds industrial employment.

The new additions to the world's stock of gold,

whether they come from the Klondike, Cripple Creek, or the Transvaal, from India, Australia, or Russia, will render bimetallism by the United States alone more difficult and more improbable than ever, and will even seriously imperil the slender chances that international bimetallism now has.

"Bimetallists have long been asking the question where the gold is to be found that is to take the place of the silver demonetized. The discoveries at Cripple Creek, in the Transvaal, and on the Klondike are a sufficient answer to this question. The mines of the world have been turning out gold of late years in greater profusion than ever before. The year 1893 marks an epoch in this respect. In the report of the director of the mint upon the production of the precious metals in the United States during the calendar year 1893, I called attention to the fact that the world's output of gold in that year was the largest in history, amounting to $155,522,000, and that it was 16.08 per cent greater than the annual average of the period of the greatest productiveness of the Californian and Australian gold mines.

"And in the report of the same series of the calendar year 1894, I remarked that the value of the world's production of gold in that year not only equaled the average value of both gold and silver in the period of 1861-1865, but exceeded it by $11,204,600, and that the probability expressed by me in 1893 that the value of the world's output of gold in 1895 and 1896 would equal that of both metals in the years immediately preceding the beginning of the depreciation of silver had been changed into a certainty by the events of 1894, since the average annual yield of gold and silver of all countries in the period 1866-1873 exceeded that of gold alone in 1894 by less than $11,000,000. If the production of gold in 1897 reaches that figure, which I confidently believe it will, of $240,000,000, it will exceed the average yearly value of both the gold and silver product of the world for the period of eight years—

1866 to 1873—which just preceded the beginning of the depreciation of silver, viz., $190,831,000—by over $50,000,000.

"Leaving out of consideration, therefore, the industrial employment of the two metals, the world now annually produces in gold alone some $50,000,000 more for monetary uses than it did in both gold and silver during the eight years (on an average) that preceded the beginning of the depreciation of the latter metal.

"On the supposition that silver has entirely ceased to be coined, the world is richer in 1897 in material for the coinage of full legal tender or standard money than it was at any former period of the world's history, and the indications are that it will grow richer in this respect in every succeeding year for decades to come.

"Hence my belief that the first effect of the new additions of gold to the stock already in existence will be an effect detrimental to bimetallism, whether national or international. There are some, I know, who think that the increased production of gold will have the contrary effect, and that it will lead to the remonetization of silver. They base their argument on this, that the increased production of gold will be followed by a depreciation of its value. This might be if the new demand for gold did not increase more rapidly than the supply. But the former is likely to exceed the latter.

"There is, in fact, at the present time, no limit to the demand for gold. The tendency of nations is toward the single gold standard. Apart from the United States, there is not, I believe, a country on the face of the earth that would not adopt gold monometallism if it had the ability to do so, with silver as a subsidiary or token coinage. There is not a country in Europe with any full legal tender silver coins but would replace them with gold coins if it could do so without too great a sacrifice. Germany would gladly put $100,000,000 in circulation, instead of its silver thalers. France and all the countries of the Latin Union would replace their full legal tender 5-franc pieces by gold could they easily get it. Russia's demand for gold is unbounded. Austria-Hungary cannot get enough, and so of every other country in Europe. Japan wants gold now that it has adopted the gold standard. Even China shows an inclination to follow the example of its conqueror, but that, of course, is out of the question. All South America is crying for gold. Chili wants it, Colombia wants it, Peru wants it. Venezuela has some but wants more. Central America wants it. Even Mexico, the last stronghold of silver, is feeling the burdensomeness of its present system in the height of its rate of exchange.

"More than this. The nations of Europe want gold, not only as currency, but as war material, for they have come to understand that gold—gold, not all kinds of money—is the sinew of war. Germany has a gold fund locked up in a fortress, and the accumulations of that metal made by other governments, ostensibly for different purposes, are really only so much war material, which the nations of Europe can no more dispense with than they can with a standing army or a navy. And where no such fund can be actually pointed to, as in England, there is felt the confidence that it can be had at any time on the credit of the nation. Then it must be remembered that all great loans are now made and must be made in gold. Only home loans are made in any other medium. This disposes of the contention that there is likely to be any depreciation in the value of gold consequent on the increased supply.

"Will the new additions to the gold stock of the world have any effect on prices? Should the increase of the world's production due to the yield of gold in the Klondike district, as well as in the Transvaal, be any way near as large as that due to the mines of California and Australia in the years immediately succeeding the discovery of the metal in those countries, it probably will, in time, especially if the new additions bear the same proportion to the already existing stock of gold in the world as did those of California and Australia. But any increase of prices that may thereby be caused will be gradual and may not be noticed for some years to come. It cannot be noticed until gold begins to depreciate in value, and of that there is no present prospect.

"Shortly after the discovery of gold in California and Australia there was a very marked rise in the general level of prices, which writers on the subject have generally attributed to the decline of the value of gold at that time. French Publicists were the first to call attention to this phenomenon. This was in 1851, 1852 and 1853. Chevalier wrote about it in 1857. In 1857 another eminent French writer published a book entitled "The Question of Gold," in which he showed the greatness of the rise, and the consequences, favorable or otherwise, which it might have for individuals or for states. The following year Chevalier took up the subject anew and endeavored to forecast the commercial and social effects which the decline of gold might have in the future. In England several statisticians noticed the same depreciation about the same time. Newmarch and Macculloch doubted it. But in 1863 Stanley Jevons demonstrated it in his essay, 'A Serious Fall in the Value of Gold Ascertained and Its Social Effects Set Forth.' Ten years later De Foville, after a long and laborious investigation, came also to the conclusion that there had been a decrease in the purchasing power of money.

"While the value of gold was thus declining there was a sudden and extraordinary increase in the supply of the metal. From 1831 to 1840 the annual production had not exceeded, on an average, 20,289 kilograms, or $13,484,000. From 1841 to 1850, after the rich auriferous deposits of the Ural, and especially of Siberia, had begun to be worked, the average annual product rose to 54,759 kilograms, or $36,393,000. The annual average was abruptly raised by the discovery of the gold diggings of California and Australia to 199,388 kilograms, or $132,513,000, from 1851 to 1855, and to an annual average of 101,750 kilograms, or $134,083,000, from 1856 to 1860. The production subsequently averaged 185,057 kilograms, or $122,989,000, from 1861 to 1865, and 195,026 kilograms, or $129,614,000, from 1866 to 1870. From 1493, that is from the discovery of America, until 1850, that is in 357 years, the quantity produced was 4,752,070 kilograms, or $3,158,223,000. From 1851 to 1870, in 20 years, the quantity of gold produced was 3,905,205 kilograms, or $2,595,996,000. This newly extracted gold, therefore, represented more than 82 per cent of the production anterior to 1850, and more than 45 per cent of the total production after 1493.

"It is easy to see that such a revolution in the conditions of production caused a decline of gold which became manifest in a rise of prices.

"The rise of prices was general at first. In 1858, according to Levasseur, the price of wheat, compared with the price in 1848 had doubled; the price of natural products, compared with the price in 1847, had increased 67.19 per cent; the price of manufactured articles compared with that of 1847 had risen 14.94 per cent; the average price of all commodities had increased 61.61 per cent. The learned writer took care to remark that the rise of prices was not due exclusively to the decline of gold. He admitted in the first place, that war and famine had caused a rise of about 20 per cent in the prices of natural as distinguished from manufactured products, and of 2 per cent in manufactured products, and that besides, speculation in 1856 had swollen all prices to the extent of 5 per cent. Leaving out of consideration these transitory causes, natural products had increased, in 1858, by 42.19 per cent, manufactured products by 7.94 per cent, all commodities considered as a whole by an everage of 25 per cent. From this rise of 25 per cent it was necessary to deduct

5 per cent in order to take into account the effect of the developments of industry and of the increase of the number of consumers. As a final result he found that the greater abundance of gold had caused a rise of 20 per cent in prices. A decline in the value of money thus amounted to 16.67 per cent.

"In 1863, Stanley Jevons reached a conclusion almost the same. He believed that the decline of gold could not be less than 15 per cent, and that it might be more. In 1863 or thereabouts, the consequences of the decline began to be less apparent than in 1858. The general rise of prices was succeeded by movements of a very different kind. Several causes which Mr. Levasseur had already drawn attention to began either to counteract or to strengthen the effects of the plentifulness of the standard metal, so that in the case of certain commodities there came a decline instead of a rise, while in others the decline became greater still.

"In 1873, when Mr. De Foville published the results of his investigations concerning prices, the movement which in 1850 was faintly outlined, became very marked and well defined. That writer showed that the prices of 1873 presented, as compared with those of half a century before, a rise of 90 per cent for foods of animal origin, of 30 per cent for vegetable foods, and 45 per cent for domestic liquors. He showed, on the other hand, a decline of prices of 35 per cent for mineral products, of 50 per cent for textiles and 45 per cent for chemical products, glassware and paper.

"By a combination of rises and declines of prices, according to the method which he called that of budget averages, Mr. De Foville came to the conclusion that there had been an increase of 33 per cent in the prices of commodities, corresponding to a decrease of 25 per cent in the purchasing power of money from the period of 1820-25 to 1870-75.

"It will be remarked that in this period of fifty years the quantity of gold produced almost trebled as compared with the 332 years between 1493 and 1825. The quantities produced amounted in 1825 to 3,926,510 kilograms, or $2,609,558,000, and in 1875 to 9,523,-696 kilograms, or $6,329,448,000. Yet the decline of gold was only 25 per cent. It must be remarked, however, that this depreciation of 25 per cent was due to a combination of causes of various kinds, and was not due entirely to the abundance of gold. Between 1825 and 1875 an economic revolution was accomplished in the world greater than most political revolutions. To describe the revolution just referred to would be to write the industrial, commercial, financial and monetary history of those fifty years.

"Judging from the effect of the gold discoveries in California and Australia in gradually raising general prices from 1850 to 1873 or thereabouts, it would be only natural to conclude that the effect of the now rapidly increasing conditions made annually to the world's product in the Transvaal, Australia, the United States, Russia and in the Klondike district would have a similar effect, provided they bore something like the same proportion to the already existing stock of gold as did those of California and Australia to the stock already on hand in 1850. Since 1871 the production of gold has been about 5,200,000 kilograms, or $3,455,-920,000, or will be by the end of the present year. Since 1886 alone the product has been about 2,718,000 kilograms, or $1,806,383,000. The gold product from 1886 to 1897 has been nearly 25 per cent of the total output of the gold mines of the world from 1493 to 1885, and the total product of gold from 1871 to 1897 has been approximately 60 per cent of the world's product of that metal from the discovery of America to 1870.

"Such an enormous production of gold since 1870 would lead one to believe that there would necessarily be caused thereby a great rise in prices. But as a matter of fact, the contrary has on the whole, been the case. A general decline of prices began in 1873, and notwithstanding the vast increase in the world's stock of gold just referred to, the decline still continues. Economists and statisticians of great merit believe that this general decline is due to what they call the appreciation of gold, although how there can be an appreciation of gold, when the world's output of the metal since 1871 has been about 60 per cent of its total product from 1493 to 1870 they do not explain.

"This vast increase in the gold stock of the world has found expression in the lowness of the rate of discount, with the facility with which municipalities and states effect loans of great magnitude at a rate of interest lower than ever before in the history of the world, and in the vast accumulation of gold and silver bullion in the great banks of the world. The fact that prices have not risen as a consequence of the increase is undoubted evidence that the causes of their decline have their source elsewhere than in the scarcity of gold or of money in general. For, as remarked above, there is now more gold available for monetary purposes than there was gold and silver before the decline of prices began. Not only this, but the substitutes for money with which every business man is familiar have vastly increased since 1873. With the development of credit that now obtains in the world the quantity of the media of circulation can have no controlling influence on the prices of commodities.

"I know it is almost a despairing view to take that, notwithstanding the vast additions yearly making to the gold stock of the world, there is no immediate prospect of a general rise of prices from that cause; and yet, considering the simple fact that the addition to the world's gold stock since 1871 has been nearly 60 per cent of the world's output of this metal from the discovery of America up to 1870, and that the product since 1886 up to the end of 1897 (an estimate of $240,000,000 being made for that year) was nearly 25 per cent of the total product from 1493 to 1885, I can reach no other conclusion. The great addition to the world's stock of gold since 1873 is a demonstrated fact, but so also is the continued decline of prices.

"The advocates of silver maintain that the decline is due to the demonetization of that metal and the consequent scarcity of money. Yet money was never more plentiful, rates of discount and interest never lower, accumulation in the banks never greater.

"These facts conclusively refute their contention.

"May not the true cause be found in the stability of the value of gold—the most desirable quality in a money metal—and in the improvement in technical processes and the cheapening of transportation—an improvement and a cheapening still going on—as well as in the almost universal substitution of machine for human labor?"

CHAPTER XXXIX.

HON. CLIFFORD SEFTON, CANADIAN MINISTER OF THE INTERIOR.

Gold seekers in the Klondike country, and in the far north region generally, will appreciate an introduction to the Hon. Clifford Sefton, Canadian Minister of the Interior. The department of the Interior of the Dominion Government is charged with the responsibility of administering all mining laws and regulations, and has immediate jurisdiction of the mounted police which is charged with the maintenance of law and order in the mining camps of the northwest gold fields west to the 141st degree of longtitude.

Mr. Sefton is a product of Manitoba where he settled with his parents in the "seventies." His father, Hon. J. W. Sefton has long been connected with the public life of the Canadian Northwest, having served as a member of the Manitoba legislature fifteen years ago. The son, the present Minister of the Interior, succeeded his father in the legislature, and later was elected to the Dominion Parliament, being a strong opponent to "separate schools" in Manitoba, an issue which has become almost world famous. Mr. Sefton, although a young man, not yet passed thirty-six years, has won distinction in the legal profession. He is an ardent and enthusiastic believer in a great future for the far northwest country, and his admirers in Canada predict for his administration a rapid development of that region. He favors liberal government subsidies for the promotion of railway construction into the rich Peace River country, and other arable districts of the northwest, and will lend his best energies to promote the settlement and development of the whole north country. He favors a liberal mining policy, but is said to lean towards plans calculated to discriminate in favor of citizens of Canada and Great Britian as against gold seekers from other countries.

CHAPTER XL.

THE PEACE-LIARD-PELLY ROUTE.

Northwest, or "Back-Door" lines of travel to the Klondike described in detail—Two and a half months from Edmonton to Dawson City—A cheap, accessible route.

And now we come to a description in detail of the most practical route to the Klondike, viz.: that by the Peace, Liard and Pelly rivers. That by the Mackenzie and Peel rivers, which is much longer, is available only when the water is open and is not likely to be extensively traveled.

The route via the Peace and Liard rivers, which is a combination of two of the lines heretofore referred to in this volume, has the advantage of being the shortest and by all odds the cheapest and most accessible line of travel to the gold fields of the far north. In addition to this it offers great facilities for taking horses and cattle through, as the country traversed abounds in good grasses, and although heavily timbered in many places, it is not rough in the sense of being mountainous.

If gold seekers decide to take this short route, the starting point will be the city of Calgary, or Edmonton, which is 192 miles further north. Edmonton may be reached by rail from Chicago or any other railway point in the United States. The Saskatchewan River is crossed at Edmonton. An excellent road runs from Calgary to Edmonton so that the traveler may chose between pack horses and the railway as to that distance of 192 miles.

The reader is requested to consult the route map which accompanies this chapter closely, in order to get a better understanding of the description of the route. From Edmonton the objective point will be the Liard

River, and there are several alternative routes, all heading northwest and converging on the Liard. When once the waters or the ice of the Liard are reached by either route the remainder of the journey is taken via Lake Frances, the portage over the great watershed to the Pelly River and thence down the Pelly and the Yukon, in boats on the water, or by sleds on the ice to Dawson City.

We will therefore now describe in detail each of these alternative routes to the Liard, pointing out when possible their respective merits and demerits, and then give our attention to that portion of the district from the Liard to the Yukon, which is common to them all.

As stated the distance from Calgary to Edmonton is 192 miles, and may be traveled by rail or by means of horses. A party taking a large number of horses and cattle will find it advantageous to go over the highway. From Edmonton there is an excellent road for wagons or sleds, according to the season, to Athabaska landing, a distance of 90 miles. Over this section many thousands of tons of freight have been hauled in the past. At Athabaska landing the traveler may ascend the Athabaska River on the ice or in boats, according to the season to Lesser Slave River, and then up this river to Lesser Slave Lake, at the west end of which there is a Hudson's Bay post. From this post a cart or wagon road, 60 miles long, leads to the Peace River. The crossing is at the junction of the Peace and Smoky rivers. The total distance from Edmonton to this crossing is 260 miles. This route has been traveled for a century by traders and is well beaten. There are several Canadian parties now en route to the Klondike over this line of travel.

Horses or cattle taken in by this route, except during the ice season are taken on the south bank of the Athabaska River from the landing to the mouth of Lesser Slave River, where they are swum across the stream and taken along the north side of Lesser Slave River and lake to the Hudson's Bay post at the head of the lake. Perhaps a better way, if horses are to be packed through during the open season, is to take the wagon road from Edmonton through St. Albert to the site of Fort Assiniboine, on the Athabaska, a distance of 85 miles, then northwest to Lesser Slave Lake, 115 miles more, and thence by the cart road to the Peace River crossing. This route is now being improved by the Government of the Canadian northwest territories under Surveyor Chalmers.

Peace River must be crossed at the Crossing, and then there is a good road or trail on the north bank of the river to Dunvegan at the mouth of the Pine River. This point is 100 miles from the Peace River crossing, and 25 miles from Fort St. John.

The favored route is by Lake St. Ann to Fort St. John or Dunvegan. This is the line of travel to the Peace River covered by Henry McLeod, C. E., when making explorations for the Canadian Pacific railway. There is a direct wagon road from Edmonton to Lake St. Ann, thence by trail to the junction of the McLeod and Athabaska Rivers, where the latter has to be crossed on the ice or by boat. From the Athabaska the trail leads to Fort St. John by way of Smoky River and Grand Prairie.

No difficulty will be experienced in crossing the Big or Little Smoky Rivers. There is a considerable amount of open country and muskegs are reputed to be conspicuous by their rarity, in addition to which good fishing can be obtained in the open season in any of the creeks and numerous small lakes along the trail. If the traveler wishes to strike the Peace River at Dunvegan, rather than at Fort St. John, he will, instead of bearing to the west after crossing the Smoky River, take a trail which leads almost directly north. In the Edmonton Bulletin, of September, 1897, mention is made of the arrival in Edmonton of S. Cunningham, who has been mining for some time in this district northwest of Lake St. Ann. He gives the distance by days' travel with loaded pack horses to Dunvegan, Peace River, as follows: Lake St. Ann to Athabasca River at junction with McLeod, four days; Little Smoky, four days; Sturgeon Lake, three days; Big Smoky, three days; Spirit River, three days; Dunvegan, two days; and says that this trail is the best one to Peace River. Mr. Cunningham adds that the Hudson's Bay Co., A. McCorrister and an Indian are establishing trading outposts at the crossing of the Athabasca.

There is an old pack trail on the north side of the Peace between St. John and Dunvegan. This trail is far enough back from the river to avoid the numerous ravines which run into the Peace Valley. On the south side of the river a trail also exists between St. John and Dunvegan. On this south trail for a distance of about 22 miles from St. John the country is much wooded, and for the remainder of the way open woods, prairie and fairly thick timber alternate. This trail lies about 20 miles south of the river for the greater portion of the distance, and the whole of this southern district is well wooded right up to the spurs of the Rocky Mountains.

"Although it was in October I passed over it, I witnessed no severe frosts, very little ice being visible anywhere, and the flora gave no evidence of having been much injured by frost. In the prairies along the creeks the grasses and plants were of as luxurious growth as in places much farther south and east. The grass was generally long and meadowlike, but as we approached Peace River it became more like the true prairie grass until extensive areas of true prairie were passed over along the tributaries of the Peace River. For a distance of six or seven miles back from the Peace River Valley there is much prairie and meadow land, with some woods and swamps scattered over it. The soil is an excellent black clay loam, as rich as I ever saw, and the growth of hay and grass bears testimony to this fact."

Dominion Land Surveyor Ogilvie, who traveled over the upper Peace River district in 1891, says:

"At Fort St. John the Hudson's Bay Co. raise potatoes and garden produce with success, and the barley and oats always ripen. They also have several bands of horses in the vicinity. These animals live on the prairie on the north side of the river winter and summer, and very seldom are there any losses, except by wolves. The fact that horses can safely winter out here speaks well for the future of the country. St. John is visited frequently during the winter months by the so-called chinook winds, which often sweep away the snow completely."

At Dunvegan the Hudson's Bay Co. has grown wheat, barley, oats, and garden produce generally for many years with great success. Mr. Ogilvie remarks that when he was there in 1883-84 he saw grain and vegetables fully equal in quality and quantity to any he has ever seen anywhere, the garden vegetables being especially fine. The Hudson's Bay Co., the Roman Catholic Mission and the Indians have many horses, which always winter out. The woods afford them shelter and on the prairies the richest grasses grow. There are also large areas where excellent hay grows. A concluding quotation from Mr. Ogilvie's report must be made, as it bears pertinently on the characteristics of the Peace River district: "Were it not for the difficulty of getting into and out of the country stock raising might be profitably engaged in. Hay is abundant and of good quality nearly everywhere, and in summer the grazing is excellent. Notwithstanding the latitude and altitude, cattle subsist with moderate help from the first of May till the middle or end of December; the rest of the year they have to be sheltered and fed. The Hudson's Bay Co. has a ranch on Spirit River, south of the Peace about 20 miles, and on the trail between Dunvegan and Grand Prairie. This was started a few years ago, and some fine stock was put on it. What the result of the experiment may be remains to be seen, but they have been kept at all the posts for many years, oxen being largely used in freighting."

In essaying to traverse the 350 miles of country which separate the Peace and Liard Rivers, the traveler has a choice of routes, though the information at his disposal is not of such a definite or particular nature as that concerning the other portions of the overland route. In selecting his course he will have, in great measure, to use his own judgment, at the same time bearing in mind that all the information contained in the government publications and that derived from the Hudson's Bay officials and Indians concur in the fact that this tract of country is passable without difficulty or danger, and that the only obstruction to be met with is the dense growth of timber, through which a trail may in occasional places have to be cut for a short distance. The Indians have trails through this section for hunting purposes.

The reader, on referring to the map, will notice that the two branches of the Nelson River take their rise in the divide, and, uniting some distance above Fort Nelson, run almost north to the Liard. Mr. W. Ogilvie, journeying south from the Liard in 1891, reached Fort St. John by traveling in a course up the west branch of the Nelson and thence packing overland. On his way he picked up a considerable amount of information as to the country, although, owing to the time of year and the delays he was subjected to, he had no opportunity of investigating for himself.

The most direct route to the head waters of the Nelson would be to take the trail running between Dunvegan and Fort St. John till it crossed the Pine River, and follow up Pine River and continue in a northwesterly direction to the forks of the Nelson River, being a distance of 140 miles from the mouth of the Pine. The head waters of the east branch of the Nelson, which Mr. Ogilvie calls the Nelson River proper, can be reached from St. John by a shorter way. A well known Indian once made a trip to Peace River from the head of canoe navigation on the Nelson, "and described his route as being southerly for one day to a lake of considerable size, thence from the lake to Peace River three days on foot, which probably would make from 50 to 70 miles from the head of this stream to Peace River. Between the lake and Peace River he crossed a ridge of hills, which he designated mountains, but they were all heavily timbered." The Edmonton Bulletin remarks, apropos of this last, that it would indicate that the greater part of the distance was not heavily timbered, and therefore passable for pack horses. A single belt of timber could very easily be cut through.

Another route which, from all reports, appears to be the most advantageous, is as follows: Proceeding up the Peace River from Fort St. John, Half-way River is reached, which has its source a little south of the head waters of the west fork of the Nelson, and runs into the Peace 40 miles above Fort St. John. There is a good horse trail up Half-way River, leading to the west fork of Nelson River, a distance of 100 miles. This trail has been much used by the Indians, and, indeed, the whole of the country around the Half-way River, from Ogilvie's description, would appear to be frequently traversed by them. Ogilvie did not pass over this trail, as he cut a path of his own to Fort St. John, but the trail, nevertheless, exists, and has been well used and therefore there can be no difficulty in packing supplies over.

Mr. Ogilvie, in speaking of the general characteristics of the ground between the Nelson and Peace Rivers, says that the timber is generally scrub, averaging two inches in thickness and eight to ten feet in height. "It may be taken," says the Edmonton Bulletin, "as established beyond question that an open pack trail exists from Edmonton to boat navigation on the west branch of the Nelson by way of St. John and Half-way River, the total distance being over 500 miles." The Indians use the Half-way and Nelson Rivers as a canoe route, there being a portage of 25 miles between the two at a point higher up than the horse trail. Mr. Frank Oliver, M. P., mentions that a party of miners took this canoe route from Peace River to the Liard about 1874. They went up Half-way River in the fall, crossed the portage in the winter and went down the Nelson in the spring.

Having reached the head waters of either the west or the east fork of the Nelson, there is no difficulty in descending to Fort Nelson and the Liard River.

The following description of the Nelson, or East Branch River, as it is locally known, taken from Ogilvie's report, will suffice to give an idea of the nature of the road: The river, for some way from its junction with the Liard, is from 200 to 400 yards wide, and capable of being navigated by stern wheel steamers as far up as Fort Nelson, 110 miles. This post is a Hudson's Bay Co. station, and as it is off the main line of travel, the only white people seen at it are those in charge of the company's business and a missionary. The Indians in the vicinity have seen very little of white men or civilized life. They have retained more of their original manners and habits than Indians generally do, and, judging from Ogilvie's experience, the less the traveler depends on them the better it will be for him. Above Fort Nelson the river continues to afford good navigation for 91 miles to where the forks are situate. The east fork is the smaller and is known as the Nelson River; the west one Ogilvie calls the Sicannie Chief River.

The east fork is very shallow, except in spring; so much so that it is only in spring there is enough water to run a canoe down. At the head it is wide and full of gravel bars, which in summer time absorb all the water. From the head of canoe navigation on this stream down to Fort Nelson takes about three or four days in high water, or say 150 to 180 miles.

The west branch, or Sicannie Chief River, was traversed by Ogilvie in his journey from Ft. Nelson to Ft. St. John in 1891, and from his report it is beyond question that the stream can be descended by canoe with facility. Ogilvie himself ascended the river in low water, and though he made somewhat slow time, he had no portages to make. We have mentioned, above, that the Indians use this west branch as a canoe route in conjunction with Half-way River.

Ogilvie observes with reference to the Nelson: "A marked peculiarity with reference to this stream is the nature of the bars in it. They consist principally of sand, and many of them are continually shifting their position. By putting a stick down to the bottom in very many places along the river the bottom can be felt in violent agitation, the sand rolling along with great force and lodging in the deep places, only to be dislodged again in time. Many of the bars are very treacherous, presenting a solid appearance which is far from real; on top of them there is a thin crust of gravel, which will not support a man, and through which he will sink in quicksand two or three feet. To cross one of these is quite an undertaking, as it is exceedingly fatiguing, if not dangerous. Much of the bottom of the river is in the same condition."

It will be seen from these observations that crossing the ice and snow in the early spring when the snow has mostly disappeared and the ice yet remains will prove the more practicable mode of travel for this section of the route.

The traveler now ascends the Liard River, which at this point and for some distance is bordered with wide alluvial flats, covered with tall, straight cottonwood and large spruce and canoe birch. The river itself is wide and filled with sandbars and wooded islands. The valley is wide and shallow and lined with gently sloping spruce clad banks. R. G. McConnell adds: "On some of the flats the Indians have built houses, and fenced in small plots for farming purposes, for which the greater part of this section of the district seems well adapted. We passed (July, 1887) one small Indian farm about 13 miles below the mouth of the Nelson and another one at the mouth of Fishing Creek, a few miles above Fort Liard, while others were noticed in the lower part of the river."

Proceeding up the Liard, the river valley for some miles is low and the hill sides are covered with forests, while the river itself spreads out and flows for some miles in a multitude of channels through a bewildering maze of islands. The journey as far as Hell Gate Canyon—40 miles from the mouth of the Nelson—is easy and after 10 miles have been traversed, the valley becomes narrow with steep sides rising up in places to a height of fully a thousand feet. The bottoms here are usually small and are chiefly wooded by members of the poplar family. In this reach the river has a steady current of about four and a half miles an hour, and varies in width from 500 yards to over a mile. In the wide portions the river is usually divided into several channels by islands and bars. Shortly before Hell Gate Canyon there is a canyon-like reach of the river about a mile in length. The stream here is narrowed down to about 150 yards in width and flows easily between vertical banks three hundred feet high.

Hell Gate Canyon is so called because it is the entrance to a wild portion of the river, where the most serious obstructions are met with. The voyageur will experience no trouble in passing Hell Gate, or the three miles of rather swift water which have next to be traversed, but above this the river is closely canyoned and riffles are met with all the way. Only some of these are dangerous, but the banks are steep, and the impossibility of getting down to the bottom of the valley compelled Mr. McConnell's party, who were coming down stream, to make a portage of four miles. On getting round this stretch of canyons a long riffle is met, and then the "Rapid of the Drowned" is reached. "Here one of the most dangerous spots on the river is formed by the water plunging, with its whole force, over a ledge of rock which curves outwards and downwards from the left-hand bank into a boiling chaudiere below. The name of the rapid originated from the drowning at this point of a Hudson Bay clerk named Brown, and a boat load of voyageurs. As the story goes, Brown, disregarding the advice of his steersman, insisted on running close to the northern bank, and the canoe plunging into the hole mentioned above was drawn under. We passed the rapid by letting our boat down cautiously with a rope to the chaudiere and then making a short portage. With a proper boat, however, no difficulty would be experienced in crossing the river above the rapid and running down close to the right bank."

For twelve miles above the Rapid of the Drowned the river is wide and shallow and filled with gravel bars, but navigation is easy. Then another narrow pass is entered where the current is swift, and riffle succeeds riffle till the Devil's portage is reached. Mr. McConnell's party had to make several short portages, but were able to use their canoe most of the way. This portion of the Liard between Devil's portage and Hell-gate, a distance of nearly 40 miles, is called the Grand Canyon, but "is more correctly a succession of short canyons, with expanded basins between filled with eddying currents. In low water the whole of this reach can be easily run in almost any kind of a boat, but in the season of high floods, such as it was when we passed through, the water forcing its way through the throat-like contractions, is thrown into a commotion too violent for any but the staunchest boat to stand."

Again the reader will observe that the ice season is by all odds the proper one for travel over this part of the journey to the Klondike.

Above the Grand Canyon the Liard makes a great bend to the northeast, all around which is a succession of rapids and canyons; and a large fall is reported in the elbow of the bend. The banks of the river are formed of almost vertical cliffs, and a portage of four miles has to be made across the bend on the left-hand bank of the river as you ascend. This portage passes over a ridge fully 1,000 feet high and the slopes are steep. In 1871 Messrs. McCullough and Thibert cleared a trail across for the purpose of hauling their boat over, and in 1887 R. G. McConnell followed their trail easily on the upper part of the portage, but the eastern portion had become gradually overgrown with brush wood, and he had to cut out a new path for himself. Mr. McConnell spent six days on the portage; but most of this time was employed in framing a boat and in crossing his outfit, which was comparatively heavy, in addition to which he had to cut a trail for some distance. Today the portage should not take more than two days at the outside.

Mr. McConnell observes that the country around the Devil's portage and Fort Halkett is probably the best moose country in North America. His party saw several, and everywhere fresh tracks in abundance were observed. Beaver are also abundant, and grizzly bear are said to be fairly common.

Beyond the portage the Liard has an average width of 400 yards, and a steady current of about four miles and a half an hour. It is bordered in places by long gravel and sand beaches, and encloses occasionally wooded islands. Various small streams come in, and 70 miles above the Nelson, at the confluence of the Smith and Liard, is the site of Fort Halkett, a Hudson's Bay trading post, which has been abandoned since 1865. Between Fort Halkett and Portage Brule the river is wide and filled with low islands and bars, some of which are auriferous. The river valley is low, lined with rows of terraces rising up to a height of several hundred feet, and clothed in unwooded portions by as luxuriant a growth of grasses and vetches as I have ever seen in any part of the country. This part of the country, judging from the luxuriance of the vegetation and the character of the soil, seems well adapted for agricultural pursuits.

The rapids at Portage Brule are about two miles long, but McConnell says that they are not very formidable. "The portage itself is nearly two miles long and leads across a nearly level, well-wooded flat, which at the upper end of the portage is only elevated a few feet above the surface of the river, but at the lower end is terminated by a sharp descent of over 200 feet. A good track was cut across when mining was being prosecuted on the Liard, and a windlass built at the lower end for the purpose of hoisting boats up the steep bank, both of which are still (i. e. 1887) in good condition."

Four miles above Portage Brule the river is again broken by several small but strong riffles, which can be avoided by making portages a few yards in length. Whirlpool Canyon, the first rapid reached, can be passed in safety by keeping to the right bank, says McConnell. Mountain Portage rapids, a little above Rabbit River, can be traversed by taking a small channel on the left-hand side of the island; the rapid itself, however, is one of the worst on the river. Cranberry rapid, some distance beyond Mountain portage, is also bad and necessitates a half mile portage along the right bank. From here to Porcupine Bar navigation is safe, and except for one small canyon the valley is wide and bottomed by long, narrow, well-wooded flats. Abandoned miners' camps are passed all the way, and the country is everywhere densely wooded, the principal trees being the white spruce, larch, birch and black pine. The spruce, which obtains here a diameter of 15 to 20 inches, is by far the most abundant and valuable. The river is here about 300 yards in width.

Between Porcupine Bar and the mouth of the Dease River there occurs but one serious rapid—the Little Canyon. It is "about half a mile long and in its narrowest place about 200 feet wide. It is easily navigable in low water, but is dangerous for small boats during floods, as the channel is very crooked, and the current, striking with great violence against the right-hand bank, is thrown forcibly back, with the production of a number of breakers running nearly lengthwise with the direction of the channel, and large enough to swamp any ordinary river boat which is drawn among them. A number of Chinamen were drowned at this point some years ago. This canyon can be run with safety by entering it nearly in the middle of the stream, which is as close to the left-hand bank as the lines of reefs and isolated rocks running out from that side will allow, and once past there making all haste to the left so as to clear the breakers below." In ascending the Liard the rapid can be avoided by a portage of about half a mile.

Dease river enters the Liard on the south, 160 miles above the mouth of the Nelson. The Liard, below the Dease, has a general width of from 250 to 400 yards, but widens out in places to over half a mile. It separates in places into a number of channels, enclosing low alluvial islands, usually well wooded. Its valley is from two to three miles wide, and is shallow, with rolling banks sloping easily up to the general level. The country is everywhere well wooded, but the trees are usually small, seldom exceeding a foot in diameter. Black pine, white spruce, poplar, and occasionally birch are seen.

Mr. McConnell, in describing the Indians he met with at the mouth of the Dease, says that they seldom ascend the Liard with canoes, as they prefer carrying their outfits along the shore, the character of the river valley permitting them to do this with greater facility than tracking a canoe against the current.

The Liard, just above the mouth of the Dease, is 840 feet in width, with a maximum velocity of 4.54 miles per hour, according to Dr. Dawson. Six miles above the mouth of the Dease the entrance to the Lower canyon is reached. The canyon is three miles in length and at high water it is said to be necessary to portage the whole of this distance, but Dr. Dawson's party lightened their boats and made four small portages over rocky points where the current was dangerously swift. Above the Lower canyon the river continues swift, the current averaging about four miles an hour and much exceeding this rate in many places. It is wide and shallow, and in places becomes a complete maze of islands and gravelly half-submerged bars. The river valley averages about two miles in width, and the higher ground is generally wooded with spruce, while the black pine is abundant on dry terraces, and groves of cottonwood of medium size often occur on the flats. However, little of this timber is of useful size or quality. Dr. Dawson remarks that when he traversed this section of the country in June, 1887, there were many wild flowers in evidence and the wild roses were rapidly coming into flower.

About midway between the Dease and Frances, a small stream enters the Liard from the southwest, and a few miles above on the opposite side of the river a small lake, reputed to be well stocked with fish, is reported. From the mouth of Dease River to the confluence of the Frances, the general bearing of the Liard is nearly due northwest, the distance following the course of the river being 45 miles.

The country is a wide, rolling plateau, with an average elevation of about 500 feet above the river. This plateau is everywhere wooded, except where intersected by grassy or mossy swamps of small area.

The Edmonton Bulletin thus sums up the route thus far: "Going carefully over all the information obtainable as to this part of the route, which includes the crossing of the Rocky mountains, the only possible obstacle to pack and cattle travel at present would be the timber, which might require to be cut through in places. On the other hand, unless the conditions are very different from what they are elsewhere in the North West, the timber would not form a very serious objection. Feed for animals must certainly exist all along, which is the main consideration, and the climate certainly cannot be severe."

Leaving the Liard the route lies up the Frances River, which, near its junction with the Liard, has an average width of 600 feet. For the first few miles above its mouth the Frances is extremely tortuous, and then, 22 miles from the Liard, the Middle canyon is reached. This canyon is about three miles in length and the river is hemmed in by broken, rocky cliffs of 200 to 300 feet in height for the greater portion of the distance. The Dawson party took their boats up along the southeast bank, making four short portages of part of their outfit, and two of both boats and load across narrow rocky points. One portage of greater length, says Dr. Dawson, on the opposite bank, would overcome all the really bad water, but the banks on that side are rougher, and the whole force of the current sets against the cliff in one place in a dangerous manner.

Above the Middle canyon the river is, in the main, bordered by quite low land on both sides for about 12 miles. The river itself is wide and deep, with a rather slack current. Proceeding further, the current becomes swifter and several streams come down from the small lakes, which the Indians say are to be found at some distance from the river. Numerous islands are met with, but there is no difficulty until the Upper canyon is reached, 39 miles from the Liard. This canyon is a mile and a quarter long and is occupied by a series of rapids, which are rocky and rather strong and have a total fall of about 30 feet. The banks rise steeply from the river to heights of 100 to 200 feet, though the rocky cliffs along the water are of inconsiderable height, scarcely anywhere exceeding 50 feet. This is the last serious impediment to the navigation of the river, and Dawson's party found it necessary to make several short portages, but with a large boat and at a good stage of the river it is possible, says Dr. Dawson, that one portage of about 1,000 feet in length, on the south bank, would overcome all the dangerous water, while the boat might be tracked up light.

From the Upper canyon to Frances Lake, a distance of 21 1-2 miles in a straight line, the river maintains a northerly direction. It is deep, with a moderate current for about eight miles to Moose Island, above which the current is again swift, averaging from four and a half to five miles an hour. It again becomes slack for a short distance below the lake. Some portions of this part of the river are much broken up by islands and gravel bars. The valley is partly occupied by terrace flats and partly of wooded hills.

Frances Lake is 2,577 feet above the sea and consists, really, of a group of lakes connected by narrow channels. Lake trout, white fish, pike and suckers are found in abundance in its waters. All the lower country around the lake is well wooded, white spruce, black spruce, larch, birch and (on the flats) cottonwood and black pine being all found. Dr. Dawson saw in July many thickets of wild roses in full bloom. These indications show that the climate is moist but not severe. Dr. Dawson remarks that the snowfall cannot be great, nor is there any indication that the total annual precipitation is very considerable.

"In general appearance the rocks of Frances Lake closely resemble those from which the rich placer gold deposits of Dease Lake are derived. * * * Several colors to the pan were obtained from surface gravel at the mouth of Finlayson River, which struck me as specially promising in aspect, and there seems no reason why some of the streams flowing across the schistose rocks into the lake or in its vicinity should not prove to be richly auriferous. This entire district well deserves careful prospecting. After my return to the coast in the autumn, I ascertained from Charles Monroe that he and some other miners had actually done some prospecting in the vicinity of the lake at the time when the Cassiar mines were yielding largely, and the more enterprising men were scouring the country in search of new fields. On comparing notes we found that he had worked for a short time at the mouth of the Finlayson, where he found the gravel to pay at the rate of from $8 to $9 a day." Geological Survey of Canada, Annual Report, 1887-8, vol. iii., pt. 1, page 113. (Dawson.)

The region between Frances Lake and Pelly River is somewhat mountainous, but the mountains at no point attain any very high altitude. The country is traversed by wide wooded valleys, of which that occupied by the Finlayson River is the principal. The climate becomes less moist as Frances Lake is left behind. "Grassy swamps are found in a number of places, and a good growth of grass is also met with, where areas have been denuded of forest by successive fires, so that should it ever become desirable to use horses on this portage, they might be maintained without difficulty."

Professor Dawson crossed this divide between the Frances and Pelly Rivers by ascending Finlayson River. He says that the lower part of the Finlayson for about four miles, near its mouth, forms a series of rapids and small cascades in a narrow rocky gorge and is utterly impassable. His party found their way along the valley with heavy packs; the canoe was brought up the stream by two Indians. Above the rapids the river is shallow, but further on it becomes a narrow and deep stream. Twenty-two miles from Lake Frances it divides into two branches, the southern of which comes from Finlayson Lake.

Finlayson Lake, about nine and a half miles long, 3,105 feet above sea level, occupies the summit of the water-shed between the Mackenzie and the Yukon. It is well stocked with white fish and lake trout. The immediate shores of the lake are generally quite low and often swampy, and the country is covered with small, poor timber, much of which has been killed by fire.

The distance from the head of the lake to the nearest point on the Pelly River, in a straight line, is about fifteen miles, but the route which the contour of the land compels the traveler to take is nearer twenty miles. White and black spruce are found, and the vegetation in the vicinity of the Pelly is abundant. The soil of the river terraces is a fine silty material, which, judging from the luxuriance of plant growth, must be very rich.

Professor Dawson took ten days to travel from Lake Frances to Pelly River, but he observes that if he had had Indian guides he would in all probability have shortened the land carriage and possibly have found a traveled Indian trail. The Hudson's Bay Company, years ago, used a trail over the divide, but beyond two abandoned caches, no trace of it was discovered by the Dawson party.

At the point where the Pelly River is reached from Lake Frances it is 326 feet wide, with a current slightly exceeding two miles and a half an hour, and a depth of seven feet. When Professor Dawson took his observations, however, the river was, he says, probably below its mean stage. The old Hudson's Bay post, Pelly Banks, was situated at this point, but the buildings have disappeared. For thirty-three miles, down to where Hoole River joins the Pelly, the navigation is unobstructed and the current is moderate. The banks are muddy, and the south bank in particular is densely wooded, and, where shady and damp, the growth of timber is small and scrubby, with much black spruce.

"Just below the mouth of Hoole River is a rapid about 600 feet long with a total fall estimated at about ten feet. There is an easy portage on the right or north bank, but a fair-sized boat might run through without danger at most stages of the water." From this rapid to Hoole canyon, a distance of ten miles, the water is swift. At Hoole canyon the most formidable rapid occurs. The river makes a knee-like bend to the north-eastward and is constricted between rocky banks and cliffs about a hundred feet in height. These render it impracticable to use the line, and the water is very rough and dangerous. Professor Dawson found it necessary to carry all his effects and his canoe to the lower end of the canyon. The distance by the river is about three-quarters of a mile, and the portage is half a mile, the highest point being one hundred feet above the river. The portage is on the south side of the river, and Professor Dawson remarks that he found traces on it of skids which had been laid by the Hudson's Bay Company many years ago, but no sign of its having been employed by the Indians, who in all this district generally travel by land, making rafts when they are obliged to cross any of the larger rivers.

Proceeding down the Pelly, which is swift in all this part of its course, Ross River is passed, twenty-three miles from the Hoole canyon, and then there follows a stretch of good water for eighty-two miles to where the Glenlyon River joins the Pelly. All the way from the Ross to the Glenlyon, the Pelly is closely bordered on the north by hills of considerable height and densely wooded. On the south the mountains are distant some six miles from the river, the intervening country being occupied by lower wooded hills and broken country. For rather more than half the distance between the Ross and Glenlyon the Pelly continues to be pretty swift and is much divided among islands and gravel bars; the remaining part is comparatively tranquil, till the Glenlyon is reached. Cottonwood, aspen, alder, spruce and willows are the prevailing trees on the river flats; and on higher ground the birch is abundant and the black pine is also found.

In the immediate vicinity of the mouth of the Glenlyon River are two rapids. The first is about two miles above the Glenlyon. It is wide and rather shallow with some rocky impediments. Professor Dawson says it is easily run with a canoe, but, at low stages of the river, doubtfully passable for a steamer, unless of light draft. The second rapid is immediately below the junction of the Glenlyon and Pelly. Here the current strikes full on the face of a rocky bank on the right of the river, and forms a heavy confused wash in consequence, but is otherwise unimpeded and deep.

From the Glenlyon River to the junction of the Pelly and Macmillan is ninety-one miles following the course of the river. Several small creeks occur, but no streams of any size. For the first twenty miles of this distance the Pelly is more than usually free from abrupt bends, and few islands are met with. There are extensive grassy slopes on the hills which border the north bank. A number of small riffles are met, but none are of a character to offer impediment to navigation, and the current averages about three miles an hour. The Macmillan River is almost as large as the Pelly, measuring 455 feet in width just above its mouth, but it has never been explored. Two prospectors told Professor Dawson that they had ascended the Macmillan for several days and that there was a large area of low land with good soil in the river basin, but that mining prospects were not encouraging.

From the mouth of the Macmillan to the confluence of the Pelly and Lewis Rivers, measured along the course of the stream, is seventy-four miles and the stream is exceedingly tortuous. Five and a half miles below the Macmillan the Pelly is 754 feet in width, with a current of 2.3 miles per hour. Thirteen miles from the Macmillan, Granite canyon is reached. The canyon is about four miles in length with steep, rocky banks 200 to 250 feet in height. In the canyon are several little rapids, but the water is deep, and with the exception of some isolated rocks, the navigation would be quite safe for steamers even at a low stage of water. As the water is much confined, Professor Dawson opines that pretty rough water may be found here during floods. After passing the ridge which is cut through by Granite Canyon, the country on both sides of the river for about fifteen miles is quite low. Wide terraces run back from the river, and these are often highly wooded and are clothed with a good growth of grass. The soil is good. The remaining distance to the mouth of the Lewis, the river is more closely bordered by low hills, the southern slopes of which are generally open and grassy, and would afford excellent pasturage. The northern exposures are pretty thickly wooded.

The country about the confluence of the Lewis and Pelly is, generally speaking, low, with extensive terrace flats. The Lewis itself is considerably larger than the Pelly and swifter, and the united rivers measure about a quarter of a mile in width, just below the junction.

The ruins of Fort Selkirk, formerly a post of the Hudson's Bay Co., stand on the south side at a short distance from the river. It was at one time the most important post of the H. B. C. to the west of the Rocky Mountains in the far north, and with the exception of Fort Yukon, it was the most western permanent post ever maintained by the company.

The total length of the Pelly from the point where it is reached at the west end of the Lake Frances portage to its confluence with the Lewis is 320 miles. On the subject of the navigability the following remarks by Professor Dawson are entitled to the greatest weight: "With the exception of Granite Canyon, where warping might have to be resorted to at one place, the river would be easily navigable for stern-wheel steamers as far up as the mouth of the Macmillan, and the latter stream is also navigable for a considerable, though unknown distance. Above the Macmillan, I believe, no serious difficulty would be met with in taking a small stern-wheel steamer of good power up to the mouth of Ross River, and possibly as far as the foot of Hoole Canyon. A line might have to be carried ashore at a few of the stronger rapids, but the chief difficulty to be encountered would be from shoal water at low stages. Where the river is widely spread and swift, a depth of three feet could scarcely be found across some of the gravelly bars. * * * Hoole Canyon is, of course, quite impassable for a steamer of any kind, and the rapid met with seventeen miles east of it, at the mouth of Hoole River, might prove to be a difficult one to surmount by warping, its fall being estimated at about eight feet. Above this point the river is again, however, an easily navigable one for small steamers to the furthest point seen by us, and possibly as far as the lakes."

Professor Dawson further reports that small colors of gold may be found in almost any suitable locality along the river, and heavy colors in considerable numbers were found by him as far up as the mouth of Hoole River. The head waters of the Macmillan and Ross and those of the Pelly itself yet remain unprospected, as well as the very numerous tributary streams of these rivers.

Such is the shortest and most convenient route to the gold fields of the far north. The whole distance from Edmonton to Dawson City may be covered easily in two or three months, and by parties going light, in less than two months. The best time to leave Edmonton is early in March, so as to reach the foot of the Rockies just as the snow disappears and the ice is yet available in the river bottoms. This will undoubtedly become the most favored route to the Klondike.

APPENDIX I.

ROUTES AND DISTANCES.

A summary of routes and distances to the gold fields on both the eastern and western slopes of the Rockies of the far north will prove of value:

NORTHWESTERN ROUTE.

	MILES.
Chicago to Winnipeg (Railway)	1,000
Winnipeg to Edmonton (Railway)	1,100
Edmonton to gold fields head of Peace River (Overland)	750
Peace River gold fields to the Klondike	800

CHILKOOT ROUTE.

Seattle to Dyea	884
Dyea to foot of Canyon	7
Canyon to Sheep Camp	5
Sheep Camp to Summit	3
Summit to Lake Lindeman	9
Lake Lindeman (length)	6
Portage to Lake Bennett	1
Lake Bennett (length)	25
Cariboo Crossing to Lake Tagish	2

WHITE PASS ROUTE.

Seattle to Skaguay	884
Dyea to Tako Arm	35
Tako Arm to Lake Tagish	20
Tagish Lake (length)	16
River to Lake Marsh	5

	MILES.
Lake Marsh (length)	20
Head of Lake Marsh to Miles Canyon	23
Miles Canyon to White Horse Rapids	2¼
White Horse Rapids	½
Foot of White Horse Rapids to Tahkeena River	13
Tahkeena River to Lake Le Barge	11½
Lake Le Barge (length)	31
Lake Le Barge to Hootalinqua River	27½
Hootalinqua River to Big Salmon River	31
Big Salmon River to Little Salmon River	34
Little Salmon River to Five Fingers	53
Five Fingers to Pelly River	55
Pelly River to White River	9
White River to Stewart River	9
Stewart River to Sixty-Mile River	21
Sixty-Mile River to Dawson City	49
Dawson City to Forty-Mile	52
Forty-Mile to Fort Cudahy	¾
Fort Cudahy to Circle City	240
Total Dyea to Circle City via Chilkoot Pass.	762
Total Skaguay to Circle City via White Pass.	759

VIA ST. MICHAEL'S AND YUKON RIVER.

Seattle to St. Michael's	3,000
St. Michael's to Kutlik	100
Kutlik to Andreafski	125
Andreafski to Holy Cross	145
Holy Cross to Koserefsky	5
Koserefsky to Anvik	75
Anvik to Nulato	225
Nulato to Narikatat	145
Narikatat to Janana	80
Janana to Fort Yukon	450
Fort Yukon to Circle City	80
Circle City to Forty Mile	240
Forty Mile to Dawson City	52

VIA TAIYA PASS.

	MILES.
Victoria to Taiya	1,000
Taiya to Cudahy	650

VIA STIKINE RIVER.

Victoria to Wrangel	750
Wrangel to Telegraph Creek	150
Telegraph Creek to Teslin Lake	150
Teslin Lake to Cudahy	650

DISTANCES FROM HEAD OF TAIYA INLET.

Head of canoe navigation, Taiya River	5.90
Forks of Taiya River	8.38
Summit of Taiya Pass	14.76
Landing at Lake Lindeman	23.06
Foot of Lake Lindeman	27.49
Head of Lake Bennett	28.09
Boundary Line B. C. and N. W. T. (Lat. 60)	38.09
Foot of Lake Bennett	53.85
Foot of Cariboo Crossing (Lake Nares)	56.44
Foot of Tagish Lake	73.25
Head of Marsh Lake	78.15
Foot of Marsh Lake	97.21
Head of Canyon	122.94
Foot of Canyon	123.56
Head of White Horse Rapids	124.95
Foot of White Horse Rapids	125.33
Tahkeena River	139.92
Head of Lake Le Barge	153.07
Foot of Lake Le Barge	184.22
Teslintoo River	215.88
Big Salmon River	249.33
Little Salmon River	285.54
Five Finger Rapids	344.83
Pelly River	403.29
White River	499.11

	MILES.
Stewart River	508.91
Sixty-Mile Creek	530.41
Dawson City	575.70
Fort Reliance	582.20
Forty-Mile River	627.08
Boundary Line	667.43

MACKENZIE RIVER ROUTE.

Edmonton to Athabasca Landing	90
Athabasca Landing to Grand Rapids	167
Grand Rapids to Fort McMurray	87
Fort McMurray to Smith's Landing	287
Smith's Landing to Fort Smith	16
Fort Smith to Fort Resolution	190
Fort Resolution to Fort Providence	167
Fort Providence to Fort Simpson	157
Fort Simpson to Fort Wrigley	134
Fort Wrigley to Fort Norman	180
Fort Norman to Fort Good Hope	169
Fort Good Hope to Fort Macpherson	274
Fort Macpherson to La Pierre's House	60
La Pierre's House to the Porcupine	20
Porcupine to the Yukon	400
Total	2,424

PEACE-LIARD-PELLY ROUTE.

Edmonton to Peace River Crossing	260
Peace River to Nelson Forks	240
Down Nelson to the Junction with Liard	120
Up Liard to Dease River	160
Dease River to Pelly River	170
Pelly River to the Junction with Lewis	220
Lewis River to Klondike	200
Total	1,370

APPENDIX II.

FACTS ABOUT GOLD.

In calculating the value of gold, one must figure on the basis of Troy weight: 24 grains one pennyweight, 20 pennyweight one ounce, 12 ounces one pound. The price fixed by the United States Government for pure gold is $20.67 per ounce. Pure gold is 1,000 fine or 24 carats. The term carat is used to indicate degrees of fineness. Gold is divided into 24 carats or degrees of fineness. Pure gold, being 24 carats fine is worth as above stated. The other degrees range in price, as to weight, as follows:

22 carat	$18.94	14 carat	$12.05
20 carat	17.22	12 carat	10.33½
18 carat	15.50	10 carat	8.61
16 carat	13.78	8 carat	6.89
6 carat	5.16		

Gold used by jewelers is seldom less than 6 carats fine. Following is the price, per ounce, according to fineness:

Gold 1,000 fine is worth	$20.67
Gold 900 fine is worth	18.60
Gold 800 fine is worth	16.53
Gold 700 fine is worth	14.47
Gold 600 fine is worth	12.40
Gold 500 fine is worth	10.33
Gold 400 fine is worth	8.26
Gold 300 fine is worth	6.20
Gold 200 fine is worth	4.13
Gold 100 fine is worth	2.06

An ounce Troy or Apothecaries' weight contains 480 Troy grains. An ounce Avoirdupois weight contains 437½ Troy grains. The grain is the unit of Troy and Apothecaries' weight, and the ounce is the unit of the Avoirdupois weight. One pound Troy or Apothecaries' weight contains 5,760 Troy grains. One pound Avoirdupois weight contains 7,000 Troy grains.

All natural gold—that is, gold extracted from rocks or washed from the beds of streams—contains some alloy, generally silver, but sometimes platinum, copper and tellurium, and it varies in amount in different localities.

APPENDIX III.

CANADIAN AND ALASKAN MINING LAWS AND REGULATIONS.

Following are the Canadian and Alaskan Mining Laws and Regulations in full:

CANADIAN.

Nature and Size of Claims.

1. Bar diggings, a strip of land 100 feet wide at high-water mark and thence extending into the river to its lowest water level.

2. The sides of a claim for bar diggings shall be two parallel lines run as nearly as possible at right angles to the stream and shall be marked by four legal posts, one at each end of the claim, at or about high-water mark; also one at each end of the claim at or about the edge of the water. One of the posts at high-water mark shall be legibly marked with the name of the miner and the date upon which the claim was staked.

3. Dry diggings shall be 100 feet square, and shall have placed at each of its four corners a legal post, upon one of which shall be legibly marked the name of the miner and the date upon which the claim was staked.

4. Creek and river claims shall be 500 feet long measured in the direction of the general course of the stream, and shall extend in width from base to base of the hill or bench on each side, but when the hills or benches are less than 100 feet apart the claim may be 100 feet in depth. The sides of a claim shall be two

parallel lines run as nearly as possible at right angles to the stream. The sides shall be marked with legal posts at or about the edge of the water and at the rear boundaries of the claim. One of the legal posts at the stream shall be legibly marked with the name of the miner and the date upon which the claim was staked.

5. Bench claims shall be 100 feet square.

6. In defining the size of claims they shall be measured horizontally, irrespective of inequalities on the surface of the ground.

7. If any person or persons shall discover a new mine, and such discovery shall be established to the satisfaction of the gold commissioner, a claim for bar diggings 750 feet in length may be granted. A new stratum or auriferous earth or gravel situated in a locality where the claims are abandoned shall for this purpose be deemed a new mine, although the same locality shall have been previously worked at a different level.

8. The forms of application for a grant for placer mining and the grant of the same shall be those contained in forms "H" and "I" in the schedule hereto.

9. A claim shall be recorded with the gold commissioner in whose district it is situated within three days after the location thereof, if it is located within ten miles of the commissioner's office. One extra day shall be allowed for making such record for every additional ten miles or fraction thereof.

10. In the event of the absence of the gold commissioner from his office, entry for a claim may be granted by any person whom he may appoint to perform his duties in his absence.

11. Entry shall not be granted for a claim which has not been staked by the applicant in person in the manner specified in these regulations. An affidavit that the claim was staked out by the applicant shall be embodied in form "H" of the schedule hereto.

12. An entry fee of $15.00 shall be charged for the first year and an annual fee of $100.00 for each of the

following years. This provision shall apply to locations for which entries have already been granted.

13. After the recording of a claim the removal of any post by the holder thereof or by any person acting in his behalf for the purpose of changing the boundaries of his claim shall act as a forfeiture of the claim.

14. The entry of every holder for a grant for placer mining must be renewed and his receipt relinquished and replaced every year. The entry fee being paid each year.

15. No miner shall receive a grant for more than one mining claim in the same locality, but the same miner may hold any number of claims by purchase, and any number of miners may unite to work their claims in common upon such terms as they may arrange, provided such agreement be registered with the gold commissioner and a fee of $5.00 paid for each registration.

16. Any miner or miners may sell, mortgage or dispose of his or their claims, provided such disposal be registered with a fee of $2.00 paid to the gold commissioner, who shall thereupon give the assignee a certificate in form "J" in the schedule hereto.

17. Every miner shall during the continuance of his grant have the exclusive right of entry upon his own claim, for the miner-like working thereof, and the construction of a residence thereon, and shall be entitled exclusively to all the proceeds realized therefrom; but he shall have no surface rights therein; and the gold commissioner may grant to the holders of adjacent claims such right of entry thereon as may be absolutely necessary for the working of their claims, upon such terms as may to him seem reasonable. He may also grant permits to miners to cut timber thereon for their own use, upon payment of the dues prescribed by the regulations in that behalf.

18. Every miner shall be entitled to the use of so much of the water naturally flowing through or past his claim, and not already lawfully appropriated, as

shall, in the opinion of the gold commissioner be necessary for the due working thereof; and shall be entitled to drain his own claim free of charge.

19. A claim shall be deemed to be abandoned and open to occupation and entry by any person when the same shall have remained unworked on working days by the grantee thereof or by some person on his behalf for the space of seventy-two hours, unless sickness or other reasonable cause be shown to the satisfaction of the gold commissioner, or unless the grantee is absent on leave given by the commissioner, and the gold commissioner, upon obtaining evidence satisfactory to himself that this provision is not being complied with, may cancel the entry given for claim.

20. If the land upon which a claim has been located is not the property of the crown, it will be necessary for the person who applied for entry to furnish proof that he has acquired from the owner of the land the surface rights before entry can be granted.

21. If the occupier of the lands has not received a patent therefor, the purchase money of the surface rights must be paid to the crown, and a patent of the surface rights will issue to the party who acquired the mining rights. The money so collected will either be refunded to the occupier of the land, when he is entitled to a patent therefor, or will be credited to him on account of payment for land.

22. When the party obtaining the mining rights to lands cannot make an arrangement with the owner thereof for the acquisition of the surface rights, it shall be lawful for him to give notice to the owner or his agent or the occupier to appoint an arbitrator to act with another arbitrator named by him, in order to award the amount of compensation to which the owner or occupant shall be entitled. The notice mentioned in this section shall be according to form to be obtained upon application from the gold commissioner for the district in which the lands in question lie, and shall, when practicable, be personally served on such owner, or

his agent, if known, or occupant; and after reasonable efforts have been made to effect personal service without success, then such notice shall be served by leaving it at, or sending by registered letter to, the last place of abode of the owner, agent or occupant. Such notice shall be served upon the owner, or agent, within a period to be fixed by the gold commissioner before the expiration of the time limited in such notice. If the proprietor refuses or declines to appoint an arbitrator, or when, for any other reason, no arbitrator is appointed by the proprietor in the time limited therefor in the notice provided for by this section, the gold commissioner for the district in which the lands in question lie shall, on being satisfied by affidavit that such notice has come to the knowledge of such owner, agent or occupant, or that such owner, agent or occupant wilfully evades the service of such notice, or cannot be found, and that reasonable efforts have been made to effect such service, and that the notice was left at the last place of abode of such owner, agent or occupant, appoint an arbitrator on his behalf.

23. (a) All arbitrators appointed under the authority of these regulations shall be sworn before a Justice of the Peace to the impartial discharge of the duties assigned to them, and they shall forthwith proceed to estimate the reasonable damages which the owner or occupants of such lands, according to their several interests therein, shall sustain by reason of such prospecting and mining operations.

(b) In estimating such damages, the arbitrators shall determine the value of the land irrespectively of any enhancement thereof from the existence of minerals therein.

(c) In case such arbitrators cannot agree, they may select a third arbitrator, and when the two arbitrators cannot agree upon a third arbitrator the Gold Commissioner for the district in which the lands in question lie shall select such third arbitrator.

(d) The award of any two such arbitrators made in

writing shall be final, and shall be filed with the Gold Commissioner for the district in which the lands lie.

If any case arise for which no provision is made in these regulations, the provisions of the regulations governing the disposal of mineral lands other than coal lands approved by His Excellency the Governor in Council on the 9th of November, 1889, shall apply.

RECENT CHANGE.

The Department of the Interior has forwarded the following notice to the Yukon:

"Clauses 4 and 8 of the regulations governing placer mining on the Yukon River and its tributaries are amended by reducing the length of a creek and river claim to 100 feet, and the length of a creek and river claim to be granted to the discoverer of a new mine to 200 feet. The fee for the renewal of an entry for a claim has been reduced from $100 to $15.

FORM "J"

CERTIFICATE OF THE ASSIGNMENT OF A PLACER MINING CLAIM.

No............

DEPARTMENT OF THE INTERIOR.

Agency................189..

This is to certify that..........(B. C.) has (or have) filed an assignment in due form dated............ 189.., and accompanied by a registration fee of two dollars, of the grant to..........(A. B.) of.......... of the right (insert description of claim) to mine in ....for one year from ....189..

This certificate entitled the said............(B. C.) to all the rights and privileges of the said..........(A. B.) in respect of the claim assigned, that is to say, to the exclusive right of entry upon the said claim for miner-like working thereof and the construction of a residence thereon, and the exclusive right to all the proceeds therefrom, for the remaining portion of the year for which the said claim was granted to the said ....(A. B.) that is to say, until the ...... day of ....189.., the said............(B. C.) shall be entitled to the use of so much of the water naturally flowing through or past his (or their) claim and not already lawfully appropriated as shall be necessary for the due working thereof, and to drain the claim free of charge.

This grant does not convey to the said........... (B. C.) any surface rights in said claim, or any rights of ownership in the soil covered by said claim, and the said grant shall lapse and be forfeited unless the claim is continually, and in good faith, worked by the said .... (B. C.) ....or his (or their) associates.

The rights hereby granted are those laid down in the Dominion Mining Regulations, and no more, and are subject to all the provisions of the said regulations, whether the same are expressed herein or not.

....
Gold Commissioner.

FORM "H."

APPLICATION FOR GRANT FOR PLACER MINING CLAIM AND AFFIDAVIT OF APPLICANT.

I, (or we)........of........hereby apply under the Dominion Mining Regulations, for a grant of a claim for placer mining as defined in the said regula-

tions, in (here describe locality) ....
......................and I (or we) solemnly swear:

1. That I (or we) have discovered therein a deposit of (here name the metal or mineral).

2. That I (or we) am (or are) to the best of my (or our) knowledge and belief, the first discover (or discoverers) of the said deposit; or,

3. That the said claim was previously granted to (here name the last grantee), but has remained unworked by the said grantee for not less than ....

4. That I (or we) am (or are) unaware that the land is other than vacant Dominion Land.

5. That I (or we) did, on the......day of......... mark out on the ground, in accordance in every particular with the provisions of the Mining Regulations for the Yukon River and its tributaries, the claim for which I (or we) make this application, and that in so doing I (or we) did not encroach on any other claim or mining location previously laid out by any other person.

6. That the said mining claim contained, as nearly as I (or we) could measure or estimate, an area of....... square feet, and that the description (and sketch, if any) of this date hereto attached, signed by me (or us) sets (or set) forth in detail, to the best of my (or our) knowledge and ability, its position, form and dimensions.

7. That I (or we) make this application in good faith, to acquire the claim for the sole purpose of mining, prosecuted by myself (or us) or by myself and associates, or by my (or our) assigns.

Sworn before me at....................this......
day of..........., 189..

(Signature.)

....

FORM "I."

GRANT FOR PLACER CLAIM.

DEPARTMENT OF THE INTERIOR.

No...... Agency............189..

In consideration of the payment of the fee prescribed by Clause 12 of the mining regulations for the Yukon River and its Tributaries by (A. B.) of ...., accompanying his (or their) application No........, dated..............189.. for a mining claim in (here insert description of locality), the Minister of the Interior hereby grants to the said........(A. B.) ....for the term of one year from the date hereof the exclusive right of entry upon the claim (here describe in detail the claim granted) for the miner-like working thereof and the construction of a residence thereon, and the exclusive right to all the proceeds realized therefrom.

The said........(A. B.) .... shall be entitled to the use of so much water naturally flowing through or past his (or their) claim, and not already lawfully appropriated, as shall be necessary for the due working thereof, and to drain his (or their) claim, free of charge.

This grant does not convey to the said......(A. B.) ......any surface rights in the said claim, or any right of ownership in the soil covered by the said claim; and the said grant shall lapse and be forfeited unless the claim is continuously and in good faith worked by the said......(A. B.)......or his (or their) associates.

The rights hereby granted are those laid down in the aforesaid mining regulations, and no more, and are subject to all the provisions of the said regulations, whether the same are expressed herein or not.

....
Gold Commissioner.

ALASKA MINING LAWS.

The Act of Congress of May 17, 1884, providing a civil government for Alaska, provides that: "The laws of the United States relating to mining claims and the rights incident thereto, shall, from and after the passage of this act, be in full force and effect in said district." The further mining laws applicable are as follows:

United States Revised Statutes.—Sec. 2318. In all cases lands valuable for minerals shall be reserved from sale, except as otherwise expressly directed by law.

Sec. 2319. All valuable mineral deposits in lands belonging to the United States, both surveyed and unsurveyed, are hereby declared to be free and open to exploration and purchase, and the lands in which they are found to occupation and purchase, by citizens of the United States and those who have declared their intention to become such, under regulations prescribed by law, and according to the local customs or rules of miners in the several mining districts, so far as the same are applicable and not inconsistent with the laws of the United States.

Sec. 2320. Mining claims upon veins or lodes or quartz or other rock in place, bearing gold, silver, cinnabar, lead, tin, copper, or other valuable deposits heretofore located, shall be governed as to length along the vein or lode by the customs, regulations, and laws in force at the date of location. A mining claim located after the tenth day of May, eighteen hundred and seventy-two, whether located by one or more persons, may equal, but shall not exceed, one thousand five hundred feet in length along the vein or lode; but no lolation of a mining claim shall be made until the discovery of the vein or lode within the limits of the claim located. No claim shall extend more than three hundred feet on each side of the middle of the vein at the surface, nor shall any claim be limited by any mining regulation to less than twenty-five feet on each side of the middle of the vein at the surface, except where adverse rights existing on the tenth day of May, eighteen hundred and seventy-two, render such limitation necessary. The end lines of each claim shall be parallel to each other.

Sec. 2322. The locators of all mining locations heretofore made or which shall hereafter be made on any mineral vein, lode, or ledge, situated on the public domain, their heirs and assigns, where no adverse claim exists on the tenth day of May, eighteen hundred and seventy-two, so long as they comply with the laws of the United States, and with state, territorial, and local regulations not in conflict with the laws of the United States governing their possessory title, shall have the exclusive right of possession and enjoyment of all the surface included within the lines of their locations, and of all veins, lodes, and ledges throughout their entire depth, the top of apex of which lies inside of such surface lines extended downward vertically, although such veins, lodes, or ledges may so far depart from a perpendicular in their course downward as to extend outside the vertical side lines of such surface locations. But their right of possession to such outside parts of such veins or ledges shall be confined to such portions thereof as lie between vertical planes drawn downward as above described, through the end lines of their locations, so continued in their own direction that such planes will intersect such exterior parts of such veins or ledges. And nothing in this section shall authorize the locator or possession of a vein or lode which extends in its downward course beyond the vertical lines of his claim to enter upon the surface of a claim owned or possessed by another.

Sec. 2324. The miners of each mining district may make regulations not in conflict with the laws of the United States, or with the laws of the state or territory in which the district is situated, governing the location, manner of recording, amount of work necessary to hold possession of a mining claim, subject to the following requirements: The location must be distinctly marked on the ground, so that its boundaries can be readily traced. All records of mining claims hereafter made shall contain the name or names of the locators, the date of the location, and such description of the claim or claims located by reference to some natural object or permanent monument as will identify the claim. On each claim located after the tenth day of May, eighteen hundred and seventy-two, and until a patent has been issued therefor, not less than one hundred dollars' worth of labor shall be performed or improvements made during each year. On all claims located prior to the tenth of May, eighteen hundred and seventy-two, ten dollars' worth of labor shall be performed or improvements made by the tenth day of June, eighteen hundred and seventy-four, and each year thereafter, for each one hundred feet in length along the vein, until a patent has been issued therefor; but where such claims are held in common, such expenditure may be made upon any one claim; and upon a failure to comply with these conditions, the claim or mine upon which such failure occurred shall be opened to relocation in the same manner as if no location of the same had ever been made: Provided, That the original locators, their heirs, assigns, or legal representatives, have not resumed work upon the claim after failure and before such location. Upon the failure of any one of several co-owners to contribute his proportion of the expenditures required hereby, the co-owners who have performed the labor or made the improvements may, at the expiration of the year, give such delinquent co-owner personal notice in writing or notice by publication in the newspaper published nearest the claim, for at least once a week for ninety days, and if at the expiration of ninety days after such notice in writing or by publication such delinquent should fail or refuse to contribute his proportion of the expenditure required by this section, his interest in the claim shall become the property of his co-owners, who have made the expenditures.

Sec. 2336. Where two or more veins intersect or cross each other, priority of title shall govern, and such prior location shall be entitled to all ore or mineral contained within the space of intersection; but the subsequent location shall have the right of way through the space of intersection for the purposes of the convenient working of the mine. And where two or more veins unite, the oldest or prior location shall take the vein below the point of union, including all the space of intersection.

Sec. 2335. A patent for any land claimed and located for valuable deposits may be obtained in the following manner: Any person, association, or corporation authorized to locate a claim under this chapter, having claimed and located a piece of land for such purposes, who has, or have, complied with the terms of this chapter, may file in the proper land-office an application for a patent, under oath, showing such compliance, together with a plat and field-notes of the claim or claims in common, made by or under the direction of the United States Surveyor-General, showing accurately the boundaries of the claim or claims, which shall be distinctly marked by monuments on the ground, and shall post a copy of such plat, together with a notice of such application for a patent, in a conspicuous place on the land embraced in such plat previous to the filing of the application for a patent, and shall file an affidavit of at least two persons that such notice has been duly posted, and shall file a copy of the notice in such land-office, and shall thereupon be entitled to a patent for the land, in the manner following: The register of the land-office, upon the filing of such application, plat, field-notes, notices, and affidavits, shall publish a notice that such application has been made, for the period of sixty days, in a newspaper to be by him designated as published nearest to such claim; and he shall also post such notice in his office for the same period. The claimant at the time of filing this application, or at any time thereafter, within sixty days of publication, shall file with the register a certificate of the United States surveyor-general that five hundred dollars' worth of labor has been expended on improvements made upon the claim by himself or grantors; that the plat is correct, with such further description by such reference to natural objects or permanent monuments as shall identify the claim, and furnish an accurate description, to be incorporated in the patent. At the expiration of the sixty days of publication the cliamant shall file his affidavit, showing that the plat and notice have been posted in a conspicuous place on the claim during such period of publication. If no adverse claim shall have been filed with the register and the receiver of the proper land-office at the expiration of the sixty days of publication, it shall be assumed that the applicant is entitled to a patent, upon the payment to the proper officer of five dollars per acre, and that no adverse claim exists; and thereafter no objection from third parties to the issuance of a patent shall be heard, except it be shown that the applicant has failed to comply with the terms of this chapter.

Sec. 2327. The description of vein or lode claims, upon surveyed lands, shall designate the location of the claim with reference to the lines of the public surveys, but need not conform therewith; but where a patent shall be issued for claims upon unsurveyed lands, the surveyor-general, in extending the surveys, shall adjust the same to the boundaries of such patented claim, according to the plat or description thereof, but so as in no case to interfere with or change the location of any such patented claim.

Act of Congress of January 22, 1880.—An Act to amend sections twenty-three hundred and twenty-four and twenty-three hundred and twenty-five of the Revised Statutes of the United States concerning mineral lands.

Be it enacted, etc., That section twenty-three hundred and twenty-five of the Revised Statutes of the United States be amended by adding hereto the following words: "Provided, That where the claimant for a patent is not a resident of or within the land district wherein the vein, lodge, ledge or deposit sought to be patented is located, the application for patent and the affidavits required to be made in this section by the claimant for such patent may be made by his, her, or its authorized agent, where said agent is conversant with the facts sought to be established by said affidavits: And provided, That this section shall apply to all applications now pending for patents to mineral lands."

Sec. 2. That section twenty-three hundred and twenty-four of the Revised Statutes of the United States be amended by adding thereto the following words: "Provided, That the period within which the work required to be done annually on all unpatented mineral claims shall commence on the first day of January succeeding the date of location of such claim, and this section shall apply to all claims located since the tenth of May, anno Domini eighteen hundred and seventy-two."

Act of Congress of February 11, 1875.—An Act to amend section two thousand three hundred and twenty-four of the Revised Statutes, relating to the development of the mining resources of the United States.

Be it enacted, etc., That section two thousand three hundred and twenty-four of the Revised Statutes be, and the same is hereby amended to that where a person or company has or may run a tunnel for the purpose of developing a lode or lodes, owned by said person or company, the money so expended in said tunnel shall be taken and considered as expended on said lode or lodes, whether located prior to or since the passage of said act, and such person or company shall not be required to perform work on the surface of said lode or lodes in order to hold the same as required by said act. [See page 43.]

United States Law.—Sec. 2323. Where a tunnel is run for the development of a vein or lode, or for the discovery of mines, the owners of such tunnel shall have the right of possession of all veins or lodes within three thousand feet from the face of such tunnel on the line thereof, not previously known to exist, discovered in such tunnel, to the same extent as if discovered from the surface: and locations on the line of such tunnel of veins or lodes, not appearing on the surface, made by other parties after the commencement of the tunnel, and while the same is being prosecuted with reasonable diligence, shall be invalid; but failure to prosecute the work on the tunnel for six months shall be considered as an abandonment of the right to all undiscovered veins on the line of such tunnel.

PLACER CLAIMS.

Sec. 2329. Claims usually called "placers," including all forms of deposit, excepting veins of quartz, or other rock in place, shall be subject to entry and patent, under like circumstances and conditions, and upon similar proceedings, as are provided for vein or lode claims; but where the lands have been previously surveyed by the United States, the entry in its exterior limits shall conform to the legal subdivisions of the public lands.

United States Law.—Sec. 2330. Legal subdivisions of forty acres may be subdivided into ten-acre tracts; and two or more persons, or associations of persons, having contiguous claims of any size, although such claims may be less than ten acres each, may make joint entry thereof; but no location of a placer-claim, made after the ninth day of July, eighteen hundred and seventy, shall exceed one hundred and sixty acres for any one person or association of persons, which location shall conform to the United States surveys; and nothing in this section contained shall defeat or impair any bona fide pre-emption or homestead claim upon agricultural lands, or authorize the sale of the improvements of any bona fide settler to any purchaser.

Sec. 2331. Where placer-claims are upon surveyed lands, and conform to legal subdivisions, no further survey or plat shall be required, and all placer mining claims located after the tenth of May, eighteen hundred and seventy-two, shall conform as near as practicable with the United States system of public-land surveys, and the rectangular subdivisions of such surveys, and no such location shall include more than twenty acres for each individual claimant; but where placer-claims can not be conformed to legal subdivisions, survey and plat shall be made as on unsurveyed lands; and where by the segregation of mineral lands in any legal subdivision a quantity of agricultural land less than forty acres remains, such fractional portions of agricultural land may be entered by any party qualified by law, for homestead or pre-emption purposes.

PLACER CLAIMS CONTAINING LODES.

United States Law.—Sec. 2333. Where the same person, association, or corporation is in possession of a placer claim, and also a vein or lode included within the boundaries thereof, application shall be made for a patent for the placer claim, with the statement that it includes such vein or lode, and in such case a patent shall issue for a placer-claim, subject to the provisions of this chapter, including such vein or lode, upon the payment of five dollars per acre for such vein or lode claim, and twenty-five feet of surface on each side thereof. The remainder of the placer claim, or any placer claim not embracing any vein or lode claim, shall be paid for at the rate of two dollars and fifty cents per acre, together with all costs of proceedings; and where a vein or lode, such as is described in section twenty-three hundred and twenty, is known to exist within the boundaries of a placer-claim, an application for a patent for such placer claim which does not include an application for the vein or lode claim shall be construed as a conclusive declaration that the claimant of the placer claim has no right of possession of the vein or lode claim; but where the existence of a vein or lode in a placer-claim is not known, a patent for the placer-claim shall convey all valuable mineral and other deposits within the boundaries thereof.

United States Law.—Sec. 2332. Where such person or association, they and their grantors, have held and worked their claims for a period equal to the time prescribed by the statute of limitations for mining claims of the State or Territory where the same may be situated, evidence of such possession and working of the claims for such period shall be sufficient to establish a right to a patent thereto under this chapter, in the absence of any adverse claim; but nothing in this chapter shall be deemed to impair any lien which may have attached in any way whatever to any mining claim or property thereto attached prior to the issuance of a patent.

United States Law.—Sec. 2321. Proof of citizenship, under this chapter, may consist, in the case of an individual, of his own affidavit thereof; in the case of an association of persons unincorporated, of the affidavit of their authorized agent, made on his own knowledge, or upon information and belief; and in the case of a corporation organized under the laws of the United States, or of any State or Territory thereof, by the filing of a certified copy of their charter or certificate of incorporation.

APPENDIX IV.

CANADIAN LAND REGULATIONS.

It is reasonable to suppose that as the mining camps increase in the gold fields of the far northwest, there will be a considerable immigration into the agricultural and stock-raising prairies adjacent thereto in Canadian territory. Enterprise in the gold districts will make farming, stock-raising, and dairy products very profitable in that region, and it is fair to suppose that cattle and horse ranches, dairy farms, and agricultural pursuits generally will at once be developed in the Peace River country, from which the mining camps in the mountains and slopes to the westward may be easily supplied, and at great profit to settlers. One may expect to see a large flouring mill established in the Peace River country before the end of another year.

On account of these prospectors it will be to the advantage of many readers to include here the land laws and regulations of Canada in respect of this territory. Here follows a summary of the regulations applicable to the free grants or homesteads, sale, settlement, etc., of the lands of Canada:

Under the Dominion Lands Regulations all surveyed even-numbered sections, excepting 8 and 26 (Hudson Bay lands), in Manitoba and the Northwest Territories, which have not been homesteaded, reserved to provide wood lots for settlers, or otherwise disposed of or reserved, are to be held exclusively for homestead. Odd-numbered sections (with the exception of 11 and 29, which are school lands) for 24 miles on each side of the Canadian Pacific Railway, may be generally stated to be railway lands, purchasable from the company, and not open for homestead. There are also other railway lands, which have been appropriated in aid of similar undertakings, and generally speaking it may be said that sections bearing odd numbers are either disposed of or reserved as grants in aid of the construction of railways.

Free grants of one quarter-section (160 acres) of surveyed agricultural lands may be obtained by any person who is the sole head of a family, or by any male who has attained the age of 18 years, on application to the local agent of Dominion Lands for the district in which the parcel applied for is situated, and by making an entry and within six months thereafter erecting a habitable house and commencing actual residence upon the land, and continuing to reside upon it for at least six months in each year for the three next succeeding years, and doing reasonable cultivation duties during that period. An office fee of $10 is levied. For lands which have been occupied an additional $10 is charged to meet inspection and cancellation expenses.

Persons making entry for homesteads on and after 1st September in any year are allowed until 1st June following to perfect their entries by commencing the performance of their settlement duties in accordance with the terms of entry in each case.

In the event of a homesteader desiring to secure his patent within a shorter period than the three years, he will be permitted to purchase it at the Government price ruling at the time of entry, on furnishing proof that he has resided on the land for at least twelve months subsequent to date of entry, and has cultivated 30 acres thereof.

The pre-emption system has been abolished, but a settler desiring to acquire a larger holding than 160 acres, and having the means to pay for it, can buy from the Government a quarter-section (adjoining his homestead, if then available), one-fourth of the purchase money being payable at the time of the sale, and the balance in three equal annual instalments with interest at six per cent per annum, or he may be able to buy from the railway company the whole or part of an adjoining odd-numbered section, as he may find expedient.

Free grants can be obtained within a reasonable distance to the west of Winnipeg, and of the line of railway. An inquiry of any of the Government land agents will, however, elicit information as to the most desirable land available for settlement.

Information respecting timber, mineral, coal, grazing and hay lands may also be obtained from any of the land agents. Homesteaders are entitled to free permits to cut a specified quantity of timber for their own use only, upon payment of an office fee of 25 cents.

It must be distinctly understood that the land regulations are subject to variations from time to time. Settlers should take care to obtain from the land agents when making their entry an explanation of the actual regulations in force at that time, and the clause of the Act under which the entry is made endorsed upon the receipt, so that no question or difficulty may then or thereafter arise.

The settler may sometimes find it convenient to buy lands partly improved, with buildings and fences upon them, of private proprietors. It very frequently happens that half-breed or other lands may be obtained on moderate terms.

The following diagram shows the manner in which the country is surveyed. It represents a township—that is, a tract of land six miles square, containing 36 sections of one square mile each. These sections are subdivided into quarter-sections of 160 acres each.

TOWNSHIP DIAGRAM.

TOWNSHIP DIAGRAM.

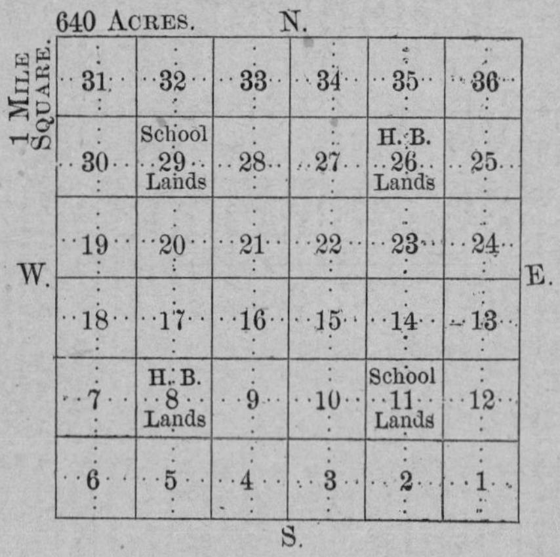

The Government makes no advances of money to settlers, and, for the better encouragement of bona fide settlement, reserve to themselves the right to declare null and void every assignment or transfer of homestead or pre-emption right made before the issue of the patent, except in cases where any person or company is desirous of assisting intending settlers, when the sanction of the Minister of the Interior to the advance having been obtained, the settler has power to create a charge upon his homestead for a sum not exceeding six hundred dollars, and interest not exceeding 8 per cent per annum, provided that particulars of how such an advance has been expended for his benefit be first furnished to the settler and verified by the local agent, or if the charge be made previous to the advance, then such charge shall only operate to the extent certified to by the local agent as having been actually advanced to or expended for the benefit of the settler. One-half of the advance may be devoted to paying the cost of the passage of the settler, paying for the homestead entry, providing for the subsistence of the settler and his family, and to erecting and insuring buildings on the homestead, and the remainder to breaking land and providing horses, cattle, and furniture, farm implements, seed grain, etc.

For the further protection of the settler it is provided that the time for payment of the first instalment of interest on any such advance shall not be earlier than the 1st of November in any year, and shall not be within two years from the establishment of the settler upon the homestead, and also that the settler shall not be bound to pay the capital of such advance within a less period than four years from the date of his establishment on his homestead.

APPENDIX V.

SUPPLIES.

The following list of supplies for one man for a year, for Klondike travel and mining, may be cut down to suit, but it contains about everything a man wants for the trip:

Flour	lbs.	400
Corn meal		20
Rolled oats		36
Rice		25
Beans		100
Sugar		75
Dried Fruits		75
Candles		20
Dry Salt Pork		50
Evaporated Potatoes		25
Evaporated Onions		5
Bacon		150
Baking Powder		10
Soda		3
Salt		20
Ginger		½
Pepper		1
Mustard		½
Coffee		25
Tea		10
Compressed Soup Vegetables		10
Soap		5
Condensed Milk	tins	24
Yeast Cakes	pkg	6
Matches		60

Butter, Extract of Beef, Tobacco, Jamaica Ginger, Evaporated Vinegar.

Gold pan	1
Granite buckets	2
Knife and fork	2
Spoons, assorted	6
Bread pan	1
Cups	2
Plates, tin	3
Whet stone	1
Coffee pot	1
Pick and handles	1
Hatchet	1
Saws, whip	1
Saws, hand	1
Shovels	1
Files, assorted	1
Axe and handle	1
Draw knife	1
Brace and bits, assorted	1
Chisels, assorted	3
Butcher knife	1
Compass	1
Revolver	1
Stove	1
Frying pan	1

Rope, half-inch, 150 feet; Nails, 20 lbs.; Pitch, Oakum, Medicine.

2 augers, 1 and 2 inch.

4 steel drills, 1 inch.

1 heavy hammer, 4 lbs.

1 single hand hammer.

Fuse and caps.

75 lbs. dynamite.

1 folding oven.

1 heavy duck tent, 12x12, wall sides (center pole may be of 4-inch piping in 4 feet lengths to serve as a stove pipe).

2 rubber sheets.

1 large cow hide, tanned with hair on, is very useful.

2 pairs heavy blankets.

1 rubber coat.
2 pairs rubber boots.
2 pairs walking shoes with nails.
10 pairs of moccasins.
1 pair snow shoes.
Socks, mitts and gloves.
3 suits underwear.
2 suits Mackinaw clothing.
Mosquito netting.
Snow glasses.
Sheath knife.

The cost of this outfit at Seattle, or Calgary, is about $150. It will require about $10,000 to equip an expedition of 50 men at Calgary, for, say eighteen months. In addition to supplies of provisions, clothing, etc., there will be an additional cost of $5,000 for, say 50 native horses; 40 buckboards fitted with wheels and bobs, harnesses, extra feed for horses, and incidentals. It will therefore require $15,000 to thoroughly equip an expedition of say 50 men for the northwest route via Edmonton and the Peace, Liard and Pelly Rivers. Such an expedition should have $5,000 of a surplus on hand for emergencies.

To sum up, parties of the following size could reach the Klondike, via the Peace-Liard-Pelly route, from Edmonton, with supplies for 18 months, at the cost given hereunder, including boats for the open season, and horses and sleds for the ice season:

Parties of 4	$ 1,500
Parties of 10	4,500
Parties of 20	8,000
Parties of 50	15,000
Parties of 100	25,000

In addition to the amounts named, such expeditions should have a surplus of from $500 to $5,000 on hand for emergencies. It will require four times these amounts to carry like expeditions, with equal supplies and provisions, by any other route now traveled. The Peace-Liard-Pelly route is being quite extensively traveled at the present time by Canadian expeditions.

Expeditions to the far north gold fields via the northwest should consist of at least four or five persons, and they will probably be more successful if composed of twenty or more. None but experienced miners should be taken, except that with the larger expeditions, carpenters, blacksmiths, boat-builders, a surveyor and a physician and surgeon should be included. It is indispensable that, even with the smallest expeditions, one well acquainted with the uses of the medicine chest should be taken. There are no dangerous diseases indigenous to the country, but scurvy is liable to prevail in the winter season, and should be guarded against carefully. Accidents are always liable to occur, and in such emergencies there should be some one at hand, with proper appliances, who knows how to dress a wound, tie an artery or put in a few stitches to facilitate healing.

There will be a great deal of prospecting for gold in the Klondike country, both east and west of the great watershed next spring and summer. This work will be best carried on by the larger expeditions, carrying with them extensive supplies. The Stewart, Macmillan and the upper branches of the Pelly will no doubt be visited, as also the mountain streams of the Liard and Peace Rivers. Should rich strikes of gold be met with on these and the many other rivers not yet explored, large parties could locate claims, and the members of such expeditions would be sufficiently close to each other to render life in the mining camp comparatively attractive. The larger expeditions could also do a profitable transportation and townsite business, as new discoveries of gold will be sure to attract others to their locations.